THE SOUTH AFRICAN NOVEL IN ENGLISH

THE SOUTH AFRICAN NOVEL IN ENGLISH

Essays in Criticism and Society

Edited by
Kenneth Parker

First published 1978 by
THE MACMILLAN PRESS LTD
London and Basingstoke
Associated companies in Delhi
Dublin Hong Kong Johannesburg Lagos
Melbourne New York Singapore Tokyo

Typeset in Great Britain by
Vantage Phototypesetting Co Ltd
Southampton & London
Printed and bound in Great Britain by
W & J Mackay Limited, Chatham

British Library Cataloguing in Publication Data

The South African Novel in English
    1.   South   African   fiction   (English) — 20th
century — History and criticism — Addresses, essays, lectures
    I. Parker, Kenneth
    823   PR9362.5

    ISBN 0-333-23529-0

---

for
Gabrielle, Philippe and Antony

Contents

Acknowledgements

The editor and publisher wish to thank the following, who have given permission for the use of copyright material:

The editor of *The Journal of Commonwealth Literature* and Oxford University Press for permission to include the articles by Ursula Edmands on Olive Schreiner from the issue of December 1969, and by Tim Couzens on Sol Plaatje from the issue of June 1973; and for extracts from the article by Michael Wade, 'William Plomer: English Liberalism and the South African Novel', from the issue of June 1973;

The British Council for permission to include Arthur Ravenscroft's article on Pauline Smith;

Evans Publishers for permission to include the chapter entitled 'South Africa's First Proletarian Writer', from Michael Wade's *Peter Abrahams*.

Notes on the contributors

Tim Couzens studied at Rhodes University, Grahamstown (South Africa) and at Oxford. He is Senior Research Officer in the African Studies Institute, University of the Witwatersrand, Johannesburg, where he was at one time a Lecturer in English.

Ursula Edmands studied at the Universities of Stellenbosch and Natal (South Africa). After previous appointments at Rhodes University, the University of the Witwatersrand and Leeds University, she is at present a Senior Lecturer in the School of Humanities and Contemporary Studies, Leeds Polytechnic.

David Rabkin studied at the Universities of Cape Town and Leeds. After completing his doctoral thesis on '*Drum* Magazine and its Effects on Black South African Writers', he worked as a journalist for 'The Cape Argus', a Cape Town evening newspaper. He is at present serving a ten-year sentence in Pretoria Central prison for 'furthering the aims of a banned organisation' [The African National Congress of South Africa].

Arthur Ravenscroft studied at the University of Cape Town and at Cambridge. After previous appointments in the Universities of Cape Town, Stellenbosch, and visiting lectureships in Africa, Europe, the West Indies, he is at present Senior Lecturer in English Literature, University of Leeds, and Editor, *The Journal of Commonwealth Literature*.

Michael Wade studied at the Universities of the Witwatersrand, Rhodes (Grahamstown), London, and Sussex. After previous appointments in the Polytechnic of North London and the University of Sussex, he is at present Chairman of the Department of African Studies in the Hebrew University, Jerusalem, Israel.

Preface

The arrival of white settlers at the Southern tip of the African continent some three centuries ago ushered in a variety of paradoxes. The most important of these would seem to be that despite the oppression of Bantu by both Boer and British (whether by war, expropriation of land, slavery, race-discrimination, or economic exploitation), South Africa has been — and will conceivably continue to be — an interdependent, multi-racial society. It is the implicit recognition of this reality — and, indeed, of the desire to institutionalise it explicitly — which lies at the heart of competing political policies and which have, in recent years, culminated in armed struggle.

The resort to armed struggle is, itself, a recognition of another paradox: that, when one examines the interactions between the three dimensions of oppression in South Africa — those of race, of class, and of nationality — one finds that a deep-seated colour prejudice, codified into an all-embracing racism, has always been resisted by a counter-vailing radicalism which specifically rejected colour and favoured a non-racial society. It is the extent to which South African novelists in English have tended to be sensitive to this latter aspiration that constitutes the core concern of this book.

There have, of course, in the past been attempts to assess the contribution of South African novelists. Of these, the two efforts which immediately come to mind are those of J. P. L. Snyman[1] and Vladimir Klima.[2] The former was based upon a thesis for the award of the degree of Doctor of Literature in the University of Potchefstroom for *Christian Higher Education* (my emphasis). The book contained an Introduction by C. R. Swart, at that time the Minister of Justice (and later still, State President of the Republic of South Africa). The imprimatur of political orthodoxy could not have been more impeccable. As a work of literary criticism it was, however, lacklustre: it seldom rose above a survey of authors, titles, and plots, although it could be argued that the writer deserved his doctorate for his tenacity in the face of so many indifferent works by now (thankfully) out-of-print writers.

Whereas Dr Snyman's book might be described as a political apologia disguised as criticism, Vladimir Klima's contribution could rank as well-intentioned but essentially ignorant political involvement masquerading as criticism. Two central assumptions underpin the book. These are, firstly, that the '. . . African viewpoint is one of the main attributes of genuine African literature and art . . .', and, secondly, that '. . . a particular emphasis had been laid upon the works written by the most advanced, gifted and progressive novelists, while lesser writers and pro-apartheid authors have been paid much less attention'.

This is not the place to enter into a discussion of the view that an 'African viewpoint' is one of the main attributes of genuine African art and literature. But, leaving aside the complexities of definition of terminology, some of the questions which require attention would seem to be: to what extent is there an 'African viewpoint'? If there is, what are its characteristics? And how, and to what extent, are these either present or absent in the works of South African writers? To what extent does the 'viewpoint' coincide with racial divisions? Most important, how does this 'viewpoint' lead, it would seem, unerringly in the direction of 'genuine' art and literature?

It is therefore a sobering experience to turn to the considered, but no less radical or committed, views of Ezekiel Mphahlele. *The African Image*[3] was published originally in 1959, and recently re-issued in an extensively revised form. While the work is not confined to South Africa, the issues raised reflect the author's long confrontation with the theoretical problems of the study of literature in Africa. A comparison of, for instance, 'The African Personality' and 'What Price "Négritude"?' in the original edition with 'Négritude Revisited', in the revised edition, will reveal the nature of the search.

The recognition that the search is political as well as literary leads to a third major paradox: that after three hundred years we are still not sure what we are searching for. The leaders of the political struggle would seem to be uncertain about what they are after, except in broad outline. No-one really knows if the objective is, say, a liberal non-racial society, a Socialist Commonwealth, a federal system of autonomous national republics, to cite a few possible options. And it would seem that the uncertainties of the politicians are reflected by the uncertainties of the novelists, who, in their turn, reflect the confusion of the peoples of

South Africa, where law, custom, and habit combine to prevent individuals and groups from discovering themselves. It is one of the great merits of the novels discussed in this book that, if their authors have done nothing else, they have tried to show how this desire for self-discovery proceeds in the face of massive obstacles.

In my attempt to make some sense of this unfolding story, I am aware of the immense debt of gratitude I owe. My primary acknowledgement must go to my contributors: their ready assent to my request to participate in the continuing debate helped to make this book possible. I also hasten to express my appreciation for the skills of (initially) Mrs Rosemary Baker and Mrs Sheila Mann, who transformed my jumble of papers into a coherent manuscript. My greatest debt is, however, to two people: to Jack Simons, for his years of wise counselling and selfless dedication in the cause of South African freedom, and to my wife, who listened patiently, encouraged gently, and commented perceptively, and who is therefore finally responsible for the fact that the book was completed.

Highgate, London
January 1978   Kenneth Parker

1. Kenneth Parker: The South African Novel in English*

Apartheid—a word with a potent appeal to the longing for racial exclusiveness. A word with a thousand meanings and no meaning, but with a curious power to change the meaning of other words.[1]

The quotation is from Harry Bloom's *Episode in the Transvaal*. It occurs almost as an aside to the musings of Lieutenant Swanepoel who is reflecting on the threat to his career in the police force, in international sport as a rugby player, and as a prospective husband, because of rumours that his sister is not white. But these reflections are short-lived: selfpity has to be postponed in the interests of an overriding need to act, since a 'riot' supervenes in the 'location' (that area on the outskirts of every South African town to which blacks are legally and compulsorily segregated). Swanepoel is responsible for the 'restoration of law and order'.

Hence, what may have been construed at first sight as tangential and as an unwarranted political intrusion into character delineation, personal motivation, and creative patterning, in its context takes on a different perspective. Swanepoel's musings and actions offer a synopsis not only of some of the major themes and concerns of the South African novel in English, but also of the environment in which the novel operates. In the language of apartheid, political protest is a 'riot', humans are 'located' and the maintenance of the system is justified as

* An expanded version of a paper read originally at The African Studies Center, UCLA, 1971.

1

the 'restoration of law and order'.

A random selection of some recent Acts of the South African Parliament will illustrate vividly the difference between inferred title and explicit intention. The Citizenship Act does not confer citizenship, but withdraws that status from certain people under specified conditions; the Industrial Conciliation Act is not designed to regulate employer-employee relationship, but splits trade unions along racial lines and provides for the reservation of jobs, by proclamation, for certain racial groups, usually in favour of whites; the Extension of University Education Act, contrary to its title prohibits qualified black students (with minor exceptions, and by prior ministerial permission) from attending the so-called 'open universities' of Cape Town and Witwatersrand; and the Publications and Entertainments Act created a mechanism for the censorship of books, films and other forms of artistic creativity where these might be construed as conflicting with the ethos of the state.

Two observations about these Acts of Parliament are in order: firstly, that they are aimed initially and specifically at the nonwhite population; secondly, that they nevertheless can be and are applicable in various degrees to all people in the country, irrespective of their race. It is important to emphasise this fact, since it has implications for the objectives which writers may set themselves.

So, how do we assess literature in the context of a society where political freedoms are abrogated, where cultural growth is stultified, and where words and their meanings (so crucial for a writer) are invariably corrupted? It was Stendhal who observed that 'politics in a work of literature is like a pistol-shot in the middle of a concert, something loud and vulgar, and yet a thing to which it is not possible to refuse one's attention'. I am also reminded of the observation by Dr Leavis that '. . . in respect of any art one takes seriously one *has* to make value-judgements, since a real response entails this; it entails forming an implicit critical sense of the human significance of the art in question, and the demand of the intelligence is that one should bring one's sense to conscious definition'.

My objective then is to offer a preliminary and tentative exploration of what is entailed in '. . . forming an implicit critical sense of the human significance of the art in question . . .', in this case the South African novel in English. While what follows is not intended to constitute a comprehensive survey, I shall try to show that there exists—indeed, has always tended to exist—a direct relation between political perspective and literary creation in South Africa. Further, that in this relation the political perspective has tended to dominate; that this relation has not been static, but that it can be defined, refined, and described by way of specific time-sequences, class patterns and cultural aspirations. In short, I hope to show that in the area of creativity no less that in other spheres we are confronted with a strange paradox: on the one hand, the existence of an abundance of the conflicts (personal as well as environmental) which potentially give rise to art; on the other, the absence of those minimum conditions of freedom which permit the growth of that art. A sense of the origins of this paradox may be obtained by resorting to a brief historical interpretation.[2]

Permanent white settlement on the southern African subcontinent dates from the latter half of the seventeenth century, when a trading station was set up at the Cape of Good Hope to provision the searoute between Europe and the East Indies. Temporary expediency soon became permanent policy, and by the time the British took the Cape by force of arms from the Dutch in 1806, it inherited jurisdiction over some 80,000 people, of whom some 26,000 were white.

From the time of the British occupation until the middle of the nineteenth century both settler groups of Boer and Briton co-existed in an atmosphere of mutual suspicion of each other's political ambitions and cultural aspirations, although this conflict was superseded by the common cause of military subjugation and economic dispossession of the original inhabitants.

With the discovery during the 1870s of the mineral wealth of the interior, and the subsequent rapid transformation of the subcontinent from an agrarian and feudal colony into an industrial mining and capitalist state, conflict between Boer and Briton increased both in degree of intensity and in scope, until these conflicts culminated in open war at the turn of the present century.

From that time onwards, the political model becomes more complex. But two characteristics predominate: firstly, the endeavour of the Boers—increasingly adopting the name 'Afrikaner'—to achieve dominance over all the other groups within the common society; secondly, the changing pattern of the white oligarchy's measures to keep the nonwhite masses (who were increasingly adopting sophisticated techniques to achieve freedom) in subjugation.

To look at this overall pattern either linguistically and culturally, or racially and nationally, the first period until the discovery of gold and diamonds has a marginal literary interest, apart from the usual official documents of civil servants and the diaries of travellers to and from the Cape, and into the interior. (It might, however, be an interesting exercise to compare English and Afrikaans' versions of the 'frontier', and even to compare the South African and North American varieties with each other.) The settler groups live as pioneers, reversing, interestingly, in the process, the usual pattern of social organisation by being, on the African subcontinent, first farmers, then herdsmen, lastly hunters. Culturally they owe their allegiance to the metropolitan countries—England, France, the Netherlands. The tribesmen, on the other hand, in the eastern areas, on the Natal coast and in the interior, maintain their cultural traditions despite undergoing, to various degrees, dispossession of land and geographical displacement, until each group (the Nama who were called Hottentot, the Khoi who were called Bushmen, and later, the Bantu-speaking nations) was defeated and forced to conform to the new foreign order. In the second period, roughly from 1870 to the Proclamation of Union in 1910, the keynote is one of rapid expansion and of institutionalising the domination of blacks by whites. Attendant on the economic transformation, four major groups of migrants either descend on or are forced into the mineral-rich interior, where they come into contact with each other in a cash nexus and proceed to lay the foundations for the situation which currently exists, and for the continuing struggle within the society for national liberation by movements of Africans, Asians and coloured (mixed race), allied to the class struggle spearheaded by socialists and communists. The first group consisted of a new wave of immigrants from Europe, chiefly from the British Isles. They came, equipped not only with the technical skills essential to an emergent mining and industrial society, but also with the pretensions of its cultural traditions.

The second group, of displaced whites, mainly from the Platteland, the rural and farming areas, was composed chiefly of Afrikaners. They were deficient not only in the skills essential to the emergent society, but they were also considered to be culturally inferior to their English counterparts. They found, consequently, that they were constrained to fit in at the bottom of the white social and economic ladder.

The third group consisted of displaced tribal Africans and migrant peasants who were often coaxed, but more generally forced by economic and legal demands, into mining and industry as sources of cheap, manual labour.

Finally, the Asians, overwhelmingly from the Indian subcontinent, entered Natal as indentured labourers on the sugar cane estates. They numbered in their ranks a small but significant group of craft workers and traders.

It is during this period, when Britain extends her hegemony over the Boer Republics of the Transvaal and the Orange Free State, that the Boers become intensely aware of themselves as a discriminated against minority and proceed to equip themselves with defence mechanisms against a 'perfidious Albion', while at the same time ensuring that 'the kaffir is kept in his place'. They systematically propound a theory of cultural uniqueness and race purity, and develop a new language which not only interprets the facts of their bondage, but also becomes the rallying-point of their resistance. Afrikaans literature, from its inception, serves as a vehicle for the enunciation of political aspirations. Novelists and poets in particular draw on the events of their group's struggles against both Bantu and Briton for inspiration, and as a consequence achieve a pivotal status in their community. To this day the literary intellectual within the Afrikaner group is invested by fellow Afrikaners with great respect, and it is against this background that those Afrikaans writers who in recent years have presumed to question the received tribal myth have been severely castigated, despite their assurance that they are working within the confines of the model created by their predecessors.

Novelists in English during this period write in a semi-scientific way about the flora and fauna of the interior, or concentrate on rather inane romantic tales. For instance, in *Leila, or Slave or No Slave* (n.d.) Mrs A. M. Carey-Hobson recounts how a slave girl turns out to be a Portuguese heiress after all, and in *An Afternoon Ride* (1897) Ann Page offers the 'Victorian' hero and heroine, both proud and wellborn, who finally surmount all obstacles to their marriage. There is little that is South African about their writing, and as far as can be ascertained, in English-speaking homes of the period, the novelists who were read included Thomas Hardy, H. G. Wells, and Arnold Bennett.

The different perspectives as between the two competing white groups are clear: while the English-speaking see their cultural heritage as being umbilically tied to that of the mother country, the Afrikaners consciously proceed to break their ties with Europe, and attempt to create an indigenous product. It is not essential to agree with the end-product of this attempt in order to acknowledge the distinction and to evaluate the contribution.

But the Wars (the Anglo-Boer Wars, or the Afrikaner Wars for Freedom, where the choice of terminology is dependent on which side you were on) is the chief source of inspiration for works of the period.[3] Perhaps 'inspiration' is out of place here, and one should say 'source of raw material'. In *An Imperial Light Horseman* (1900), Harold Blore describes the exodus from Johannesburg to Natal, and the Siege of Glencoe, but the technique is episodic and there is little attempt at creativity. In Arthur Laycock's *Steve, the Outlander* (1900), the hero is wounded, goes to hospital and there meets the girl who has betrayed him, who now suffers remorse and hopes to do penance. *The Despatch Rider* (1901) is merely a convenient peg on which to hang a description of the Siege of Ladysmith. The author, Ernest Glanville, like his contemporary writers, shows little sign that the conditions and the ingredients for the rise of the novel in England had affected his self-consciousness about his own attempts. Glanville is one of the most prolific writers of the time. Between 1888 and 1927 he wrote some twenty novels, all under the imprint of reputable English publishing houses such as Methuen, Chatto, Constable, and Cape. Someone ought to assess the critical reception of these novels in England at the time. To what extent were novels of the period instrumental in influencing views about Southern Africa? What impressions are conjured up in the mind by titles like these, all by Glanville—*Among the Kaffirs*; *The Lost Heiress*; *A Fair Colonist*; *The Commandant*; *The Diamond Seekers*; *A Beautiful Rebel*? Or by titles such as *The Gun Runner*; *A Romance of the Cape Frontier*; *The King's Assegai*; *A Veldt Official*; *A Secret of the Lebombo*; *A Border Scourge*; to name only a few at random taken from some forty-five works written by Bertram Mitford between 1894 and 1913?

The point about the importance of the critical reception can be illustrated by the case of *The Dop Doctor*, published in 1909 by Clothilde Graves under the pseudonym Richard Dehan. Benefiting from favourable reviews engendered partly by its own qualities and partly by the context of the imminent grant of dominion status to the Union of South Africa, the novel ran to twenty editions and impressions in five years. In its portrayal of the Siege of Mafeking the author tries to reveal the horrors of war and the reactions of ordinary people under emotional and military stress. Some reviewers even tried to compare the author with Balzac, although some years later Francis Brett Young was perhaps closer to a more objective comment when he described it as '. . . a crude, violently sentimental narrative of a woman who called herself Richard Dehan . . .'[4]

Two general points seem in order at this stage. Firstly, the novels are invariably disappointing. The charge of emotionalism and sentimentalism levelled by Brett Young can be applied generally, but it must be added that a minor theme of all these works is a crude jingo-feeling. I am prepared to concede that works written in close proximity to a conflict as vicious as the one between Boer and Briton could not be expected to be dispassionate. Yet, and this is the second point, it is noteworthy that no great saga about this war has yet been written, particularly since to this day, the effects of the war still loom large in the relationship between the two white groups.

It is only with Olive Schreiner (1855–1920) and, to a lesser extent, with Pauline Smith (1883–1959), that the novel takes creative root: so firmly, in fact, that the root gave rise to most of the dominant themes and strains which have exercised creative writers to this very day.

The tradition which begins with Olive Schreiner I shall call 'liberal-concerned'. Its chief characteristics appear to be marked creative sensibility allied to and informed by a deep compassion. Spanning the past century, it cuts across colour lines and class origins and coincides in literary terms with that period in political development when white rule consolidates itself, but where some members of the dominant group as well as writers from the dominated group articulate demands for the amelioration of discriminatory practices. Although they reveal a rich variegation of positions, the writers of this early post-Schreiner period would seem to subscribe to a shared set of values, notably the notion of 'equality before the law' (although the actions of the policy were calculated to keep the dispossessed in subjugation by means of the twin forces of colonial rule and 'baasskap' or overlordship). The definitive statement is, I think, the one made by the magistrate in Laurens van der Post's *In a Province* (1934), who observes that he is not trying to defend the utility of custom, since:

. . . it's useless, and because it's useless, it's cruel. But what worries me is, can we, humanly speaking, call that murder? You see, I myself haven't much faith in an abstract conception of justice. It seems to me that between the psychological habits of people, and their conception of justice there is, or should be, a very close bond. We wouldn't, with a mediaeval mentality, be able to tolerate twentieth-century justice; if we were able to, we would abuse it: and it would, of course, be worse than the other way round. Yet that's precisely what we are trying to inflict on these people. In their case it's doubly cruel, because we won't allow the black people to enter into the system of living for which our justice was obviously devised. By refusing to do so we imply that they are psychologically and racially in a different class. Yet we proceed very illogically to inflict our system on them as if they were like ourselves. I wouldn't hesitate for a moment to punish them. But you see, I feel that indirectly we have a terrible responsibil-

ity in cases like these. We forbid them the sort of life their law
demands, and give them our law without the sort of life that our law
demands.[5]

Between the end of the Second World War and the end of the sixties,
as the present government entrenched itself and as the struggle for
equality and emancipation took on an increasingly extra-parliamentary
nature, writers tended towards a literary denunciation of apartheid,
while yet hoping to influence the nature and pace of political change. It
is the view perhaps best expounded by Alan Paton in *Cry, the Beloved
Country* (1948) and *Too Late, the Phalarope* (1953), and by Jack Cope
in, among others, *The Golden Oriole* (1958), *The Road to Ysterberg*
(1959), *The Rainmaker (1971)* and *The Student of Zend* (1972).
Perhaps the most striking feature of these novels is the recurrent
themes—often almost indistinguishable from clichés—of which some
of the more obvious are that: all Afrikaners are baddies; all blacks are
goodies—unless they are politicians, in which case they are corrupt; all
priests are goodies, although white priests and Anglican priests in
particular, are better goodies than black priests; all black creative
artists are potential genius material; the 'problem' (that is, apartheid)
is capable of simple solution if we all decide to be nice to each other in
our personal relationships—a sort of South African 'only connect';
industrialisation has destroyed the self-contained albeit quaint and
picturesque life of the blacks, who, in their 'natural state' have a 'heart
of white'.
'Liberal-concerned' writers feel that they have a role to play in the
attempted political solution. Hence they argue in favour of gradualism,
fear revolution, and are terrified of the possibility of majority rule. They
demand 'assurances' that 'civilised standards' will be 'respected',
meaning by such demands that the artificial imposition of alien grafts
be continued—at a time when these very grafts are being undermined
in their countries of origin. Critically, the South African cultural critics
arrive at their conclusions because they live in a society that offers them
all the privileges that a white skin confers, while at the same time
insulating them against the disabilities that a black skin imposes. But it
is also this position of privilege which isolates them, rather than any
myth that 'whites cannot portray black people'. They may choose to
mix—and the choice is theirs—with their black cultural counterparts
at a party or a discussion in those comparatively balmy days between
the forties and sixties, but they will deny that this mixing is not, in fact,
between equals.
It is my impression that one of the reasons for the development of the

notion of black consciousness stems not only from the desire to assert an identity, but precisely to reject this cultural gesturing on the part of the diminishing band of white liberals. Perhaps the sharpest focus on the dilemma these writers create for themselves can be seen when white writers judge the work of their black counterparts. Essentially their response comes down to a formula: how interesting (charming, quaint, competent, fascinating) in view of his colour and therefore his lack of opportunities. And the yardstick for the choice of adjective is the degree of 'bitterness' displayed by the black writer. Should the black writer be too 'radical' for the sensibilities of his critic, then the critic falls back on the view that 'politics and literature should not mix', but really meaning that that particular kind of politics should not be brought into literature. Instead of interpreting, let me quote the first editorial of the magazine which is effectively the mouthpiece of this view. I refer to the quarterly, *Contrast*, then edited by Jack Cope and having on its Editorial Board and amongst its Advisory Editors virtually the cream of the white South African literary establishment—Alan Paton, Nadine Gordimer, Dan Jacobson, Uys Krige, Guy Butler, W. H. Gardner. 'In a policy-ridden country . . .', the Editorial stated, '. . . here in the first place is a magazine with no policy. Its aims may be difficult just because they are so simple—to keep out of the rough and tumble of parties and groups and yet to cross all borders and to hold a balance even between conflicting opinions'.[6]

It is salutary to compare the views of the *Contrast* editorial with that of the Johannesburg *The Classic*, which was originally edited by the late Nat Nakasa, and which stated in its first editorial that it was as '. . . non-political as the life of a domestic servant, the life of a Dutch Reformed Church predikant or that of an opulent Johannesburg business man. If the daily lives of these people are not regulated by political decisions, that will be reflected in *The Classic*. If however, the work they do, if their sexual lives and their search for God are governed by political decrees, then that will also be reflected in the material published in *The Classic*. After all, these stories and poems and drawings and sculpture will be about the lives of these people.'[7]

The response of *Contrast* typifies the general point I have been trying to make. In an editorial, 'Taking Stock with The Classic', the *Contrast* editor observed that '. . . this may be good sociology, but is it good literary criticism?' In another editorial, under the heading 'The Liberal Conscience', the following appears:

Politics at any level are compounded of dense irrational impulses ultimately beyond analysis. Out of the web can be picked a single strand, an effect of liberalism on the art of the writer. Guilt is held to originate from infantile fears. As such it is a natural and normal attribute of the human psyche and without the process of guilt, remorse and expiation our society would degenerate to the jungle. Guilt felt by the English-speaking liberal writer in terms of the South African scene arises from intense and probably unrealised anxieties. We wronged the Boer-Afrikaner and therefore we deserved to be punished. At the same time we affront his language and denigrate his cultural status and so justify our own loss of dignity as part of a nerveless minority. Towards the black man the liberal guilt is an expression of a deeper complex of anxieties—fear of darkness equated with sin; fear of the defeat of our sexual potency implied in our surrender as a politically impotent group; fear of death and destruction as the punishment earned by our own injustice and those of our forebears towards the black and coloured races. Now, particularly, the continued enjoyment of ease and privilege based on a moral injustice throw burning coals on the conscience. Dissociation is impossible except in momentary acts of expiation or in physical flight . . . The prayer of the South African writer to his or her Muse should be in the first place for a vision penetrating beyond the silhouettes to the man and woman of reality, a sensuous identity with this world and people. He may then beg for time and inner stillness to perfect his craft, to weigh every word and syllable and pause so that their effect is to strike like iron to the readers' heart; to strive for style which our work lacks, and hold not to the forces of truth only but to its mood and inward spirit.[8]

From this statement of the creed of the 'liberal conscience' we can deduce at least three central features. The first is the rejection of involvement with the political because of the purported irrationality of politics. The argument here would seem to be perverse. One would have thought that the contemporary writer's interest in the irrational would have been a sufficient professional inducement to attempt to elucidate the nature of South African political reality. The second feature relates to the sub-Freudian musings. I am not competent to comment on the validity of the assertion that guilt originates in infantile fears—but even if it does, it would seem to have little relevance for our concern. The issue is not one of guilt, but one of power relationships. Thirdly, there is the question of the 'prayer', which amounts to no more than the well-known liberal South African solution: continued enjoyment of the physical benefits of the country while trying to keep alive the remnants of a European (hence, in the context essentially inappropriate) solution to the critical and creative problem. One prefers the old-fashioned conservatism of Van der Post's comments earlier on to this more 'sophisticated' capitulation.

Alex la Guma expressed a clear alternative for the writer. He observed, at the African-Scandinavian Writers' Conference, in response to a comment by Wole Soyinka that '. . . when it comes to the position of writers in South Africa, we find that we are in the same position as any ordinary person. The South African artist finds himself with no other choice but to dedicate himself to that movement which must involve not only himself but ordinary people as well.'⁹

What, one may ask, happened to the vision of Olive Schreiner, who had written that:

> . . . there is a subtle and very real bond which unites all South
> Africans, and differentiates us from all other people in the world.
> *This bond is our mixture of races itself.* It is this which divides South
> Africans from all other peoples in the world, and makes us one . . .
> Wherever a Dutchman, an Englishman, a Jew and a native are
> superimposed, there is that common South African condition
> through which no dividing line can be drawn. The only form of
> organization which can be healthily and naturally assumed by us is
> one which takes cognizance of this universal condition . . . Difficult
> as it may be, it is at once simpler and easier than the consolidation of
> any separate part. It is the one form of crystallization open to us, the
> one shape we shall assume . . . if the South Africa of the future is to
> remain eaten internally by race hatreds, a film of culture and
> intelligence spread over seething masses of ignorance and brutality,
> inter-support and union being wholly lacking, then, though it may
> be our misfortune rather than our fault, our doom is sealed; our place
> shall be wanting among the great, free nations of earth.¹⁰

It is this affirmation in Schreiner, and its absence in Alan Paton, that constitutes one of the major differences between the two writers. Whatever his political and public pronouncements, Paton's novels are 'romantic'; in them he articulates the view that it is still possible to offer the blacks a 'square deal' by way of a magnanimous change of heart.

Martin Staniland characterised the Paton position as an 'appear-ance-reality dichotomy' where 'the traditional though partial solution to this problem in South Africa has been to deny its necessity, to regard the African as a temporary inhabitant of the city. The real life of the African is said to be in the Reserves, the real life of the white in the towns; thus the philosophical problem is dispersed rather than resolved.' Staniland observed that *Cry, the Beloved Country* is important in two respects:

> first, because it represents the climax of his tradition in which revulsion and nostalgia mingle; second, because whatever crudity of its characterization . . . it attracted a hearing for the South African novelist which was not necessarily attentive to writers of Paton's views . . . it is a powerful statement of one position, but to generate this force a certain amount of cheating takes place. Why does the one African politician have to be presented as corrupt? Why are only Anglicans seen to be decent? And why do all black Africans have to appear passive, leaving the limelight of philanthropy to their white superiors.[11]

One could reply, cynically, to Staniland, that if there were no passive blacks like Msimangu whose text is, 'It is the law, mother; we must uphold the law', there would be no white philanthropists like Arthur Jarvis. Paton's next novel, *Too Late, the Phalarope* (1953), is based on a similar kind of cheating. Peter van Vlaanderen is portrayed as a young Greek god, endowed with all the virtues associated with that stature—as well as with the associated fatal flaw essential as to his downfall. Van Vlaanderen's fatal flaw is lust. Not lust *per se*, but lust for a black woman. In other words, what would merely under most circumstances be construed as a biological urge, becomes, in the context of South Africa, transformed into cosmic importance. The hero talks of the prohibition of such acts across the colour line as 'the greatest and holiest of laws'. And let us be clear about the law that he is talking about. It is not the Act of the South African parliament which prohibits 'immorality' (sex between members of different racial groups) but something which he sees as an immutable spirit of the law as articulated by the white South African tribal mythmakers. In addition, Van Vlaanderen is not shocked by the fact of his lust; it is the *object* thereof, the black out-of-work servant, that horrifies him. In the end he is discovered and has to atone, but it is still a confidence trick, which cannot be invested with national or cultural significance. Even Paton realises this when he makes the police captain observe: 'I know of an offence against the law, and, as a Christian, of an offence against

God; but I do not know of an offence against the race'.

This obsession with inter-racial sex, and its reputed consequences, was first made fashionable by Sarah Gertrude Millin in *God's Stepchildren* (1924). Her Rev Andrew Flood arrives in South Africa in the 1820s to bring the benefits of western, Christian civilisation to the tribesmen. But Flood soon comes to the, for him, horrible realisation that these tribesmen were not as naïve and ignorant as he had expected. Not only do they possess totems equivalent to the one he is trying to hawk, but they actually mock him and consider his product an inferior version for their needs. So in order to sell his product, Flood 'goes native' and as a supreme token of his sincerity marries a local woman. The drift of the novelist's argument is important. Its underlying assumption seems to be that black South Africans should of necessity want what their white counterparts have, because the product of the latter is somehow better. In other words, the onus is placed on the blacks to alter. Yet, paradoxically, blacks are discriminated against because, it is claimed that they are racially incapable of making that change. Refer here to Van der Post's magistrate, to Paton's Msimangu, to the conflict between the 'blood-brothers' Tom Erskine and Kolombe Pela in Cope's *The Fair House* and even to that between the mine *induna* Xuma and his mine-boss, Paddy in Peter Abrahams' *Mine Boy* (1946).

Then there is the question of sin. Flood did not sin in a theological sense, nor even in a legal sense. He married the Hottentot woman in proper Christian union. His sin is seen as being against the white race. And so the rest of the novel encompasses four generations of Flood descendants to prove that what started off as a merely unconventional act becomes transformed into a mortal sin which has to be expiated. And how is this done? Barry Lindsell, Flood's great-great-grandson, wants to commit suicide—not because his skin colour denies him the 'benefits' of white South Africa, but because he wants to atone for the sin that Flood and his descendants committed against the white races!

This obsession with 'sex across the colour bar', as it is so quaintly referred to in South Africa, remains one of the dominant themes in the novel. To demonstrate the 'health' of the theme, as well as its context, I need refer only to John Coetzee's second novel, *In the Heart of the Country*,[12] where the white sheep farmer (inevitably!) seduces the wife of his black foreman in order to assuage the loneliness and pain of his wife's death. Driven mad by this act, his daughter retaliates by killing her father and inviting the foreman and his wife to share the farm house with her. Before the new tenants are inevitably forced out of their new abode, the foreman completes the circle by (again, inevitably!) raping the daughter. And of all this—delectable of ironies!—in the developing conventions of the post-modernist novel.

One has, it seems, to try to account for this continuing interest. Is the novelist's concern with inter-racial sex not disproportionate when one considers all the other alternatives which might fruitfully benefit from imaginative investigation? It seems to me that it is only in the case of Mrs Millin that the author's objectives are clear: she wants to show the inescapable effects of inter-racial sex, not only for the individual, but for society as a whole. And these effects are, in her view, uniformly debasing, a threat to the very fabric of the civilisation whose values she espouses. To that extent Mrs Millin occupies a unique place among the ranks of writers in English in that she makes racism a respectable topic in the novel.

I am less certain about some of the other novelists but I wonder if, for instance in Coetzee's novel, cited above, anything fundamental would have been lost if the dimension of inter-racial sex had been excluded. There appears to be a great need for a sense of balance, and once again one returns to William Plomer's *Turbott Wolfe*[13] which was first published in 1925, and was reissued only in 1965, with a long introduction by the author's lifelong friend Laurens van der Post. Since the novel is discussed elsewhere in this book, I simply draw attention to the question of race and sex as Plomer sees it. Wolfe comes to Africa neither to preach or convert, nor to escape; he is not shackled with either moral guilt or intellectual arrogance. Plomer can therefore make his hero perform the unforgivable task—that of measuring the white man against Africa, instead of the other way round. Thus, when Wolfe falls in love with the black girl, he sees this development as neither a cosmic nor a racial sin—he was merely '. . . afraid of falling in love with her'. Which would seem to be a perfectly adequate description for an eminently normal relationship!

But what is a normal relationship in South Africa? How is individual behaviour affected by the codes of the dominant groups? Is it possible for the individual to behave decently? Ultimately, can one deduce from the choices made by individuals any universal or generalising significance? The two novelists who have, in their separate ways explored these issues most effectively are Nadine Gordimer and Dan Jacobson. Since Miss Gordimer's work is discussed in greater detail later, I shall restrict my comments here to Dan Jacobson's novels in which there is a South African dimension.

In his first novel, *The Trap* (1955), Jacobson deals with a single episode. A white butcher of Scottish origin and a black farmworker join forces to steal sheep from an Afrikaner farmer. When the conspiracy is about to be discovered, the white man decides to become a police informer. Thus, while the police deal with the black man, the white man not only goes free but assists the sheep farmer in a brutal assault on the black man, while the police stand by.

Perhaps the most important point about *The Trap* is the author's stance. Since incidents of the kind outlined above are fairly normal, he seems to be saying they really are the equivalent of (say) a street brawl observed from the safety of a passing bus. But equally, therein lies the problem: by dismissing the incident as 'normal', South Africans recognise the measure of their acceptance of certain codes. White South Africans, like the farmer Van Schoor, want to know the truth of what goes on on his farm. But to acquire that truth will destroy his relative innocence, murder his peace and shatter his beliefs. Similarly, the temporary help, the black man Setole, rejects those aspects of the white man's world which are useless to him: if the society organises itself in such a way that Setole cannot use his knowledge except to minister to the white man's needs, then he, Setole, would rather not use it at all. Negative it may be; but the rebellion is militant and radical. Finally there is McLachlan, who persuades himself that he is guilty of betraying the white race by enlisting the help of the black man Willem—and that he can atone for this 'crime' by betraying his partner. Jacobson portrays two central issues—the way Willem is betrayed because of his colour, and the way McLachlan is an alien to both Boer and Bantu—rather well.

These issues occur again in the next novel, *A Dance in the Sun* (1956).[14] Once again the novel focuses upon a single episode. Two 'liberal' student hitch-hikers find themselves in the village of Mirredal (vale of myrrh!). Because the hotel is full, they take refuge in the guest house of the Fletchers, which becomes the base not merely for the surface events but for the symbolic conflict between the largeness of the narrator's ideals and aspirations and the narrowness of the world. As the narrator observes:

Growth here in Mirredal was a bitter and constricted business. The only thing that was not constricted was the sky and the space of earth. There was an immensity of space above my head, and the night gathering above could not hide the great sweep of earth away from my little summit, a lavish generosity of space given unconditionally to drought and silence. (p. 35)

Jacobson here encapsulates some of the major parodoxes of living in South Africa. First of all, the narrator knows and admits that he knows. Despite the admission of constriction, there is the admission that there are wider possibilities. But how to reach out to these when we can so casually be routed out of one's way to end up in Mirredal? And is this what three centuries of civilising have produced? Hence, when the African Joseph appears out of the inevitable Karroo storm, it is impossible for the students to establish any real human relationships with him. Then there is Fletcher who, like McLachlan in *The Trap*, becomes detribalised. Indeed, he goes further—he marries an Afrikaner woman as an earnest of his deep desire to become one. But he can never be one, because to be an Afrikaner is to belong to a cultural group as well as to a racial category. Only Nasie Louw (and I suspect that in this highly symbolic novel the pun on Nasie [Nation] is intentional) in all his perversity can begin to relate to the blacks. But Nasie is a fractured being. He is the father of Joseph's sister's child (his sole act of assertion of individuality) but he cannot bring himself to recognise a black person as his equal.

Finally, in this novel, there is the manner in which the author exposes the emptiness of the South African variety of liberalism when the narrator and his friend make it clear that they will not accept Joseph's offer of payment for the information he needs—simply because they will not accept money from a 'kaffir'. Their liberalism is, in the end, little different from Fletcher's open racialism. The only one who triumphs is Joseph, because he manages to force Fletcher to reengage him. A small triumph, but then, in its context, a not unimportant one.

The most important of Jacobson's works for our purposes is, in many ways, his fourth, *The Evidence of Love*.[15] At a superficial level it is Jacobson's contribution to the exploration of the theme of inter-racial sex. But to characterise it thus would be to reify it quite unforgivably. It is at one and the same time much more complex, thematically and artistically, than his previous novels, and his most searching investigation into the conflicts between the demands of freedom and the obstacles of convention and of obsolete customs. Simply stated, it is the story of Kenneth Makeer, a coloured (mixed-race) boy who escapes the drudgery of apprenticeship as a bricklayer to his humble father because of the friendship of Miss Bentwisch, a heiress to a diamond fortune. She pays for him to go to England to study law. Miss Bentwisch is also the link to Isabel Last, a young 'liberal' (South African variety) whose father had come from England and who now, as a 'self-made' man, could offer advice to Kenneth and his father to accept their position in the scheme of things. But both Mr Last and Miss Bentwisch are disappointed when Isabel rebels against their teachings by going to England instead of marrying one Martin Bullevant. Later, when Miss Bentwisch dies, Kenneth has an identity crisis in London. He seeks out Isabel, finds and rescues her from the language school where she works as a secretary (and from the thinly disguised advances of the proprietor!). They fall in love, but Kenneth conceals from Isabel the vital bit of information that, in the context of the South African way of life, he is not white. Bullevant finds out, goes to London to rescue Isabel, but her return to Lyndhurst (Jacobson's Kimberley) is not a great success because some time after her return she encounters Kenneth's darker brother Peter. This triggers anew her love for Kenneth which scandalises her father to such an extent that he enables her to return to England to marry Kenneth. So far, so good, but then we are faced with one of the oddest conclusions to a South African novel. Jacobson makes his married couple return to South Africa after a few years, only to be arrested for contravention of the Immorality Act, which forbids miscegenation. They are tried, found guilty, and given short jail sentences each. Mr Last promises Mr Makeer that he will pay his trip to England to visit Kenneth and Isabel when they return there after their release.

Despite its faults (particularly those of the ending, and of the portrayal of the character of Kenneth), the novel does highlight some important issues: firstly, that in the peculiar context of South Africa it is not only Kenneth, but also Isabel, who needs to struggle for freedom. Secondly, that the question of individual freedom is tied very closely to the notion of self-identity; thirdly, that Isabel and Kenneth can achieve individual identities only by the recognition that they complement each other, are incomplete the one without the other, but that the very nature of the South African experience forces upon the individual a choice which makes it impossible to live in South Africa and to be free at the same time.

This realisation by Jacobson throws into sharp relief a central concern, which, for the moment, can be formulated as follows: if you are white, is living in South Africa compatible with notions of freedom? Since white privilege is dependent upon black dispossession, to what extent can white South Africans think themselves as being free? Or is the notion of whites being entrapped in their privilege, corrupted by their superiority, merely sophistic? The evidence of one's senses would seem to suggest that the question is irrelevant. The majority of white South Africans seemingly do not feel that they are not free. In addition, they strenuously deny the charge that they oppress their black compatriots. And, superficially again, one would suppose that the overwhelming majority of blacks, given their present conditions, would happily settle for the ways of white folks. Because, for blacks the formulation of the problem is essentially and qualitatively different. They are aware of their oppression, and their efforts are concentrated upon two related objectives: firstly, how to maintain personal dignity, integrity, in the face of the white society's restrictions; secondly, how to achieve freedom—a form of political association that will enable people to be free to be themselves, irrespective of the rather weary categories of race or colour. Since the work of one of the pioneers of this issue, Solomon T. Plaatje's *Mhudi*, is considered elsewhere in this volume, I want to pass to a novel by Peter Abrahams which exemplifies some of these complexities. *Wild Conquest*[16] is an endeavour to explain the origins, course, and nature of black-white conflict on the subcontinent. The Boers are portrayed as the representatives of white attitudes, while the Matabele are characterised as embodying the aspirations of the blacks.

Abrahams begins by describing the effect upon a Boer family, the Jansens, of the news of the abolition of slavery. Refusing to submit to such an unacceptable restriction upon their way of life, imposed by an alien government, the Jansens link with other farmers to flee the Cape Colony in search of 'freedom'. After a middle section in which he describes the life of the Matabele nation before the arrival of the Trekkers, Abrahams devotes the final part of the novel to an investigation of the collision between Boer and Matabele, and its outcome.

The differences between *Mhudi* and *Wild Conquest* are quite stark. I suspect that this may be traced to their different social standpoints. Where Plaatje immersed himself in the political life of his country, saw his writing as an adjunct to the political process, Abrahams would seem to be primarily concerned with his position as a novelist, with the notion of the freedom of the artist. And having left South Africa as a ship's stoker around 1939, arriving in England in 1941, it must be said that he escaped living through the particularly sophisticated forms and degrees of oppression of the past thirty-odd years.

My case is not that understanding is dependent upon lived experience, but simply the registration of the absence of this dimension in Abrahams—at a time when both oppressors and oppressed reformulate their objectives and methods of struggle in the aftermath of the end of the Second World War and of the coming to power in South

Africa of the Nationalist Party. Abrahams had codified his standpoint in the revealing report, *Return to Goli*,[17] published the year after *Wild Conquest*. 'For years', he stated, 'I have found the burden of oppression by both (white and black) wearisome and stifling. Now I would be rid of it. As a writer, my work demands this liberation if I am to see more clearly, to understand more wholly. As a human being it would add a completely new dimension of both pain and joy to the business of living.'[18] One is drawn to the reluctant but inevitable conclusion that Abrahams here is little different from other foreign journalists sent to South Africa. He can forget that he is:

> . . . in a small house in Orlando with no electricity and with the awful bucket lavatory system . . . [because] . . . talk ranged far and wide: books, science, education, philosophy, the whole wide range. We might have been a group of young men of any nationality, anywhere in any of the cultural capitals of the world . . . The rather naïve touches that my friends had shown earlier fell away. They became civilised, sophisticated, and shrewdly urbane. Each had his own views on the subjects under discussion and argued for them as civilised men do throughout the world.[19]

Remarkable, the blinding revelation. Despite his blackness, the author's recollection of the impress of discrimination is as naïve as his creation, Kasper Jansen, who '. . . wondered what they (the slaves) thought, and as he wondered, a great realisation shook him. He had never thought of them as people with thoughts and feelings. Never wondered what went on under those dark brows. What had they been thinking all this time?'[20] Abrahams, the black novelist, would seem to be as full of conventional attitudinising as Jansen, his white creation, and as (not too paradoxically) other people who make the case for putting 'both sides of the argument'. And so he proceeds to encapsulate what he tried to do in *Wild Conquest*—to tell:

> . . . the story of the Afrikaans-speaking whites [which] began as one of the most heroic quests for freedom of modern times. These people so loved freedom that their journey in search of it—the Great Trek—is the outstanding epic of heroic enterprise and high endeavour in modern South African history. . . . Whatever else might be said of that epic journey, it was an undoubted testimony of a people's love of freedom.[21]

One cannot refrain from observing that Abrahams here is simply wrongheaded. There is no logically justifiable way in which a people who flee in order to continue their desire to enslave others because of colour can be said to be in quest of freedom. And rather than being an event of epic proportions, it was (even by African rather than by world yardsticks) a relatively modest affair compared to (say) the Mfecane. Instead of being lovers of freedom, it was the unmitigated desire to impose their own impress upon the original inhabitants that motivated the Trekkers. Their attitudes to indigenous peoples are made clear not only in the fictional portrayal of the Trekboer Sarel Siljay in *Mhudi*, but indeed in the legal and constitutional provisions of the ethnocentric Republics the Trekkers established in the lands they had wrested from the Bantu by force of superior arms. And Abrahams is not ignorant of these facts. One of the main strands he explores in *Wild Conquest* is how the Jansen family are typical Boers — and how they are driven by the desire to destroy. Indeed, he sees their intervention as paradoxically beneficial in that they destroy the might of the bloodthirsty Matabele. The western liberal 'humanist' is here at odds with the proletarian and early socialist in him. The desire to demonstrate, by the elaborate balancing of white characters with black characters, that underneath their skins people are the same, is otiose. The writ of liberal humanism does not operate in the context of South Africa. The remarks by the Matabele general, Gubuza, towards the end of the novel, indicate the extent to which the author romanticises reality:

> For myself, I have often thought and wondered about the coming of these people. Sometimes I thought their coming might bring new wisdom that would put an end to our fighting. I thought that they might come in peace. If they had come thus, I, Gubuza, would have gone to them and said, 'Wise men from the seas! I come to sit at your feet that I might learn wisdom'. I would have gone to them and said that! But they came in the name of war! They came speaking the old language of blood and wrath, the old language of war. Oh, where are my hopes! They came with new ways and new weapons but no new wisdom![22]

The sentiments are trite, as contrived as the coincidence which enables Gubuza and his white alter ego, Paul, to die side-by-side.

My purpose is not to deny the existence of such sentiments as those placed in the mouth of Gubuza, but precisely the opposite: to draw attention to the persistence of the notion of the white man as missionary and mentor, of the black man as a suitable case for instruction, and (if need be, chastisement). Mrs Millin had noted it with approbation; Van der Post had expressed a sharp-edged ambivalence. In more recent times, Paton in *Cry, the Beloved Country* and Jack Cope in *The Fair House* would attempt their own 'sophisticated' version: it was preferable to receive the British rather than the Boer hand of friendship. And all this rests upon the validity of the view that blacks would actually wish to avail themselves of this new 'wisdom'. There is a strong sense that Abrahams not only misrepresents his Boer and his Bantu, but in that order to be fair to the former, he patronises the latter. Abrahams does not seem prepared—in the novel, at any rate—to recognise that what is of overriding importance is the power relationship: how those in power can continue to maintain their position; how those without power can evolve strategies for the acquisition of power. The novels which deal with this new theme have at least three important general similarities: firstly their focus shifts from a concern with the individual to a concern with large groups. Even when the novelist concentrates upon a simple individual or a small number, they are seen much more sharply as having identities only because this derives from the group; secondly, these words generally date from the early sixties. In other words, they coincide with and attempt to describe some of the consequences of the adoption by the liberation movements of increasingly non-violent forms of political struggle; thirdly, they portray the nature and extent of the state's response. They vividly show that a choice between *verligte* or enlightened (a choice example of how a word can become a casualty in the context of South Africa) and *verkrampte* or bigoted is no more than a debate about methods for the modernisation of oppression.

An early version of this new concern was Harry Bloom's novel, which has appeared under various titles: *Episode*; *Transvaal Episode*; *Episode in the Transvaal*, being some of them. It is based to a considerable extent upon the author's experience as a defence counsel in the Defiance Campaign of 1952, when blacks agitated peacefully for the repeal of unjust laws. It is, superficially, the story of how a 'riot' occurs and is dealt with by the police. The spark for the 'riot' is an old washerwoman who is accused by one of her white clients of being a collar short in the wash. When payment is refused, the washerwoman tears the clothes to shreds and dumps these into the river. When the police try to arrest her, she assaults the sergeant in a most painful place, is herself set upon by his assistants, and so sets off the inevitable chain of events which leads to the destruction of a 'model location'.

This notion of the 'model location' is important. White town and black township live as part of, but apart from, each other. Like Siamese twins, they cannot escape each other. Like captor and captive, their relationship is one of unresolved love-hate. As the author observes, for the white town to talk of its black counterpart as a 'location' is '. . . itself a significantly unique use of the word, for it denotes not a place where people live, but where something is found'. (p. 13) And the 'something' to be found consists of people: people who minister to the needs of the white town; people totally at the mercy of the location superintendent, whose official position—indeed, his power, rests upon a neat irony: as the representative of the might of the white state, it is his task to administer *apartheid*. But, in order to do so, he finds himself surrounded by and in close contact with precisely the people he is enjoined to keep at a distance. In addition, as a great believer in the benefits of the system of *apartheid*, he busies himself with social welfare schemes and other reforms to 'improve' the lot of the township's inhabitants. He is dumbstruck, later, when he finds out that they consider him to be a tyrant. And one way the township people used to overcome the tyranny was to mock it. No-one could do this better than Andries Gwebu, Bachelor of Arts, official interpreter, and the bane of the Superintendent's life. The relationship between the two, the Superintendent Du Toit and the interpreter Gwebu, encapsulates vividly both the political and personal dimensions of living in South Africa. To illustrate the former: the Superintendent had promulgated a new rule to forbid climbing through the fence which encircled the location. The best way of communicating this new rule was to announce it at a meeting. When he spoke, his

> . . . short announcement was translated sentence by sentence by Gwebu. But Gwebu took wings. He made a piece of soaring oratory out of Du Toit's dull officialness. He brought the language of bye-laws to life with images and metaphors. He spoke with gestures. pauses, looks, silences, and thunder. When Du Toit spoke of the danger of climbing through the fence near the railway line, Gwebu pictured it in terms of maimed children and decapitated cattle. When he warned that the pass laws would be strictly enforced, Gwebu painted a picture of a serene smiling community all happily free from the worry of arrests, and on wonderful terms with the police because they were properly documented. As with everything he said, there was a dual meaning, two images imperfectly superimposed, leaving a shadowy outline of doubt. Darting between the legs of the hyperbole was a lively midget of sarcasm, running ahead, falling back,

waiting, overtaking. When he spoke, it was always doubtful what he himself believed. (pp. 73–4)

And so, inevitably, Du Toit is trapped:

He hated Gwebu ... what started as a need for advice to avoid mistakes became a bickering, uncomfortable, involved, but indissoluble relationship. The antagonism between them was never stronger than the forces that held them together. (p. 74)

But vitality, exuberance, irreverence even, in the face of apartheid is not enough. Gwebu can only supply a momentary antidote to a deep-seated disease that needs a new kind of radical treatment. And this arrives in the form of the motor mechanic, Walter Mabaso. Soon

... the conception of a new type of leader found its way into people's minds. Mabaso did not claim leadership, nor did anyone claim it on his behalf. But there was something about the way he worked that gave people the idea of him. There was sympathy, a respect for the work of the location people, a refusal to blame, censure, or patronise, and most of all, a bold new way of speaking about the location's grievances ... After the ferment of the night, after the strange experience, people turned to Mabaso with his appeal for planning, loyalty, patience, and work, and the promise only of slow, far-off rewards. It seemed as if the location came of age that night ... (p. 138)

This new maturity is soon put to the test. When the Superintendent announces that all women should carry passes, they refuse. This loss of authority and of personal humiliation (the Superintendent is forced to flee the wrath of his questioners at the meeting at which the new regulation is announced) becomes the signal for the white town's vengeance. The Superintendent's technique of subjugation by confidence-trick is supplanted by Lieutenant Swanepoel's method of naked violence. This the location-dwellers accept as the inevitable price they have to pay for destroying the hitherto-existing relationship between itself and the town. The most important price they pay is Mabaso's death. It appeared

... that a little way outside Nelstroom the van had a breakdown and it was necessary to open the door to get the tools. Mabaso, it seemed, jumped out and tried to escape. That was how he came to be shot a number of times in the back. Or so they said. (p. 329)

But to have a scapegoat was not enough. The town also required proof that its belief in the notion of white infallibility was still valid. This it obtained by its acceptance of the police story of the attack on the superintendent. That is why, after the event, for the Superintendent of the town

> . . . looked the same as usual, as if nothing at all had happened. He saw some neighbours watering their gardens, housewives shaking carpets out over the sides of their stoeps: people were walking in the street carrying briefcases and parcels, cars sped by on their way through to the bushveld: there was an ox-wagon laden with peaches creaking slowly past the front of the house: some children playing about on bicycles. The town had put on a great big air of innocence. (pp. 333–4)

But, in the end, neither guile nor force will sustain false innocence. Mabaso's significance for the location is not his death, but the example of how a political man inspires others to acts of heroism.

The novelist who seems to show this process at work with considerable skill is Alex la Guma. All his novels appear to deal with the problem of how people with limited choices (Michael Adonis, Joe in *A Walk in the Night*,[23] Ma Pauls in *And a Threefold Cord*[24] are good examples) continue to display a considerable range of human responses despite the massive efforts to brutalise them. How to live 'normal' lives on a minimal scale becomes a question of power-relationships and of moral behaviour in active operation. La Guma had tried to deal with the matter in *The Stone Country*,[25] which is, superficially, the story of a fight to the death between two inmates of a prison. Into this world of the Casbah Kid (who is to hang), of Josef, of the Turk and Butcherboy, the collector of tribute (sworn enemies to each other), of Solly the habitual offender, comes George, the political 'criminal'. Just as Mabaso in *Episode* acts as the spur in the location-dwellers' self-recognition, so George, because of his political awareness, brings a touch of humanity to this prison, whose façade

> . . . had been brightened with lawns and flowerbeds; the grim work of an executioner hidden behind a holiday mask. The brasswork in the castellated main door was polished to perfection, and the flagged pathway up to it kept spotless, as if at any moment it would receive some dignitary or other. It waited like a diseased harlot, disguised in finery, to embrace an unsuspecting visitor.[26]

The writing here is raw, the symbolism obvious, but the point comes across with considerable force: white South Africa is both a prison that brutalises and a whore which infects the unsuspecting. How to break the hold of these twin symbols is the basis for La Guma's most recent work, *In the Fog of the Seasons' End*.[27] It is the story of three men (two 'coloured' or mixed-blood and one black) who continue to work for a banned political organisation, despite the enormous risk and dangers. But this story of Elias Tekwane, who is tortured to death by the Security police; of Beukes who escapes with a bullet wound in the arm, and of Isaac who crosses to freedom in a neighbouring state, is primarily the story of ordinary people. La Guma keeps on insisting that no-one is particularly heroic. Most of them are not even terribly clever. Each one has his or her particular immediate problem or idiosyncrasy: Beukes cannot bear to be parted from his brown paper parcel which contains his emblems of civilised behaviour—his pyjamas; Bennett, who has risen just sufficiently on the ladder of limited possibilities to fear losing all by helping Beukes; the doctor who helps briefly because it allows him to indulge in nostalgia for the time when he was a liberal student with a 'conscience'; and Tommy, who shelters Beukes but continues to be his own person. Where Joe in *A Walk in the Night*, maintains his integrity by observing things at the water's edge, Tommy survives by dint of his single-minded concentration upon his ballroom dancing.

David Rabkin has drawn attention to some of the ways in which this novel differs from La Guma's previous work. Rabkin argues, convincingly, that:

> . . . in this novel, character is the exhibition of alternative responses to the political situation. The rich variety of what La Guma earlier described as 'the human salad', is replaced by a set of typical figures: the frightened middle-class coloured person, the worker who assists the political organisers, the simple people who help out of personal friendship, and the committed politicals themselves. Personal details are largely subordinated to this scheme. Where characters are provided with a personal history, its function is to illustrate how they came to adopt their present stance. The characters are necessarily static, since the author's concern is here not with the quality of their response, but with the actions that flow from the choices they have *already made*. The novel is permeated with a sense of a new era, a post-political phase in which, with the battle lines already drawn, the action has become mechanical. Whatever one may think of La

Guma's analysis of the political situation, it is clearly not one which will readily assist the novelist's art.[28]

Rabkin's observations about La Guma as a particular case can be related to the South African novel in English as a general case. Oddly enough, the most obvious question is not about the fact of the form's survival; I am sure that it will continue to do so. But what will it be worth? If, internally, the political climate becomes increasingly hostile to creative writing, what accommodations will authors seek with their political masters? And for how long will authors in exile, unable to interact with the reality of South Africa, be able to write convincingly from their position as exiles? One suspects that, with honourable exceptions, novelists inside the country will increasingly resort to exoticisms of one kind or another—they will, as in a bygone age, cater for the wishes of a public interested in the quaint. One also suspects that the majority of novelists in exile will become increasingly propagandistic: the novel as an arm of the struggle for political power. The question of whether the fog of the seasons' end will be transformed into zephyrs of freedom's spring must, for the novelist, for the time being remain open.

2. Ursula Edmands: Olive Schreiner*

Olive Schreiner's *The Story of an African Farm*, published in 1883,[1] had the distinction of being the first novel written by a colonial to be warmly and widely acclaimed in Britain. Its author was a remarkable woman whose lack of formal education had not hampered her intellectual growth, nor her eagerness to challenge conventional attitudes (particularly towards women), outworn beliefs, and old ideas. She was lionised in London during the 1880s, but to English readers she is little more than the writer of a minor Victorian 'problem novel'. She wrote two other novels, *Undine*[2] and *From Man to Man*,[3] neither of which was intended for publication. They were edited and posthumously published by her husband, and have remained relatively unknown. In South Africa, however, she established a second reputation. She became one of the prominent public figures in Cape Society at the turn of the century, the friend of Cecil Rhodes, Saul Solomon, Paul Kruger, and later of the young J. C. Smuts. Her advice on politics and social questions was sought and listened to with respect, although her refusal to compromise on matters of principle inevitably lost her many political acquaintances. Her championship of minority groups, whether Coloured people or the Jews, prostitutes or underpaid working women, won her gratitude and admiration from every section of the South African community.

Whatever she did was done with intensity and passion. If she could not become totally involved in what she was doing, she felt that her activity was not worthwhile. She once said that her novels were 'written

* From: *The Journal of Commonwealth Literature*, no. 8, (December 1969) pp. 107–24.

in blood', an accurate if rhetorical description of the agony creative work caused her; and an English journalist, hearing her address a political meeting was convinced 'that if Mrs Schreiner had ordered them to storm Government House, they would have thrown themselves on the bayonets'.[4]

Olive Schreiner was born in 1855. She was the ninth child of pioneering missionaries, whose endeavours to civilise the heathen on the Eastern frontier of the Cape Colony were conspicuously unsuccessful, but who clearly endowed their daughter (and most of their children) with both passion and intelligence. In spite of his own orthodox Christianity, her father apparently never discouraged Olive from her critical questioning of his beliefs. Her mother felt that the only way to survive in the wilderness to which a momentary impulse of religious fervour had brought her, was to uphold at all costs the rigidly conventional standards of her own English childhood. Olive, always a nonconformist, never forgot an early experience of being whipped for a Dutch exclamation in a moment of excitement. English was the language of civilisation for Mrs Schreiner, in spite of her marriage to a German, and she meted out barbarous punishments for trivial misbehaviour. On one occasion which Olive liked to recall, she shocked an assembled group of sedate adults by demanding that they proceed at once to take the precepts of the Sermon on the Mount literally. In spite of her outrageous behaviour, or because of it, her parents evidently regarded her as a remarkable child whose talent for amusing the family by telling stories was praised and encouraged.

Three of the Schreiner sons were sent to Cambridge where they all distinguished themselves. Will, the youngest, later succeeded Cecil Rhodes as Prime Minister of the Cape Colony. But Olive was not given any formal education at all, and was allowed to do much as she liked as an adolescent. It was assumed that she would eventually become a governess and help to support her parents as all the older Schreiner children were expected to do. She thus spent a number of years reading widely; mainly political philosophy, economics, theology, and history; and whenever possible she liked to discuss her somewhat haphazard and undisciplined ideas. Many people later remembered the ardent and beautiful girl with 'wonderful eyes' who dominated the conversation wherever she was. Olive's ideas were usually the most advanced in her circle, and her behaviour was unconventional enough for it to be talked about years later. The most flattering and also the most perceptive comment on this period of her life was written after her death by the Rev Zadoc Robinson, who had known Olive's parents and had watched her grow from a precocious child into a fascinating young woman. He wrote:

> There is no doubt that Olive was a strong attraction. She had everything that makes for charm in a social gathering. Her eyes, her voice, which in laughter became music, her gay mirthfulness of disposition, the ready and easy flow of language, with ideas that seemed to come to her lips with a gladsome speed, and fulness, made her conversation sparkling and suggestive . . . In all this there was never anything frivolous or shallow. You felt that she had *read* and *thought* . . . Olive was a fine flower that expanded nobly in a soil that could contribute nothing to her growth.[5]

When Olive was seventeen, she became a governess on an isolated Karoo farm. She had been away from the Eastern Cape only twice: once to visit the newly-discovered diamond fields near Kimberley and once to spend a few months in Cape Town, in those days still a quiet and unexciting little town. Almost immediately after this visit, she began to write a novel, and before it was finished, she was planning two more. Eventually, only *The Story of an African Farm* was completed to her satisfaction.

Olive recorded the progress of her novels in a note-book, in which she also noted her recurrent attacks of asthma, a malady from which she suffered all her life. Frequently she was almost crippled by the attacks, and often she was unable to work for long periods. At such times she was gripped by moods of intense despair. Passages such as the following abound in her letters:

> Why does every one cling to me? Why do they all follow me? God knows, I am so weak, and not a human soul puts out its hand to help me, only to demand love from me, and I am bankrupt, I am dying, I have nothing more to give.[6]

When she was well, could breathe in comfort, and was working hard, she was often correspondingly elated. Then she could write:

> You know, we must love every one in this world . . . I wish I were large and strong and could put my arms round all the tired lonely women in the world and help them.[7]

Perhaps her most accurate attempt to sum up her characteristic blend of strong emotional identification with people and causes, and her equally strong rejection of stupidity and excessive demands on her time and sympathy is contained in a letter she wrote to Havelock Ellis, one of her closest friends:

> You know, darling, when I say I'm happy . . . I think you think I mean something like what is ordinarily called happiness. I don't think the feeling I call 'happiness' has much likeness to that. It means that *I am for a time in a condition to master my own feelings and keep them from rending me.* I don't think you know what feeling is to me, how it can rend even my physical structure . . . I still pray like when I was a little child that I might not feel too much . . . Life is a battle to be fought, quietly, persistently, at every moment.[8]

Her abrupt and often violent changes of mood, reflected in her letters, continued throughout her life, making her a difficult and unpredictable person to live with, the terror of landladies and the joy and torment of her many friends. While she was a governess, however, neither these moods nor her asthma, nor the excessive demands of her employers prevented her from writing. Not only was she a capable teacher but she had to act as a shop assistant and a general mother's help. The members of the local farming community vied eagerly for Miss Schreiner's services, little realising that they were providing her with a unique insight into the Afrikaner society she was later to describe so penetratingly.

In 1881 *The Story of an African Farm* was completed. The manuscript was sent to a friend in Scotland, and Olive began to make plans to leave South Africa. In November 1881 she arrived in London, half determined to enter a medical school or nursing college. 'It seems to me', she wrote at this time, 'that a doctor's life is the most perfect of all lives; it satisfies the craving to know, and also the craving to serve. A nurse's life is sweet but not so perfect'.[9] Nothing came of this plan, however, mainly because she was very quickly absorbed in literary and intellectual life. By 1883, the unknown young South African was one of the most sought-after women in London. Oscar Wilde discussed her opinions with Yeats; Herbert Spencer met her at a party, but failed to impress his one-time disciple, who found him 'tall and lank' and his conversation singularly uninteresting. Rider Haggard came to tea with her, as did Philip Marston, Eleanor Marx, George Moore, Arthur Symons, and Edward Carpenter. Symons was so impressed that he wrote a detailed account of his first meeting with her beginning:

The day of days, today I met Olive Schreiner ... our talk, such communion of souls, such revelation, as I never believed possible on earth.[10]

Gladstone, who had expressed admiration of her novel, met Olive at lunch, and editors and publishers begged her to write reviews, articles, or stories for them. She became a popular spokesman for the rapidly emerging Women's Movement, and for that section of the working class which was beginning to demand education and better opportunities generally. Mary Brown, a social worker in Lancashire, tells how she asked a 'working-woman' what she thought of Olive's novel. With a far-off look in her eyes she said, 'I think there is hundreds of women what feels like that but can't speak it, but *she* could speak what we feel.'[11]

To this period, that is 1883–9, belongs Olive's intimate friendship with Havelock Ellis. When she met him, he was still a young medical student, obviously flattered and stimulated by her enthusiasm for his research into the psychology of sex, a subject still very much in its infancy. Olive had always been interested in 'woman' and 'the sex question', and under Ellis's influence she abandoned for a time her work on *From Man to Man*. Instead she planned to write an extended treatise on 'sex'. Eventually this project was so long deferred that no one knew whether she had actually written the 'sex book' or not. She made constant reference to it, sometimes hinting that it had been destroyed during the Anglo-Boer war, sometimes that she had lost the manuscript. But it seems fairly certain that most of what she wanted to say about women and sex was eventually incorporated in *Woman and Labour*.[12] One of Olive's biographers, D. L. Hobman, describes how this book, with its plea, 'Give us labour and the training to fit us for labour', [13] and its claim, 'We take all labour for our province',[14] moved and inspired a whole generation of young women who were trying to rebel against genteel late-Victorian conventions. She read the book, she says, on a train journey through Italy:

When I arrived in Florence I had become an ardent convert in the cause of feminism. No other book, before or since, has ever had so sudden or so lasting an influence on me as this one; and I have since heard from some of my contemporaries that the effect on them was equally startling.[15]

In Cape Town, much later, when women started to campaign for their rights, Olive's advice and active support were much in demand. Without her inspiration the movement would have lacked a good deal of its impetus and certainly most of its eloquence. Only when it became clear that the leaders of the Women's Enfranchisement League did not want to include non-white women in their campaign, did she leave them. The principles on which she acted, and from which she did not waver, were that *all* women must work together, and that freedom is not divisible.

In 1889, when *The Story of an African Farm* had been a best-seller for five years, Olive returned to South Africa, declaring that she could not work in Europe and that she needed to renew her contact with African soil and sunshine. She soon found that the sunshine she craved had been purchased at the expense of intellectual stimulation. But she was not averse to playing the role she was to fill for the next thirty years—that of South Africa's 'wise woman'. Her opinions and predictions were sought, discussed, and not infrequently acted on by politicians and editors both in South Africa and England.

She lived for some time in Matjiesfontein, a tiny village in the Karoo, a day's train journey from Cape Town, and it became customary for eminent visitors to South Africa to visit her there. The local inhabitants soon grew used to seeing Olive, dumpy and unfashionably dressed, striding up and down the station platform, deep in animated conversation with cabinet ministers, lawyers, or foreign journalists. Rhodes was a frequent visitor, and at first Olive returned his obvious admiration, feeling that he was the least hypocritical politician she had met. When it became clear that he was not the idealist she had imagined, she withdrew her friendship dramatically. She later wrote of this occasion:

> I never gave up all hope of him [Rhodes] till one day on Matjiesfontein station, when he and Slievewright and Logan were talking together. I didn't even say goodbye to them. I just went back to my house.[16]

In 1894 she married Samuel Cronwright, a young farmer whose opinions on politics coincided with her own. The marriage was hardly a conventional success: Olive and her husband spent more than half their married life apart. Cronwright agreed to take his wife's name ('It would be so beautiful', Olive had written to him shortly before the marriage, 'if we could have one name. People would know it was because I had written books.'[17]). He remained on his farm and later became an attorney, while Olive searched hopefully and unsuccessfully for a place where she would be free of asthma. Cronwright-Schreiner believed he had married a 'genius' whose implicit duty it was to produce at least two more 'great novels' to consolidate the success of *The Story of an African Farm*. He was bitterly disappointed when Olive did not finish *From Man to Man* or her 'sex book', after assuring him time and again that she only needed another few months or weeks to do so. To him it seemed as if Olive did nothing, not even, as he somewhat petulantly observed, the housework. After her death he seemd to be determined to prove that his wife had, in fact, written more than most people realised and he tried to gain the recognition for her as a novelist that he felt she deserved. Not only did he write an incredibly detailed biography, *The Life of Olive Schreiner*, but also edited an interesting but incomplete selection of her letters: and he published with copious notes and lengthy introductions, both *Undine* and *From Man to Man*. Having done this, he commented: 'And so I complete my contribution to the study of a genius . . .'.[18] He had certainly provided a great deal of information about Olive's background and her daily life, but what his *Life* and his other notes most obviously lack is a consistent interpretation of her career and personality. He failed to see, for instance, what was the strongest trait in his wife's character—her need to be actively identified with a cause. She needed to feel that her writing was producing positive practical results, that it was helping the weak and the oppressed. When she herself was ill, and felt she might be dying, she wrote:

> It isn't the pain and weakness one minds, it's the not being able to work. My one novel especially [*From Man to Man*] I would have liked to finish. I feel that if only one lonely struggling woman read it and found strength and comfort from it one would not have lived quite in vain. I seem to have done so little with my life.[19]

When she felt she could no longer contribute anything towards a cause, she began to lose interest in it. This was demonstrated clearly after the Anglo-Boer war. During the war she had taken the side of the Boers against the British, whom she regarded as oppressors of a brave, struggling little community. In 1906, however, she wrote:

> All my real interest has gone from the Boer question. They are more than able to take care of themselves . . . As soon as I know people or causes have no *need* of me, it's wonderful how my heart can loosen itself from them.[20]

She did not usually accept change in such a cheerful spirit, and often complained when the people with whom she had been identified no longer seemed to need help. When her friend, Emily Hobhouse (whose work in the detention camps during the war had made her a heroine of the Boer community) was leaving South Africa, Olive wrote to her:

> It seems sad that you are really going away from Africa, and yet I feel it's best. I would go too if I could. That is, I feel I could do much more in Europe than I can here. No one needs me here now except the Natives . . . and that is indeed hard and stern work that calls to all the bravest souls in South Africa for many years to come.[21]

It is not surprising, even though Cronwright appeared to think so, that Olive should have written no fiction after her return to South Africa in 1889. The country, torn apart by racial and ideological strife, was heading rapidly for war with Britain. Olive, whose brother was Attorney-General and later a member of Rhodes's cabinet, was concerned not with artistic but with political matters. She did, however, write one story, *Trooper Peter Halket of Mashonaland*,[22] a political tract aimed at exposing the barbarous methods Rhodes was using to open up the land north of the Limpopo. With effectively controlled irony (a device she has used nowhere else) she pin-points the colonial fraud as practised in Southern Africa: the uncritical adherence to a double standard which allows 'civilized Christians' to kill, rob, and exploit 'niggers' who 'probably don't care if they're alive or dead'. Peter Halket, not yet twenty-one, who often remembers his English childhood and his hardworking mother, sits next to his campfire in Mashonaland one night:

> . . . [he] considered his business prospects. When he had served his time as a volunteer he would have a large piece of land given him, and the Mashonas and Matabeles would have all their land taken away from them in time, and the Chartered Company would pass a law that they had to work for the white men; and he, Peter Halket, would make them work. He would make money.[23]

A stranger, whom the reader soon realises is Christ, comes to his fire, and Peter tells him about the good times he has had in Africa:

> I had two huts to myself, and a couple of nigger girls. It's better fun having these nigger women than the whites. The whites you've got to support, but the niggers support you! . . . I'm all for the nigger gals.[24]

Peter is finally persuaded to join the stranger's 'company', even though he will not make any money that way. He eventually gives his life for another when he is shot by his infuriated captain for allowing an African 'spy' to escape. His action, by a final irony, is interpreted by his fellow-troopers as evidence of 'bush-madness'.

The frontispiece of the original edition was a photograph showing three Africans dangling from a tree, watched by a group of white men in nonchalant attitudes. 'Did you hear of the spree they had up Bulawayo way, hanging those three niggers for spies?' Peter is made to ask the stranger. 'I wasn't there myself but a fellow who was told me they made the niggers jump down from the tree and hang themselves.' 'I was there', the stranger replies, 'I was with those men.'[25] To this indictment, even Rhodes had no answer.

In 1898 Olive wrote a fervent anti-war pamphlet, *A South African's View of the Situation*,[26] in which she pleaded for an end to the growing war-fever. If war came, she felt, it would be because Britain had betrayed the trust she had inspired in South Africa and which she had, until now, deserved. Britain had many faults, but her one redeeming virtue had always been that she stood, 'for freedom, not only for herself, but for humanity'.[27] If she allowed unscrupulous men like Rhodes to provoke a war, she would lose the respect and love of all loyal South Africans. When war was finally declared on the Republics of the Transvaal and the Orange Free State, Olive's idealism suffered its greatest blow. She was unable to conceal her bitter disappointment, and lost no opportunity of disparaging the British or of supporting the Boers. She spent the war years in a small Karoo town, Hanover, which was placed under martial law by the British. Lord Milner, the High Commissioner, issued special instructions that Olive was not to be molested, but she felt that her freedom was unnecessarily and cruelly restricted. Not surprisingly, she had a nervous breakdown, from which her recovery was painfully slow.

In spite of ill-health, she managed to complete *Woman and Labour* and *Thoughts on South Africa* during the war. The latter, a collection of essays, includes chapters on the half-castes (a group whose existence was usually ignored in those days, and of whom no one had written as sympathetically and honestly as Olive did), on the Africans, on the English-speaking South Africans, and on the Boers. Each essay outlines the history of the group, analyses its distinctive contribution to the complex South African society and predicts its future development in the unified community which, according to Olive, would inevitably develop. The analysis, at all times compassionate and penetrating, still retains a great deal of its relevance, though Olive could not, of course, foresee the changes which would occur in the twentieth century. She wrongly predicted that Afrikaans would never flourish as an independent language, and thought that the Boers, whom she regarded as hardy but primitive survivors of the seventeenth century, would be assimilated within fifty years into the 'great English-speaking South African people'.[28] This new race would be imbued with the best liberal tradition of its Dutch and English forefathers, a prediction which has, unhappily, not been fulfilled.

After the war, Cronwright was elected to the Cape Parliament as a 'Native Representative', and Olive joined the Women's Enfranchisement League. In 1909 Britain proposed to unite South Africa under a central government, and a National Convention was called to discuss the form this government should take. Olive, who favoured federation, was asked for her views by the editor of a Transvaal newspaper. He sent her a list of twelve questions, which she answered at length in a pamphlet, *Closer Union*.[29] The document contains her most eloquent plea for Justice and equality of opportunity for all members of society. In answer to a question on the political representation of the non-white races, she wrote:

> I am of the opinion that where the Federal Franchise is concerned, no distinction of race or colour should be made between South Africans. All persons born in the country or permanently resident here should be one in the eye of the State . . . South Africa must be a free man's country. The idea that a man born in this country . . . should in this, his native land, be refused any form of civic or political right on the ground that he is descended from a race with a civilisation, it may be, much older than our own, is one which must be abhorrent to every liberalized mind. I believe that any attempt to base our national life on distinctions of race and colour as such will, after the lapse of many years, prove fatal to us.[30]

Asked to comment on 'the Native Question', which she rightly considered the 'root question' in South Africa, she wrote: 'They [the Africans] are the makers of our wealth, the basic rock on which our State is founded'.[31] For lasting peace and progress in South Africa, there would have to be:

> . . . inter-action of distinct human varieties on the largest and most beneficent lines, making for the development of humanity as a

whole, and carried out in a manner consonant with modern ideals and modern social wants . . . We in South Africa are one of the first peoples in the modern world . . . to be brought face to face with this problem in its acutest form. On our power to solve it regally and heroically depends our greatness. If it be possible for us out of our great complex body of humanity . . . to raise up a free, intelligent, harmonious nation, each part acting with and for the benefit of the others then we shall have played a part as great as that of any other nation in the world's record.[32]

Such statements have earned for Olive Schreiner her reputation as a prominent spokesman for the liberal cause in a society whose members are notoriously devoted to sectional interests.

In 1913 Olive left South Africa again, hoping to renew her friendships in England, and to regain some measure of physical and mental energy by revisiting her favourite Italian resorts. War overtook her, however, and it was not until 1920 that she was able to return to the Cape, where she died shortly afterwards.

It is easy to concur in the judgement that Olive Schreiner was a remarkable woman. Her friends have been quick to say, and her writing shows, that she was a passionate, often inspiring person, warm, sympathetic, highly intelligent, and capable of tremendous altruistic enthusiasm. What is more difficult to assess is the value of her literary work. All her life she regarded herself as an artist, and she was deeply concerned about the nature and function of art. Yet many critics have felt that her talent had exhausted itself when she had written *The Story of an African Farm*, and that everything she wrote after that was inferior. Such a judgment is possible only if one persists in regarding her as a novelist working within the nineteenth-century English tradition. This view does not take into account her concept of art or of the artist's function in society, nor her frequently stated aims. That she wrote three novels at the beginning of her career did not make her a novelist, nor did she ever regard herself as one.

When Olive was seventeen, she first read the *Essays* of Ralph Waldo Emerson, and he remained the writer whose ideas had most influence of her own work. In 1884 she wrote to Havelock Ellis:

I always feel (I did from the first moment I opened his book) akin to Emerson . . . His value . . . is that of stimulation. He brings new thought . . . but he makes all thought live and throb which is the work of true genius.[33]

Emerson believed that art should serve a purpose. The artist, an individual peculiarly endowed with acute perception and imagination should not keep these gifts to himself. He had a duty to make others aware of social circumstances. This doctrine, stressing responsibility and duty, appealed to the daughter of Protestant missionaries. The artist, declared Emerson, 'is the liberating god',[34] and Olive expanded this definition in a letter to Cronwright:

> Art is the little crack in the iron wall of life which shuts one in awful isolation through which the spirit can force itself out and show itself to its own like-minded fellow-spirits outside, or rather creep through the cracks in their terrible walls that shut in the individual life and say, 'You are not alone'.[35]

Emerson emphasised that the role of an artist was particularly important in a society without a firmly established literary tradition. He hoped that the great American poet of the future would involve himself in the social and political life of his own times; that he would 'celebrate the dazzling geography' of his own country; that he would write about the negroes, the Indians, 'the wrath of rogues and the pusillanimity of honest men'.[36] Olive must have felt she could and ought to be such a poet. South Africa, as well as New England, had its 'dazzling geography', its social complexities, its rogues and honest men, afraid to say and do what they knew to be right. These are the things she wrote about in *The Story of an African Farm*, which she began after reading the *Essays*, and they are the themes of most of her later work.

Emerson had a low opinion of fiction, and attached no great importance to the novel as a literary form. What mattered to him were the 'symbols' an artist used, by which he meant words, images, and ideas. Here too, Olive followed his lead. 'All art is symbol, and these (allegories) are pure symbol',[37] she said, explaining why she so frequently used allegory. Even *Woman and Labour*, a book intended to present a logical analysis of the position of women, includes an allegory in each section, because she felt that argument alone was not sufficient. She judged her work by its moral effect on her readers, and so, because the allegories were easy to understand and made a direct appeal to the general reader, she concluded that they were of more importance than *The Story of an African Farm*.

The allegories she valued so much are contained in three volumes.[38] They are for the most part poetical fragments, each dramatising a particular contemporary problem in a deliberately rhetorical manner. For instance, 'Three Dreams in a Desert' allegorises the 'woman question'. A 'dreamer' speaks:

> I thought I stood on the border of a great desert, and the sand blew everywhere. And I thought I saw two great figures like beasts of burden of the desert, and one lay upon the sand with its neck stretched out, and one stood by it. And I looked curiously at the one that lay upon the ground, for it had a great burden upon it, and the sand was thick about it, so that it seemed to have piled over it for centuries.[39]

The figure on the ground is 'woman', she that bears men in her body. She cannot rise, nor can the man who stands next to her, leave her. 'I saw a broad band passing along the ground from one to the other, and it bound them together.' Only when the woman staggers to her knees will there be progress, and then the man 'will stand close to her, and look into her eyes with sympathy'.

It is their consistently prophetic and declamatory tone that marks the allegories most strongly. Olive had been hailed as a prophet of a changing world by reviewers in 1883, and a prophet, of doom or of hope, she intended to remain. Thus in 'The Sunlight Lay Across My Bed', one of her favourite allegories, she describes a dream in which she meets God. He shows her a vision of Hell, a vast hall, in which 'fair men and women are feasting on wine', oblivious of the destruction they are creating for themselves. 'Powerful' was the favourite adjective of contemporary reviewers for this particular story, but a modern reader might well sympathise with Olive's ironic mother who told her daughter she 'didn't know *what* it was about'.[40]

Olive Schreiner's novels have a common theme, which is explored with varying success in the three books. Each novel describes the development of a particularly gifted young woman who is frustrated by her environment and the society to which she belongs. The three heroines, Undine, Lyndall and Rebekah, are forced to pay a high price for their attempts to challenge the conventions. Lyndall and Undine both die young, having forfeited all happiness, and Rebekah, whose initial idealism was even greater than theirs, becomes completely disillusioned. Neither *Undine* nor *From Man to Man* can be regarded as a good novel, but Olive did not intend them for publication. *Undine*, which was written before *The Story of an African Farm*, is little more than a highly romanticised version of her own early life.[41] It describes her childhood, her adolescence (the scene of which is transferred from Cradock in the Eastern Cape to 'England', a country in which luxuriant roses bloom whenever the deep snow chances to melt), and an unhappy love affair she had at sixteen. The best parts of the novel are those in which she reports, with a sharp eye for detail, on life at New Rush, the town established near the diamond diggings, where Undine ends her short career. In the descriptions of the multi-racial community and of the manners in the crude, bustling mining camp, one can detect the beginning of Olive's real int erest, which was sociological analysis rather than story-telling. On her arrival in New Rush, Undine walks down the main street, looking for lodgings:

> Alone . . . though the street was so thronged with the streaming crowd of niggers and diggers returning home from work that they kicked up the red sand into a lurid cloud above their heads — stark naked savages from the interior, with their bent spindle-legs and their big-jawed foreheadless monkey-faces, who — though they were going home to fire and meals, could hardly get out of their habitual crawl — colonial niggers half-dressed, not half-civilized, and with some hundred per cent more of evil in their black countenances than those of their wilder brethren — great muscular fellows, almost taller and stronger than their masters, the white diggers, who formed a thin sprinkling in the crowd and who, in spite of the thick dust that enveloped them, might be distinguished by their more quick and energetic movements.[42]

From Man to Man was Olive's most ambitious project and also her least successful one. She intended to put into this book (which she had begun to write before she left South Africa in 1881) everything she had ever felt or thought about being a woman, and as her ideas were constantly changing, so the novel grew and was revised time and again. (She was apparently working on the manuscript on the night of her death.) It tells the story of two sisters: Rebekah, intellectual and virtuous, and Bettie, beautiful but not very intelligent. Through her own ignorance and the negligence of her parents, Bettie is seduced at a very early age, and has a depressing career as a 'fallen woman'. Rebekah is an exemplary mother and wife, but her habitually unfaithful husband systematically destroys all her happiness. There is little development in the novel, and most of the book consists of Rebekah's thoughts on the subjects that interested her creator: human rights, the position of women, the cruelty of men, the race problem in South

Africa, and the proper education of children. Olive appears to have used this book as a confidential diary, and allowed herself to express in it attitudes she ruthlessly suppressed in her published work. Rebekah, for instance, tells her sons that all people are equal in the sight of God ('it isn't the colour or the shape of the jaw that matters'), but a few lines later she suddenly says: 'I've tried to like coloured women, and do all I can to help them, and then they jeer at me! . . . it's as if a knife ran into me under my ribs'.[43]

In comparison with the other two novels, *The Story of an African Farm* is entirely successful. It is basically a reworking of the material already used in *Undine*, but in this novel Olive was able to create a convincing fictional world, to transform her own painful experience into part of a meaningful pattern, in which suffering is seen to be inevitable, not merely undeserved personal misfortune. The novel tells the story of a group of people living together on a lonely Karoo farm. The two main characters are Waldo and Lyndall, whom we see first as children and later as young adults determined to overcome the limitations of their environment. Although the book ends with the death, first of Lyndall and then of Waldo, it is not a conventionally 'tragic' story: the tendency is rather to show that without a struggle nothing worthwhile can be achieved.

The novel begins with a description of the farm by moonlight. The moon lends an 'oppressive beauty' to the scene and 'quite etherealises' the stunted vegetation, the ugly farm building and the parched square of sandy earth which is the only garden. By daylight, however, the farm and its surroundings are seen to be 'less lovely':

> The plain was a weary flat of loose red sand sparsely covered by dry karoo bushes, that cracked beneath the tread like tinder, and showed the red earth everywhere. Here and there a milkbush lifted its pale-coloured rods, and in every direction the ants and beetles ran about the blazing sand. The red walls of the farmhouse, the zinc roofs of the outbuildings, the stone walls of the 'kraals', all reflected the fierce sunlight, till the eye ached and blenched. No tree or shrub was to be seen far or near. The two sunflowers that stood before the door, outstared by the sun, drooped their brazen faces to the sand; and the little cicada-like insects cried aloud among the stones of the 'kopje'. (p. 4)[44]

The 'red walls of the farmhouse' shelter Tant' Sannie, the Boer woman who owns the farm, her small 'English' step-daughter, Em, and Em's orphan cousin, Lyndall. In one of the outbuildings lives Otto, the German overseer, with his son Waldo. The kraals provide shelter for the labourers, blanketed Africans, and for the privileged house servants, the 'yellow Hottentots'. This farm is not the peaceful, gabled homestead often associated with the Dutch-South African way of life, nor are its inhabitants the easy-going, generous folk of popular tradition. The African farm, as Olive Schreiner presents it, is a place where a complex mixture of races and nationalities live together in a harsh environment, where the heat and drought are matched by intellectual barrenness, deliberate idleness, and the frustration of every impulse towards 'the finer life'. The only white woman the children know is Tant' Sannie, who:

> . . . sat on a chair in the great front room, with her feet on a wooden stove, and wiped her flat face with the corner of her apron, and drank coffee, and in Cape Dutch swore that the beloved weather was damned. (p. 5)

Otto, the German, who tries to uphold Christian values, and refuses to acknowledge either racial or cultural differences:

> . . . stood out at the kraals in the blazing sun, explaining to two Kaffir boys the approaching end of the world. The boys, as they cut the cakes of dung, winked at each other, and worked as slowly as they possibly could, but the German never saw it. (p. 6)

Waldo, herding sheep, struggles with ignorance and loneliness, trying to understand the mysteries of religion; and Lyndall, who craves beauty, knowledge, and freedom, has to be content with finding dew 'diamonds' in the leaves of an ice-plant.

The routine of the farm is broken up by the arrival of a tramp, an Englishman who calls himself Bonaparte Blenkins and claims kinship with the Duke of Wellington. Explaining why he has come to Africa, he tells Otto:

> I had money, I had lands, I said to my wife, 'There is Africa, a struggling country; they want capital; they want men of talent; they want men of ability to open up that land. Let us go.' (p. 31)

He represents a type whom Olive Schreiner particularly detested, the would-be exploiter of colonial simplicity. Both he and Tant' Sannie are cruel to the children, but where she is merely stupid and can be excused, Bonaparte is shown to be vicious. In an incredibly short time, and in spite of much initial hostility from Tant' Sannie, he establishes himself as a sadistic tyrant, and almost succeeds in destroying the little good that had existed on the farm. Not content with usurping Otto's position as overseer, he persuades Tant' Sannie to dismiss the selfless old man for 'ingratitude'. The description of his dismissal is painful in its accuracy:

'Be near my house tomorrow morning when the sun rises [Tant' Sannie shouts], my Kaffirs will drag you through the sand. They would do it gladly, any of them, for a bit of tobacco for all your prayings with them.'
    'I am bewildered, I am bewildered', said the German, standing before her and raising his hand to his forehead, 'I—I do not understand.' . . .
    'Go, dog,' cried the Dutch-woman, 'I would have been a rich woman this day if it had not been for your laziness. Praying with the Kaffirs behind the kraal walls. Go, you Kaffir's dog!'

Otto turns to the Hottentot woman for enlightenment, 'she was his friend, she would tell him kindly the truth' but:

. . . The woman answered by a loud ringing laugh.
    'Give it to him, old missis: Give it to him!'
    It was so nice to see the white man who had been master hunted down.
    The coloured woman laughed, and threw a dozen mealie grains into her mouth to chew. (p. 63)

Bonaparte next destroys a little machine which Waldo had made, the first evidence of his latent artistic ability, and applies his own form of censorship to the only collection of books on the farm:

Whenever you come into contact with any book . . . of which you comprehend absolutely nothing, declare that book to be immoral. Bespatter it, vituperate against it, strongly insist that any man or woman harbouring it is a fool or a knave or both . . . Do all that in you lies to annihilate that book. (p. 89)

It is only when he tries to court Tant' Sannie's niece that the Boer-woman throws him out, and he disappears from the story.

The second half of the novel, after Bonaparte's ignominious departure, seems at first to have only a tenuous connection with the earlier section. The children have grown up; Lyndall has left the farm; and there is a new manager, Gregory Rose. Two long, allegorical chapters mark the shift in emphasis from story-telling and detailed description of day-to-day events to a greater concentration on the mental development of Lyndall and Waldo. 'Times and Seasons', the first of these chapters, charts a child's development in terms of his changing attitudes towards religion and science; and the second, 'Waldo Stranger', is an allegory on the nature of truth. A passing traveller tells Waldo that Truth is like a white bird from whose wing one feather occasionally drops onto a high mountain peak. The bird can be glimpsed only by those who persevere in the right way throughout life, giving up all worldly desires, so that dying, they may say:

Where I lie down, worn out, other men will stand, young and fresh. By the steps that I have cut they will climb; by the stairs that I have built they will mount . . . when the stones roll they will curse me. But they will mount, and on *my* work; they will climb, and by *my* stair! And no man liveth to himself, and no man dieth to himself.' (p. 148)

The didactic and rhetorical tone of these two interpolated chapters may have been acceptable to a Victorian audience accustomed to being edified by their fiction, but they are, in fact, unnecessary and tedious. Olive Schreiner, never a particularly economical writer, does not seem to have realised that her theme ('no man liveth to himself') emerges perfectly clearly from the development of the novel itself.

The rest of the novel is concerned with the fate of the characters who leave the farm to challenge the world beyond its boundaries: Lyndall, Waldo, and also Gregory. Both men are in love with Lyndall and it is through their love that they gain some insight into the nature of life. Waldo is at first reluctant to leave. He argues that nothing is worth doing because 'the universe is so large, and man is so small'. Lyndall replies with an argument based on Emerson's essay, 'Self-Reliance':

But we must not think so far; it is madness, it is a disease. We know that no man's work is great and stands forever. Men have set their mark on mankind forever, as they thought; but time has washed it out as it has washed out mountains and continents . . . Mankind is only an ephemeral blossom on the tree of time . . . (p. 204)

Waldo is persuaded that he should find work, and not merely gaze up at the stars, and sets out to look for 'the finer life'. Inevitably he is disappointed. He has not had sufficient education and is not articulate enough to make his way in the demanding modern world. When he returns to the farm, he learn's of Lyndall's death. For her, also, the struggle against her limitations has been too great. She was a 'woman, young, friendless, the weakest thing on God's earth', whose only asset in the eyes of the world was her beauty. She had wanted freedom, but not on the terms it was offered: marriage to a man she did not love. She had, however, agreed to go away with her 'stranger', and had borne him a child, which died soon after birth. Gregory, who had searched the countryside for her, arrived just in time to watch her die, too weak to return to the farm. Waldo now has nothing left to live for, and 'goes out to sit in the sunshine'. To a casual observer his life may seem to have been of small account, but he has known his father's goodness, Em's compassion, Lyndall's exciting ideas, and has lived in close contact with nature. To him, life seems 'a rare and very rich thing'. Neither he nor Lyndall has been successful, but their lives had value in that they had shown the way to others.

The barriers which seemed so insurmountable to Waldo and Lyndal in 1880 have largeley been overcome, but Olive Schreiner's achievement does not really lie in a discussion of once topical problems. What she has done in *The Story of an African Farm* is to create a lasting symbol of South Africa: the lonely farm, hauntingly beautiful by moonlight, harsh and demanding in reality, where everyday life becomes a drama played out in a tense multi-racial society; where the individual must conform or engage in bitter struggles against sometimes overwhelming odds. It is this vision that marks the novel as an original one, and as a success, in spite of its occasional lapses in style and tone.

The answer to critics who have wondered why Olive Schreiner did not write more novels, is implicit in the foregoing discussion. Her interest lay in sociological analysis, and in political prediction, not in plot-making or creation of character. She spent life observing and commenting on the real life counterparts of the characters she had first observed on the African farm, analysing their behaviour, predicting their future, and working for the time when 'soul shall not thrust back soul . . . when men shall not be driven to seek solitude, because of the crying out of their hearts for love and sympathy'. (p. 295)

3. Arthur Ravenscroft: Pauline Smith*

This passage of magisterial self-importance appears in Arnold Bennett's *Journals* under 11 October 1909:

> Last night I began talking to Pauline Smith about her work, though I had some difficulty in getting *her* to talk. She gave me a notion of a half-formed scheme for a novel—nothing really but a dim idea. I enlarged it and straightened it out for her, and by my enthusiasm lighted hers a little, indeed much. I poured practical advice into her for an hour, such as I don't think she could have got from any other living man, and such as I would have given my head for 15 years ago. I told her exactly what to think about today and it was arranged that she should report to me to-night how far she had proceeded and that we should go further with the plot. After dinner to-night she began to read. It is true it was one of my books. I gave her a chance and waited for her to put the book down. Then after half an hour I said: 'I shan't let Pauline read any more of my books. She doesn't do anything else.' She smiled and murmured: 'Just let me finish this.' I played a sonata, and then ostentatiously waited. No sign. She kept on reading till 9.30, and then went straight to bed.[1]

Bennett's exasperation at Pauline Smith's elusiveness does suggest that although he advised and greatly encouraged her writing (and she in turn felt gratitude and affection), she was not in the relationship of a studio pupil to him. She had certainly learned to value his judgment

*From: A Review of English Literature, vol. IV, no. 2 (April 1963), pp. 55–67.

when they first met in the previous winter and he had persuaded her to show him all that she had yet written—a few sketches of Scottish village life, some children's stories, and the opening chapters of a novel. But her own account, despite its deference and humility, shows that his judgment really confirmed her own instinctive reaction:

> His damning of those opening chapters gave me a confidence in his judgement which no praise could have won, and brought me so overwhelmingly a sense of relief and release that it was as if he had broken down for me an imprisoning wall and drawn me out into the open air. I destroyed my novel and never afterwards regretted it.[2]

Bennett's kindly interest undoubtedly liberated what small confidence Pauline Smith ever felt in her own powers. It is ironical to reflect that so retiring a personality and so single-mindedly honest an artist would probably have written even less than she did had it not been for the hectoring of a self-confident and prolific writer. Yet the friendship that developed between Bennett and the shy, frail young woman showed a warm generosity in him that enabled her to persevere with her writing in the face of constant and debilitating ill-health.

Pauline Janet Smith was born on 2 April 1882[3] in the village of Oudtshoorn on the Little Karoo plateau in the south-west of the Cape Province. She was the elder of two sisters; a younger brother died in infancy. Their mother, Jessie, was a Scotswoman of great charm and beauty, and the father, Herbert Urmson Smith, who had gone to South Africa from England for the sake of his health, was the first resident physician in the Little Karoo. His practice extended over some 2000 square miles between the Zwartberg Mountains in the north and the Outeniqua Mountains in the south, though it was centred in Oudtshoorn. Dr Smith was frequently called out to patients in the remoter valleys where the people were almost entirely Afrikaans-speaking, read (if able to) only the Bible, and lived an austere, patriarchal, peasant life.

As a child Pauline Smith sometimes accompanied her father on these excursions by Cape cart, and at an early age learned much about the people, their ways and, especially, their speech. She must have been an extraordinarily sensitive child, for out of her vivid memory of the people and places of her childhood, reinforced by later visits to Oudtshoorn, especially, in 1913–14 and 1926–7, were to grow the Little Karoo stories and novel.

For a 'colonial' Englishman in a predominantly Afrikaans area Dr

Smith seems to have been unusually intelligent, unaffected and sympathetic, and Pauline and Dorothy Smith grew up in life-long friendship with the daughters of both the Anglican rector, the Rev Alfred Morris, and a Dutch Reformed pastor, the Rev Stegmann.

Pauline's first school was primitive, upstairs in a grey stone house where 'school was "taught" round a yellow-wood table in a small, bare, scrubbed room', that 'looked down upon a bare sun-baked yard'.[4] It was followed by a regime of governesses at home. When Pauline was about 11 years old she attended the Girls' High School, but illness interrupted her education and it was many months before she went to school again, in Scotland and later England.

The volume of children's stories and verses, *Platkops Children*,[5] conveys the happy and relaxed flavour of the childhood the Smith sisters had in Oudtshoorn in the eighteen-eighties and nineties. The book is dedicated to Dorothy as 'These memories of our South African Childhood', and in an unpublished letter Pauline Smith says: 'You will find the book very simple and childish—for the first of the stories were in fact written for my sister when ill-health cut short my schooling in England and we were parted.[6] With language and spelling intended not only to be juvenile but at times also to convey the vocabulary and pronunciation of South African English, these sketches tell of a peaceful village life in a remote 'colonial' province where the children are startled by the apparition of 'a perlite English boy in a welwet suit an' leather gloves', by an itinerant showman who makes a momentous ascent in a balloon, by the discovery of bath taps in a Scottish house during a visit to Britain. The children climb trees, play innocent games with stink lilies, invent games and rudimentary theatricals, observe weddings, and visit Afrikaans farms. The juvenile convention assumed for the telling of these stories is largely unconvincing: the tricks are obvious and repetitive, there is little artistry. But they do tell unpretentiously of a pre-industrial way of life that has disappeared, and my experience is that young American and South African children at any rate still find them engrossing.

When Pauline Smith was in her twelfth year the two sisters were taken to school in Britain. In 1898 Dr Smith died suddenly in London having just arrived from South Africa to visit them. Pauline's delicate health was already causing anxiety and interfered constantly with her formal education. When the sisters finally left school, they and their mother led a somewhat wandering life among their relations in England and Scotland and on various visits to the Continent where they stayed at modest pensions and formed part of a 'rather conventional English circle'.

At long intervals in these years Pauline Smith was struggling to write, but although her sketches of Scottish life were published in *The Aberdeen Free Press*, she had no confidence in her own ability. She was conscious of being confined by painful mental as well as physical bonds, and her vital emotional existence seemed to her to belong to the past, to the Little Karoo she had left as a child and to her sorrowing memories of her father's intelligent and affectionate companionship:

> All my happiest memories [she was to write some thirty years later] and my most formative impressions were those of my South African childhood and my father's companionship. For the rest none of the adventures of youth and none of its attributes, so wonderful to me in others, had ever been mine. In all our wanderings I had remained strangely inexperienced in life, and in literature I knew myself to be ill-read. Of all these shortcomings I was painfully aware, and in company the shyness and self-consciousness they caused me made me awkward and silent.[7]

It was in December 1908, at an unpretentious hotel in the hills above Vevey in Switzerland, during one of the Smith visits abroad, that Pauline Smith first met Arnold Bennett and found in his insistence and approval the stimulus she needed. She was then twenty-six.

It is clear that Bennett burst dazzlingly into the narrowed lives of Mrs Smith and her daughters. His bumptious yet genuine and painstaking interest in Pauline as soon as Mrs Smith told him that she 'wrote a little', won her deep gratitude and forced her to struggle intermittently for eighteen years with a by no means facile pen, and produce a novel and ten short stories of tragic and mature power. If her own account of the effect exaggerates Bennett's stature, it also reveals her own modesty and sense of new enlargement:

> Until now in the varying yet narrow circumstances of my life, this world had been beyond my reach. Such taste and feeling as I had for English letters had come not from intelligence but from the deep impression made upon me in my South African childhood by the beauty and simplicity of the Old Testament stories (whose country and people were so like my own): by the spell cast upon me by *The Ancient Mariner* read aloud to me one Sunday morning when all the rest of the world was at church: and by my accidental discovery of *The Vicar of Wakefield*. Later at school in England had come a wider acquaintance with English classics, and a deeper appreciation of my father's insistence upon a just use of words, but no change in the 'set'

which my mind had taken in childhood. And after leaving school a fatherless wandering life had made my reading so haphazard that much of the best in modern literature was still unknown to me. But here now, in this quiet room, by one of the moderns himself, was the world of modern literature, in France and Russia as well as in England, revealed to me.[8]

Her gratitude to Bennett and admiration of his novels did not, however, significantly influence the conception and artistry of her own stories, and there are many signs that she was never blinded to what a passage like the following (despite its defensive tone) shows her to have felt as a fundamental difference of moral outlook between them:

> The fact that our worlds lay apart was accepted by us both. . . . He liked to impress me, even through my fears with its [his world's] gaiety and riches, its wit if not its wisdom, its rush and glamour and importance, as he himself, sometimes perhaps against his better judgement, was so eagerly impressed . . . His response to the glamour of wealth, as to the romance of the big hotel and the successful business, was, indeed, strangely like the innocent unenvious wonder of a child whose memories of starved unlovely days made this new world in which he had now an established place a fairy tale of his own planning at last come true.[9]

As a result of the first meeting, Pauline Smith went to stay with Arnold and Marguerite Bennett in their cottage at Fontainebleau in the autumn of 1909. In the winter she hurried back to England when she heard that her sister Dorothy was ill. In the spring of 1910 she re-joined the Bennetts in Paris and travelled back with them to the same hotel in Vevey. Here she had one of her frequent attacks of acute neuralgia. By the time they moved on to Florence she was daily discussing her creative ideas with Bennett and straining herself to write in earnest. But her weak throat was affected by the cold Florentine winds and in the depression of oncoming illness she made little progress. More than once she would have given up in despair had it not been for Bennett's faith in her writing ability. While they were in Florence her friendship with the Bennetts was more intimately reinforced by Dorothy Smith's engagement in London to Bennett's old friend Alexander Webster.

In Florence Pauline Smith had a serious attack of quinsy followed by a dangerous ear infection and had to be moved to the Casi di Cura of the Blue Nuns. After nearly two years of widened horizons, this illness forced her back into a contracted life and after returning to England she saw much less of the Bennetts. She did stay with them again in Essex, just before sailing to South Africa in the summer of (apparently) 1913. This visit seems to have had a greater impact on her creative imagination than her first return to the Little Karoo in 1905. She was in England once more shortly after the outbreak of the 1914 war.

By now her home was in Dorset. It was later to be permanently shared by Dorothy Webster and her son Alexander Paul, for Alexander Webster died in 1920 after a forty-eight-hour illness.

From now on Pauline Smith saw Bennett chiefly during periodic trips to London when she continued to consult with him over her writing, and he virtually became her agent in business matters. Soon after she had completed her short story 'The Pain', Bennett put into Poole harbour with his yacht and persuaded her to go with him on a short cruise along the coast. She showed him the manuscript. He posted it off to Middleton Murry who published it almost immediately in *The Adelphi*. It was followed at intervals by others. In February 1925, the first collected edition of the stories appeared as *The Little Karoo*.[10] The next year *The Beadle* appeared, which she had been working on for more than ten years.[11] It deserves to be much more widely known than it is.

When Bennett once promised to arrange a lunch for Pauline Smith with any author she would name, she at once named 'George Bourne' (George Sturt), the author of *Change in the Village*. 'But of my talk that day', she writes, 'I remember not one single word: it is George Bourne's, of country fairs he had known in England in his youth, that lingers still in my memory.'[12]

When one looks at her writings it is obvious why she should so readily have asked to meet the author of *Change in the Village*. For what fired Pauline Smith's imagination as she pondered over her memories of the isolated Afrikaner people of the Little Karoo was not a condescending interest in rural quaintness, but a rich, warm comprehension of the grey tones in which life and the will of God were revealed to them. That she, of English origin, should have been able to grasp this is in itself remarkable, but the lasting value of her artistry lies not in the sure, concrete details with which she presents their daily lives, but in the realisation, through these details, of an organic community, with a way of life, identity, and consciousness of its own. The sympathetic intimacy with which she presents an insulated, entirely pre-industrial culture and the sensitivity and emotional logic with which she senses where stresses within individuals and between individuals and the community are likely to occur, rank her work, despite its small extent, with that of the George Eliot of *Silas Marner*. She has little of George Eliot's massiveness of intellect, but her austere art, superficially so simple, but in reality wise and imaginative in the fullest sense, explores the mentally claustrophobic limits of the Little Karoo people with fine precision and an accurate penetration to the common humanity that lies beneath their regional and racial peculiarities.

These peculiarities are there, convincingly and throughout; they are encompassed within her understanding of an elemental human condition, yet their rendering is one of the means, not the end, of her art. This is no mere regionalism, though there is evidence that some of her admirers have found her 'charm' as a writer to extend no further. And it is all too easy to be captivated by the exoticism to the non-South African reader of the setting of the stories, and by what a *New York Times* reviewer refers to as Pauline Smith's 'almost Biblical eloquence'.[13] This is chiefly the level on which they have been praised. But 'biblical' is not a useful critical term.

There are echoes, sometimes for specific purposes (as in the story 'Ludovitje'), of biblical cadences and phraseology, but on the whole they occur in order to show how life in the Little Karoo resembles for its people that of Israel in the Old Testament. To this extent the dialogue of Pauline Smith's stories is 'biblical', but she is clearly less interested in echoing the Bible than the accents of the leisurely, metaphor-laden language actually used by her people. To do this in English for Afrikaans speech, she tries to give their dialogue a distinctly un-English flavour by such means as literal renderings of Afrikaans exclamations and endearments. ('No, what!', 'Now look now', 'My little springbok', 'My little heart-thief'), by the use of Afrikaans sentence patterns which invert normal English word order ('Say for me now . . .', 'After you will I send . . .') and occasionally by the insertion of an untranslated Afrikaans expression, such as 'a-le-wêreld'. The biblicality is only part of this translation of colloquial Afrikaans speech, which contributes so largely to the authenticity and immediacy of her characters.

The faithful recording of actual speech is at the centre of her artistic method and has its counterparts on other levels too. Real geographical names are interchanged or but slightly altered, many of the surnames of her characters are well known in the Oudtshoorn district, and the description of Platkops village and its hospital in 'The Pain' is still recognisably that of Oudtshoorn, even after fifty years of change. Yet the art is not flat representationalism. With locality and mode of life firmly rooted in her actual experience of it, Pauline Smith goes on to probe the emotional lives of individuals whose desires, whether selfish or generous, are delineated with profound imaginative insight. The 'simple' setting of a homogenous community primitively close to a reluctant soil enables her to concentrate fully on an order of human experience shorn of incidental elaborations. Her narrative techniques are shaped by this environmental severity. What gives the language of *The Little Karoo* and *The Beadle* their real eloquence is a rigorous critical faculty which forbids excrescence, irrelevance or slackness. The description, for instance, in 'Desolation' of the terrain over which Old Alie and her grandson travel to Hermansdorp:

> Throughout the first day it was in the Verlatenheid, with frequent outspans, that they journeyed. And here, from sun-up to sun-down they met no human being and saw in the distance only one white-washed and deserted farmhouse, bare and treeless in the drought-stricken veld. Every *kuil* or water-hole they passed was dry, and near every *kuil* were the skeletons of donkeys and sheep which had come there but to perish of their thirst. Of living things they saw only, now and then, a couple of *koorhan* rising suddenly in flight, or a lizard basking lazily in the sun. And once, bright as a jewel in that desert of sand and stone, they came upon a small green bush poisonous to sheep and cattle alike.

Turned off the land, old Alie stands between the child and destitution. She makes for the village where fifty years before she worked happily as a mattress-maker and now hopes to resume her trade. But the village too is blighted by drought and where she expected to find the pleasant cottage of her youth there now stands an impersonal orphanage. The passage conveys the grim ironic pathos of the story: the signs of calamitous drought are listed with remorseless exactness, culminating in the final irony that the only green bush in the desolate immensity is poisonous.

Within the narrow compass, the range and depth of human emotions explored is impressive. The theme of 'The Pain' is the tender old-age love of Juriaan and Deltje which through their fifty hard, childless years together has been the one sure sensuous fact of their existence, threatened only once—by the foreign efficiency of the Platkops hospital. When Deltje finds that their enforced lying apart brings pain to their hearts more unendurable even than her physical pain, they steal away at night and return home with a deep content to await her death. This is the most tender of all the stories, though human capacity for selfless devotion occurs as a theme also in 'Desolation' and 'The Pastor's Daughter', and supremely in the nature of Andrina's love of the easy-going Englishman in *The Beadle*.

Pauline Smith handles the relationship between Andrina and the Englishman with fearlessness and a stress upon the sanctity of sex that cannot fail to remind one of D. H. Lawrence. Whether Andrina is in narrowly realistic terms a successful creation is perhaps beside the point. She is treated as completely innocent and childlike, and the very sparseness of her physical and mental environment makes genuine and moving the touching into life of her emotional and spiritual potentialities, even by an irresponsible Englishman from across the mountains. Her naïve trust is emphasised in order to show the unspoiled generosity of her nature, contrasted with her aunt Johanna's bitter righteousness and inability to forgive an old wrong, and with the beadle's tortured moroseness that conceals his unexpiated sin. The flowering of Andrina's love coincides with her admission to church membership and she interprets the joy her love brings her as a sign of God's mercy and bounty. In her poverty she can give the Englishman only her body and this she does unselfconsciously with the same sacramental intensity that accompanies her other means of administering to him.

> It was not compassion that he aroused in her now. It was not tenderness. With the strange disturbing, physical response of her quivering body to these passionate caresses there went an exultant, overwhelming, primitive desire to minister to his needs. And in the thought of service to him there was for her now no absolute cleavage between the joy of her body and the joy of her soul. Together they made for her, in the outpouring of her love, in the humility of her spirit, in the innocence of her mind, a glory that had no shame.

As this passage indicates, Pauline Smith conceives Andrina's passion in terms of a complete correspondence between her wondering acceptance of a divine gift, her compulsion to give herself fully and the joy of her new sensuous experience.

Though the Englishman is identified with an arrogant world 'which sent out judges and administrators to its colonies', he is not merely callous. He cossets himself with semi-imaginary invalidism and makes that the moral excuse for his actions, but without being a villainous seducer. Incapable of fathoming Andrina's fatalistic acceptance of God's will (whether it brings pain or joy) he misreads it as an admirable 'emancipated' courage. He needs to justify his actions before his own conscience, and Pauline Smith sets forth his morally self-deluding arguments with an ironic sympathy that shows a grasp almost as sure of this kind of sophisticated mind as of the 'simpler' minds of the Little Karoo people.

He had taken nothing from Andrina which she had not been willing to give. He had given her nothing which she had not been eager to have. He had done her no harm. Again and again, as if in argument with an opponent, he insisted upon this—he had done her no harm.

Despite his desertion and her desolation, she joyously looks forward to the birth of the child that will be her comforter.

Their relationship and the exploration of its enriching effect upon Andrina do not constitute the whole core of the novel. This again lies in the setting of the Aangenaam valley and the nature of the forces that work upon its inhabitants. The bitter feud between Johanna Steenkamp and the beadle, Mijnheer van der Merwe's stern patriarchy, his wife's beneficence, the comic, well-intentioned matrimonial manipulation of Tan' Linda of the post office, and the canny motives behind Jan Beyer's wife-seeking—all these form a skilfully integrated pattern both for the characterisation of a people and for the working out of Andrina's fate.

One of Pauline Smith's creative strengths is her ability to present the warping, through a variety of pressures, of human feeling into perverse self-torture and cruelty to others: a father in anguish over dangers to his child but unable to prevent them because he is too proud to acknowledge that she is, illegitimately, his; an outcast finding peace and love but destroying both in the same kind of fit of demented rage that had driven him thousands of miles from home. In *The Beadle* one sees it particularly in the beadle's treatment of Jacoba Steenkamp, whose forgiveness of his ancient infidelity twists his conscience-stricken mind into uttering the cruel words that hasten her death. A tubercular miller dies without being able to articulate the tender words that will wipe out the effect of his self-pitying outbursts of rage against a timid wife whom he had loved dearly before his illness. One of the most powerful of the stories is 'The Father', which unfolds the process by which Piet Pienaar acquires, and tries to push a holding of farmland to the river bank by scrimping and piecemeal purchase. This passion is frustrated by Mijnheer van Reenen, a shrewd landowner with a reputation for 'evil-living'. Pienaar gradually becomes so unhinged that he convinces himself of the illegitimacy of his only son, 'whose birth had closed Aantje's womb to those other sons for whose creating he had married her'. His delusion leads to an attempt upon his son's life so that he may triumph over the combined mockery of himself by God, Mijnheer and Aantje.

Pauline Smith has nothing to say about black-white racial tensions in South Africa. 'Ludovitje', the least successful of her stories, is the only one which, on a mystical–religious plane, deals specifically with relations between Afrikaner and African. But her grasp of the situation is summed up with caustic economy in this passage from *The Beadle*:

> When the last of the dishes was cleared away, the great Bible was placed before Mijnheer. From a drawer in the sideboard Andrina brought the psalm-books—one for each person round the table and one for the Englishman among the rest. From the kitchen quarters came the native servants, crowding in the doorway without entering in the room and squatting down there on the floor. The chapter was read. The psalm was sung. Jantje, slipping from his chair, walked up to his grandfather's knee and repeated his evening prayer. From the doorway came the indentured children and they too, at their master's knee, repeated a prayer. 'Make me obedient to my mistress, oh Lord', prayed Spaasie in her rough, hoarse voice. 'Make me to run quickly when my master calls', prayed Klaas.

Her art deals uncompromisingly with the passions of an obscure community. It is never likely to be 'popular', but its influence is to be found in the work of subsequent South African writers, both in English and Afrikaans, among them Alan Paton. Ten months before Pauline Smith died at Broadstone in Dorset, on 29 January 1959, a group of South African writers acknowledged their indebtedness by presenting her with an illuminated scroll as 'a tribute of our admiration'. More widely, her stories form a small but living contribution to the specifically English literary tradition inspired by the best qualities of English puritan fidelity.

4. Tim Couzens: Sol Plaatje's *Mhudi**

One of the first novels written in English by an African, *Mhudi*, which was published in 1930 but probably largely written about 1917 or 1918, has not been considered worthy of major critical attention. In 1952, J. Snyman could dismiss the book fairly quickly and attack Plaatje for a lack of imagination:

> In *Mhudi* (1930), Plaatje deals with the times of Mzilikazi, and especially with the war between the Matabele and Barolong. He has examined the causes of this war and finds that its origin lay in the murder of Mzilikazi's tax-collectors by the Barolong. He shows also that the Matabele had justification for some of their deeds. Plaatje takes pride in his people, and attempts here to interpret to the reading public 'one phase of the back of the native mind', as well as to gain sufficient money to arrest the lack of interest of his people in their own beliefs and literature, by collecting and printing Sechuana folk-tales which are in danger of being forgotten through the spread of European ideas. Although *Mhudi* would seem to be authentic, it lacks the spontaneity of Mitford's Untuswa series. The reader is aware that the writer is recounting events which occurred a hundred years ago, and it seems as if Plaatje is unable to span the gap and live in the period about which he is writing. Little fault can be found,

*From: *The Journal of Commonwealth Literature*. vol. viii. no. 1. (June 1973) pp. 1–19; this article is a development of ideas which Dr Couzens originally expressed in another article, 'The Dark Side of the World: Sol Plaatje's *'Mhudi'*, English Studies in Africa* (Johannesburg), XIV, 2(1971).

however, with his account of life at Mzilikazi's kraal in the Matabele capital.[1]

Martin Tucker remains somewhat non-committal:

Plaatje's novel, *Mhudi: An Epic of South African Native Life a Hundred Years Ago*, written at least ten years before its publication by Lovedale Press in South Africa in 1930, is an attempt at blending African folk material with individually realized characters in the Western novelistic tradition; the result has been both admired and denigrated by commentators. Plaatje's story of the two Bechuana natives who survive a raid by warring Zulu tribe, fall in love (one episode describes the admiration which the hero inspires in his female companion when he subdues a lion by wrenching its tail), and triumph over the mistreatment they endure from the Boers whom they have aided, is leavened by the humour and sense of proportion. Although the novel contains idyllic scenes of native life, the hero Ra-Thaga, and Mhudi, who becomes his wife, are not sentimental Noble Savages but peaceful citizens forced to accept the harshness of the invading white world.[2]

Tucker says too that 'Plaatje is not highly regarded by his fellow African writers today'. Janheinz Jahn has categorised *Mhudi* as being 'hedging or half-and-half' writing and as 'mission' literature:

No hard-and-fast line, of course, can be drawn dividing 'apprentice' and 'protest' literature. Between them there is a wide field of 'hedging' or 'neutral' works. For, to avoid having to approve their tutelage, many writers glorified the traditional life of the tribe and the tribal chiefs and heroes: this can be interpreted as a form of indirect protest. The novel *Mhudi*, for instance, by Solomon Tzhekisho Plaatje (1877–1932), is a love story which has as its background the battles between Mzilikazi's Ndebele and the Baralong.[3]

Jahn has also written of *Mhudi* that it is 'weak in comparison with other works, for Plaatje tries to individualise his characters in the European fashion and thus the African pathos of the dialogue becomes empty'.[4] When critics largely ignore the social-historical milieu from which a work springs, the unfortunate situation can arise that a book is written off for its poor 'quality of writing' or for what at first sight seem to be clichaic ideas. Not only do arbitrary and vague (and often ethnocentric) ideas of 'taste' lead to hasty dismissals, they also conveniently allow the critic to avoid the book. *Mhudi* seems to be such a novel, which has been neglected for the lack of a little extra research.

To characterise *Mhudi* as in any way being 'neutral', as Jahn does, may be in the interest of categorisation, and may be the reasonable expectation set up by works of Plaatje's contemporaries, but it certainly cannot seriously be maintained in the light of Plaatje's character, his beliefs, his actions, and his other writings. This article argues that a study of these matters throws new light on *Mhudi*.

Since biographical information on Plaatje is not easy to come by, it seems desirable to quote a pen-sketch which Plaatje probably played a large part in writing:

Mr Sol T. Plaatje was born at Boshof and educated at Pniel Lutheran Mission school. Married Elizabeth, daughter of the late Mr Mbelle, and sister of Mr I. Bud Mbelle, of Pretoria. Was interpreter to the Court of Summary Jurisdiction under Lord Edward Cecil. Rendered much service to the British Government during the siege of Mafeking in the Anglo-Boer War. Was editor of *Koranta ea Becoana* and *Tsala ea Batho*, Kimberley. Was war correspondent during the Anglo-Boer War. Foundation member and first geneal secretary of the South African National Congress when Rev J. L. Dube was president. Went abroad twice on deputations in 1914 and 1919. Toured Canada and the United States during 1920–3. Founder and president of the Diamond Fields Men's Own Brotherhood. On attaining fifty years of age, in 1928, a group of Bantu, Coloured and Indian admirers started a Jubilee Fund and purchased his residence, 32, Angel Street, and gave it to him as a present in appreciation of his lifelong unsalaried work in the Non-European cause. Mr Plaatje is now engaged in writing Sechuana Readers for native schools. He is the author of the famous book *Native Life in South Africa*. Has also written *Mhudi*—a novel, *Sechuana Proverbs and their European Equivalents*, *The Mote and the Beam*, *Native Labour in South Africa*, also *Sechuana Reader in International Phonetics* (the latter in conjunction with Professor Daniel Jones, M.A., University College, London). The latest of Mr Plaatje's books is the translation of Shakespeare's works in Sechuana. Is one of the best writers and speakers among Africans in S.A.[5]

A founder member of the African National Congress (he refused its presidency on one occasion), a writer of famous political book (*Native Life in South Africa*) and of two linguistic texts, Plaatje, the uncle of

Z. K. Matthews, was in the forefront of the political defence of his people throughout his life and was certainly no Uncle Tom of the missions. Indeed, in a letter to the Administrator of Rhodesia in which he attacks the hypocrisy and knock-kneed quality of English liberals (particularly John Harris, the Secretary of the Aborigines Protection Society), he describes himself with characteristic humour and irony:

> I am exceedingly sorry to encroach upon your precious time but, as the following lines will show the above controversy [between Harris and the Rhodesian Government] is of intense interest to me and the natives of the Union; you will perhaps be surprised to hear that I, a native of natives, immensely enjoyed reading the sound thrashing administered to Mr J. H. Harris by the logical pen of His Honour Sir Drummond Chaplin.[6]

In this article I would like to examine three major issues relating to Plaatje's work in general and to *Mhudi* in particular: (1) the question of his language use, attempting a partial defence of it; (2) his distinctive ideas of history, the portrayal of which is virtually unique in South African literature; (3) the question of whether *Mhudi* is something more than a lovely idyll with black heroes or an historical romance. I argue that *Mhudi* is a sensitive political novel, in which the historical moment of the 1830s was a carefully selected model for Plaatje's own situation in the period after Union and the Natives Land Act of 1913.

Janheinz Jahn talks of Plaatje's 'padded "Victorian" style',[7] and it is true that Plaatje uses 'poetic' archaisms such as 'jocund lambs', 'eligible swains', and 'native gallantry', but these tend to be absent when Plaatje reaches the more significant moments in his narrative and, in any case, the phrases often seem to be used with that distinctive sense of irony which is seldom far from the surface in all of Plaatje's writing (as, for instance, in the probable pun in the last of the examples cited). This irony manifests itself in Plaatje's frequently used technique of reinforcing his argument by couching it in his opponents' own terms — whether their language or their beliefs. The technique can be illustrated by his use of a European (Scottish) proverb to illustrate the throwing-off from their land of two related 'native' families, described in his book *Native Life in South Africa*.

> The father-in-law asked that Kgobadi should try and secure a place for him in the much dreaded 'Free' State as the Transvaal had suddenly become uninhabitable to Natives who cannot become

servants; but 'greedy folk hae long airms', and Kgobadi himself was proceeding with his family and belongings in a wagon, to inform his people-in-law of his own eviction without notice, in the 'Free' State, for a similar reason to that which sent his father-in-law adrift.[8]

The passion here is in no doubt, for his hatred of the Natives Land Act is implicit in all Plaatje's public actions after 1913, and the irony is savage. It is the irony of adopting what many South African whites would call the 'cheeky Kaffir' stance, by answering the opponent in his own language. To miss Plaatje's tone, and often his irony, will almost inevitably lead to patronising his language. It would be well to remember that the great linguist Daniel Jones, in his preface to *A Sechuana Reader* which he and Plaatje compiled, found Plaatje in possession of 'unusual linguistic ability'.

For his use of Biblical and epic language, though perhaps not completely successful, Plaatje does at least give a justification, whether adequate or not. In the introduction to his *Sechuana Proverbs* he writes: 'The similarity between all pastoral nations is such that some passages in the history of the Jews read uncommonly like a description of the Bechuana during the nineteenth century'.[9] There is here a concept of decorum, and the use of the metaphor of the Garden of Eden at the beginning of the novel to describe African traditional life is not accidental—for he is showing an idyllic society about to be shattered by forces which were the genesis of South Africa's problems, as Plaatje saw them after the Natives Land Act. What is more, Plaatje comments on the limitations of his own use of language within the novel itself. He says of the speech of Chief Moroka:

His speeches abounded in allegories and proverbial sayings, some traditional and others original. His own maxims had about them the spice of originality which always provided his auditors with much food for thought . . . The crowd pressed forward and eagerly hung on to every word, but it is to be regretted that much of the charm is lost in translation.[10]

Plaatje was fully aware of all the problems of 'translation' which still beset the African writer, but once his decision was made he did not fuss unnecessarily about it. One of his minor themes, however, is the tragedy which frequently arises because of the lack of communication through mutual ignorance of respective languages, whether between man and man, or man and beast or nature.

But Plaatje does not simply use clichaic English of suitable decorum.
Part of the richness of literature lies in deviation. And Plaatje frequently
gives us a fresh idiom, stemming often from 'translation'; for example,
his description of lions as 'making thunder in the forest',[11] or when one
speaker rebukes another for dissenting, by saying 'his speech was the
one fly in the milk'.[12] The language of the novel abounds also in
localised South African imagery. Most interesting in the field of the
figurative use of language, however, is his deliberate distribution of
proverbs.

In discussing proverbs in both their oral and written form, Ruth
Finnegan has written:

> In neither case should they be regarded as isolated sayings to be
> collected in hundreds or thousands on their own, but rather as just
> one aspect of artistic expression within a social and literary context.[13]

It is noticeable that in *Mhudi* there is a marked increase in the number
of proverbs used by speakers during the crucial debate amongst the
Barolong about whether they should help the Boers (five proverbs in
five pages,[14] three of them given to the man who is the ideal of justice,
Chief Moroka, whose 'allegories and proverbial sayings 'were both
original and traditional). This debate reveals one of the major themes of
the book; that the whites would scarcely have survived without the aid
of the blacks, and the heightening of the language through proverbs,
showing the traditional wisdom of the debaters, is both functional and
significant. There is also, in the same scene, interesting confirmation of
another of Ruth Finnegan's suggestions:

> Though proverbs can occur in very many different kinds of contexts,
> they seem to be particularly important in situations where there is
> both conflict and, at the same time, some obligation that this conflict
> should not take on too open and personal a form.[15]

A conflict situation arises in the debate, but is de-fused through a
humorous proverb:

> Some were for letting the Boers stew in their own juice, as the
> Barolongs had perforce to do years before; others were for combining
> with the Boers against the Matabele; some again were for letting the
> enemy well alone as long as he remained on the far side of the Vaal
> River—that river of many vicissitudes and grim histories—yet

many believed that a scrap with the Matabele with the aid of the Boers would give each one an opportunity of avenging the blood of his relations before he himself joined his forefathers. Such were the conflicting views that found expression among the waiting throng. One grizzly old man with small jaws and very short teeth, touching his shins said: 'Oh, that I could infuse some youth into these old bones and raise my shield! I would march against the vampires with spear in hand. Then Mzilikazi would know that among the Barolong there was a man named Nakedi—just as the pack of lions at Mafika-Kgo-coana knew me to their cost.'

One man raised a laugh among the serious groups. 'What a truthful thing is a proverb,' he said. 'According to an old saying "Lightning fire is quenched by other fire". It seems a good idea then to fight the Matabele with the help of the women, for they always kill in their attacks. If Sarel Siljay's women had not helped the Boers, they would not have defied Gubuza's army and Schalk would not be here to tell the tale.'[16]

The 'sense of detachment and generalization inherent in proverbs'[17] is clearly in evidence, mixed here with laughter in its conflict-avoiding function.

Plaatje's relationship with proverbs has yet one more interesting aspect. At the Matabele victory celebrations after the defeat of the Barolong near the beginning of the book, one man, Gubuza, stands out against the rest in warning of the possible consequences. His pessimism is rebuked by another speaker but Mzilikazi defends Gubuza.

If Gubuza had not spoken I should have been very sorry. You see a man has two legs so as to enable him to walk properly. He cannot go far if he has one leg . . . For the same reason he has two eyes in order to see better. A man has two ears so as to hear both sides of a dispute. A man who joins in a discussion with the acts of one side only, will often find himself in the wrong. In every grade of life there are two sides to every matter.[18]

In this idiomatic passage, which is Plaatje at his very best, the near-proverbs express the idea of the two-sidedness of arguments. The idea seems to interest him. In his collection of Sechuana proverbs Plaatje writes:

The reader will here and there come across two proverbs that appear to contradict each other; but such anomalies are not peculiar to Sechuana . . . The whole truth about a fact cannot be summed up in one pithy saying. It may have several different aspects, which taken separately, seem to be contradictory and have to be considered in connexion with their surrounding circumstances. To explain the connexion is the work of a sermon or essay, not of a proverb. All the latter can do is to express each aspect by itself and let them balance each other.[19]

It seems to me that he extends this idea into both the theme and technique of the novel. Although the book is clearly an epic praising the Barolong, through the technique of shifting perspective, we come to have a certain sympathy with the Matabele; we see, in fact, the final battle through their eyes not through those of the favoured victors (this is a technique which is probably reinforced by his translation of several Shakespearian plays, for though the crimes of Claudius and Macbeth are very similar, our response is different, but only because of the amount we see of their inner thoughts). The technique, then, in the novel, is of shifting perspective; what both sides are given through this technique is a reinforcement of one of the major themes — that there *are* two sides to every argument.

The merit of Plaatje's novel also lies in other directions. Because South African written history has been dominated by white historians and most of South Africa's imaginative writers have been white, South African history and literature usually display a bias of historical interpretation which seldom escapes complete ethnocentricity. Writers have endlessly extolled the courage of the Voortrekkers and the 1820 Settlers, but Plaatje is one of the few, and certainly one of the very earliest, who dealt with the events from 'the other side', from the side of the people who had to face dangers just as great, if not greater, for they ultimately came into contact with a people who had the advantage of those conveniences of civilisation, the horse and the gun. (Indeed, without these two benefits, with, according to some historians, the Bible as a supplement, it is difficult to see how the whites could have survived at all in South Africa.) In *Mhudi*, the Great Trek is put into perspective, and is seen as a mere part of a much greater complex of events and activity. So that, in *Mhudi*, the whites appear only a third of the way through the book, and the course of South African history had already been as much determined by interaction amongst the blacks as anything the whites could do in the future. In other words, the blacks *made history* in South Africa as much as, if not more so than, the whites. Plaatje perceived that the Boers were simply a fourth force added to the existing groups of Barolong, Matabele and Korannas — not to mention Griquas, Bakwena, Bangwaketse, etc. The world of the novel is that of the relatively peaceful tribes inhabiting the areas around Transorangia who are, after the initial idyllic setting, thrown into turmoil as a result of the 'Mfecane;, the great upheaval caused by the transformation of the tribes of Northern Natal into the Zulu military state, when tribes were sent fleeing all over Southern Africa and the effects of the upheaval were felt in areas as far distant as present-day Tanzania. J. D. Omer-Cooper has written of the 'Mfecane': 'It far exceeds other comparable movements such as the sixteenth century migration of the Zimba and Jagas and it positively dwarfs the Boer Great Trek'.[20]

Life before the 'Mfecane', though not without its inter-tribal conflict, was fairly peaceful, and it is this life which Plaatje is describing at the beginning of the novel. The introduction of the terrible and warlike Matabele is clearly meant to be a contrast to the picture of the relatively peaceful Barolong — relatively peaceful because Plaatje's image of the Barolong has two sides to it. In his *Sechuana Proverbs* he took pains to describe his disagreement with prevailing historians over the character of the Bechuana, particularly the Barolong:

> Historians describe the Bechuana as the most peace-loving and timid section of the Bantu. Their statements, however, do not seem to be quite in accord with the facts; for, fighting their way South, from the Central African lakes, some of the Bechuana tribes become known as 'the People with the Sharpspear'. And if I am not much mistaken they were the only natives who indignantly, though vainly, protested against the 'South African Defence Act which debars Native citizens from joining the Citizen Volunteer Force' . . . But the proverbial phrases in this book do not seem to support the view that they are by nature far from being bellicose.[21]

Most of their proverbs, he points out, are of hunting or the pastoral and not concerned with war, but it is his clear intention to show that though the Barolong love peace they are brave if war is necessary. His concern here is not unreasonable. The leading historians of his time were explicit. G. W. Stow, for instance, wrote of the Barolong in 1905:

> They seem however to have possessed the same natural timidity as the rest of the Bechuana, and as a race were not a whit more warlike

than the cowardly Batlapin themselves, who, as we have seen, were only brave when they found their antagonists weaker than themselves, or when they had defenceless women and children to deal with.[22]

The historian Theal concurred in 1915:

> It is impossible to give the number of Moselekatse's warriors, but it was probably not greater than twenty thousand. Fifty of them were a match for more than five hundred Betshuana.[23]

Plaatje's motive in showing the Barolong to be courageous when necessary was not only to counter white prejudice but also to indicate that the exclusion of his people from the army was one more sign of the inequality existing at the time of writing. (The whites' ability both to admire and condemn the bravery of the Zulu war-machine is a fascinating exercise in double standards; the whites' pride in 'bringing peace' yet their contempt for the Tswana 'cowards' is a similar contradiction and forces Plaatje to defend on two seemingly contradictory fronts.)

In keeping with this view of history, in which blacks contribute as much as whites, Plaatje does not sentimentalise the Boers as so many writers have done. Rather he views central South African history more in terms of what someone once described as 'a clash of rival cattle cultures'. De Kiewiet describes it in terms which would probably have appealed to Plaatje:

> The native wars, from major campaigns to unheralded skirmishes, were spectacular phases in a lengthy process of encroachment, invasion, extrusion, and dispossession. For the most part of the wars were not caused by the inborn quarrelsomeness of savage and warlike tribes, but by the keen competition of two groups, with very similar agricultural and pastoral habits, for the possession of the most fertile and best-watered stretches of land.[24]

Plaatje gives a view of a Boer search-party in *Mhudi* which few white writers would ever have thought of at the time.

> The search party looked foolish as they brought no news, but the climax of their incompetence came a few days later when a Basuto chief sent an ultimatum to the effect that the Boer party had killed two

of his men and maimed two more who were peacefully hunting on the
Vaal River . . . But thanks to the intercession of Chief Moroka, a
satisfactory compromise was effected.[25]

The only Boer who is sympathetically dealt with in *Mhudi*, Phil Jay, is
described by the heroine, Mhudi, as 'the one humane Boer that there
was among the wild men of his tribe', and even he, despite the general
sentimentality used to describe him, is illiterate.

Not only is Plaatje able to correct what he ragards as a mistaken bias
in history, he is, at the same time, able to defend many traditional
customs and beliefs of his people and to establish them as a coherent
system within the novel. He praises his own people for the same things
that Edward Blyden praised Africans for in his *African Life and Customs* (1908) — for their religions and socialism, their system of marriage, and the absence of orphans and prostitutes. From the beginning
of the book he emphasises the religion of his people, with the ancestral
spirits at its core, and contrasts it with the broken-down Christianity of
the Boers. And throughout the book he contrasts the basic justice of the
traditional society with the arbitrary, dictatorial justice of Mzilikazi
(and, implicitly, of modern whites, as we shall see). In Chapter Fifteen
of *Mhudi*, Chief Moroka is seen to dispense justice in a manner far
superior to any of the other characters, including white men, and the
function of the chapter is somewhat similar to that of Chapter Ten in
Chinua Achebe's *Things Fall Apart*—in both books justice is established as central to the society and is given a central place in the book.
De Kiewiet has described the tragedy of the whites' failure to see any
merit in African society:

At least two generations of settlers grew up in ignorance of the
ingenuity and appropriateness with which the natives in their tribal
state met the many problems of their lives, in ignorance of the
validity of many of the social and moral rules which held them
together. European society most easily saw the unattractive aspects
of tribal life. It saw the superstition and witchcraft and cruelty. But it
failed to see, or saw only imperfectly, the rational structure of tribal
life, the protection which it gave the individual, the comfort which it
gave his mind, the surveillance which it kept over the distribution of
food and land. European society condemned as stagnant and unen-
lightened a way of life in which happiness and contentment were, for
the native not difficult to find. Between soldier and settler, missionary and magistrate there was an unvoiced conspiracy against the

institutions of the tribe.[26]

Plaatje has clearly chosen to describe a time when these values and customs were most coherent, most unified, strongest, and yet also a time of transition when these values are about to change or disappear. He chooses a period where he can analyse both the values and the genesis of the causes of their disappearance.

It is Plaatje's view of history, then, which directs him to choose this particular period for his novel. But there is a possible further reason for his choosing this time. Omer-Cooper points to it:

> The events of the Mfecane have moreover impressed themselves indelibly in the consciousness of subsequent generations. The memories and traditions of this period serve to maintain the sense of identity of peoples who were vitally affected by it, influencing attitudes within and between groups in many complex ways. In the context of white rule, this heritage has helped many peoples to keep alive a sense of pride and independence of spirit. Together with other factors it has contributed to that great reservoir of largely inarticulate feelings and attitudes which underlies the emergence of modern African political movements.[27]

Plaatje returns to a time when (in the face of a common enemy, the Matabele) there are the beginnings of inter-tribal unity, when the seeds of the alliances of 1917 were first sown, when the possibility of a nationalism transcending tribalism was first conceivable (linked naturally to Plaatje's interest in the South African Native Congress). In this period of the 1830s Plaatje discovers 'a sense of pride and independence of spirit' whose incarnation is the heroine, Mhudi. Vladimir Klima has admirably hinted at these aspects of the novel:

> The novel is remarkable for memorable portraits of Negro characters (mainly female ones are well characterised), and for Plaatje's original interpretation of historical facts. Both the Zulus and the Boers are shown as violent invaders but the author's compassionate detachment helped him in presenting a well-balanced historical fresco in which human fates can easily be traced. Mhudi's love story is especially successful and would provide a good piece of reading even outside the historical framework of the novel.[28]

Mhudi, however, is not a novel interesting only for its concept of history and its defence of traditional custom. It is also a document relevant to the time it was written in, relevant to that period immediately following the Natives Land Act. It is also a comment on the conditions which resulted from that Act. Plaatje attacked the Act directly in his best-known book *Native Life in South Africa*, and in his pamphlet on the legal disabilities of Africans. I believe that *Mhudi* and *Native Life in South Africa* should be read in conjunction for they were not only written within a short time of each other, but they also show Plaatje's consistent and persistent preoccupations. The Natives Land Act was devastating in its effect, rendering homeless large numbers of Africans throughout the Union and causing untold hardship. *Native Life in South Africa* is an explicit, and *Mhudi* an implicit, attack on the Act and the hardship it caused. *Mhudi*, I believe, is a political novel relevant to 1917 or thereabouts.

South African history largely revolves around two problems: land and labour. The whites have usually solved both problems simultaneously: take land away from the Africans and they then need to sell their labour. The labour shortage can often be helped, too, by the levying of a tax. And, throughout Plaatje's writings, a single theme constantly recurs — the loss of the land the African loves and needs. 'To lose land', writes De Kiewiet, 'was to lose the most important foundation upon which tribal life was built.' (So Plaatje's defence of traditional custom described above is an integral part of what follows.)

In *Mhudi* Plaatje's people are deprived of their land (after refusing to pay taxes) by the Matabele; in *Native Life in South Africa* they are deprived of their land by the whites. It seems to me, therefore, that Plaatje intends *Mhudi* to be, in addition to the true perspective of history discussed above, a model for events including and after the Natives Land Act of 1913. For, in *Native Life in South Africa*, the whites are described in exactly the same terms as are the Matabele in *Mhudi*. The Natives Land Act, for instance, is called 'the plague Law', 'this Parliamentary land plague', 'the land plague' and 'the plague Act'. Furthermore, he quotes with approval a speech by Dr A. Abdurahman:

Now let us consider the position in the Northern Colonies, especially in the misnamed Free State. There a very different picture is presented. From the days that the voortrekkers endeavoured to escape English rule, from the day that they sought the hospitality of Chief Moroka, the history of the treatment of the blacks north of the Orange River is one long and uninterrupted record of rapine and greed, without a solitary virtue to redeem the horrors which were committed in the name of civilization. Such is the opinion any impartial student must arrive at from a study even of the meagre records available. If all were told, it would indeed be a bloodcurdling tale, and it is probably well that the world was not acquainted with all that happened. However, the treatment of the Coloured races, even in the Northern Colonies, is just what one might expect from their history. The restraints of civilization were flung aside, and the essentials of Christian precepts ignored. The northward march of the voortrekkers was a gigantic plundering raid. They swept like a desolating pestilence through the land, blasting everything in their path, and pitilessly laughing at the ravages from which the native races have not yet recovered.[29]

In *Mhudi* the Matabele are described as continuing 'their march very much like a swarm of locusts', and Chief Moroka later asks for help 'to rid the country of this pest'. Both the whites and Mzilikazi levy taxes and give little in return, and both have systems of justice arbitrary in the extreme. The Matabele in *Mhudi* are particularly loathsome because they are 'impartial in their killing',[30] women and children are not spared. In *Native Life in South Africa* the whites share this trait:

When the Free State ex-Republicans made use of the South African Constitution — a Constitution which Lord Gladstone says is one after the Boer sentiment — to ruin the coloured population, they should at least have confined their persecution to the male portion of the blacks — and have left the women and children alone.[31]

The implicit comparison in *Mhudi* is explicit in *Native Life*:

'This', says Mr Ludorf, 'caused the Natives to exclaim: "Mzilikasi, the Matabele King, was cruel to his enemies but kind to those he conquered; whilst the Boers are cruel to their enemies and ill-treat and enslave their friends".'[32]

If there are doubts that Mhudi provides a model for the situation created by the Land Act they should be assuaged by the dedication of the novel, to 'Our beloved Olive, One of the many youthful victims of "A Settled System"', a dedication very much against the land settlement scheme. Indeed, the whole theory that *Mhudi* is a model for 1918 can be checked by reference to pages 105 to 111 of *Native Life*, where

the whole background plot of *Mhudi* is specifically recounted as
leading up to and foreshadowing the Land Act.

What makes the behaviour of the Boers worse is the hospitality and
generosity with which they are originally received by the Africans, in
Mhudi and, according to Plaatje, in history. The leader of the Korannas
for instance, says that for any man who enters his dominion: 'My home
is his home, my lands are his lands, my cattle are his cattle, and my law
is his shield'.[33] And when the Boers arrive, 'the Barolongs informed the
Boers that the country round about was wide and there was plenty of
land for all'. The Boers' hospitality does not show up well when
Ra-Thaga tries to drink water from a vessel in the Boers' camp.[34] Not
only has the Boers' subsequent behaviour shown ingratitude towards
original hospitality but it is shown to be even worse: for in *Mhudi* they
even plead for help from the Barolong when hard-pressed by the
Matabele. Their subsequent unification with the Barolong and Griquas
against the Matabele also has its ulterior motive. 'Of course,' explains
Plaatje in *Native Life*, 'Boers could not be expected to participate in any
adventure which did not immediately lead to land grabbing.'[35] The land
in question is not only vital in itself; it leads to another important
problem, that of labour. As I have remarked, it has been a frequent
device in South African history to cure labour problems by the confis-
cating of land, and allowing the Africans nothing to sell but their
labour. This labour problem, too, has its model in *Mhudi* in the Boers'
treatment of their Hottentot servants, as in the following episode:

> Outside one of the huts close by she observed a grizzly old Boer who
> started to give a Hottentot maid some thunder and lightening with
> his tongue. Of course Mhudi could not understand a word: but the
> harangue sounded positively terrible and its effect upon the maid was
> unmistakable. She felt that the Hottentot's position was unenviable,
> but more was to come. An old lady sitting near a fire behind the
> wagon took sides against the maid. The episode which began rather
> humorously developed quickly into a tragedy. The old lady pulled a
> poker out of the fire and beat the half-naked girl with the hot iron.
> The unfortunate maid screamed, jumped away and writhed with
> pain as she tried to escape. A stalwart young Boer caught hold of the
> screaming girl and brought her back to the old dame, who had now
> left the fireplace and stood beside a vice near the waggon. The young
> man pressed the head of the Hottentot girl against the vice; the old
> lady pulled her left ear between the two irons, then screwed the jaws
> of the vice tightly upon the poor girl's ear. Mhudi looked at Phil's

mother, but, so far from showing any concern on behalf of the
sufferer, she went about her own domestic business as though
nothing at all unusual was taking place. The screams of·the girl
attracted several Dutch men and woman who looked as though they
enjoyed the sickly sight.[36]

'Africa,' Plaatje writes in *Native Life*, 'is a land of prophets and
prophetesses.'[37] And the idea of *Mhudi* being a model for a future time
fits neatly into the prophetic strain of much of the work. In fact, in a
crucial prophecy, Mzilikazi specifically points to it. In one of Plaatje's
most interesting and skilful adaptations of an oral literature technique,
Mzilikazi takes a folktale from the past and says it applies to his own
fate. He then says that his own story applies to the Barolong in the
future:

The Bechuana know not the story of Zungu of old. Remember him,
my people; he caught a lion's whelp and thought that, if he fed it with
milk of his cows, he would in due course possess a useful mastiff to
help him in hunting valuable specimens of wild beasts. The cub grew
up, apparently tame and meek just like an ordinary domestic puppy;
but one day Zungu came home and found, what? It had eaten his
children, chewed up two of his wives, and in destroying it, he himself
narrowly escaped being mauled. So, if Tauana and his gang of
brigands imagine that they shall have rain and plenty under the
protection of these marauding wizards from the sea, they will gather
some sense before long.

Chaka served us just as treacherously. Where is Chaka's dynasty
now? Extinguished, by the very Boers who poisoned my wives and
are pursuing us to-day. The Bechuana are fools to think that these
unnatural Kiwas will return their so-called friendship with honest
friendship. Together they are laughing at my misery. Let them
rejoice; they need all the laughter they can have to-day for when their
deliverers begin to dose them with the same bitter medicine they
prepared for me; when the Kiwas rob them of their cattle, their
children and their lands, they will weep their eyes out of their sockets
and get left with only their empty throats to squeal in vain for mercy.

They will despoil them of the very lands they have rendered unsafe
for us; they will entice the Bechuana youths to war and the chase,
only to use them as pack-oxen; yea, they will refuse to share with
them the spoils of victory. They will turn Bechuana women into
beasts of burden to drag their loaded wagons to their granaries . . .[38]

The folktale is seen a model for Mzikazi, and Mzilikazi in *Mhudi* is seen as a model for the twentieth-century black South African. Thus the folktale here is used not merely for its quaintness but for its model-like functions, a use which illuminates the technique of the whole novel.

There is a further and, I think, conclusive proof of this model-like function of the novel. Implicit in the model of *Mhudi* is the warning that, if a people like the Matabele oppress other peoples long enough, the oppressed will eventually unite and overthrow their oppressor, in open conflict if necessary—that such oppressors are, in a phrase from *Native Life*, 'courting retribution'. The whites are being warned in *Mhudi* that the kind of thing they are doing, as described in *Native Life*, could lead to ultimate revolution. What confirms it, I think, is his use of Halley's comet. Halley's comet appeared in 1835, and, though the Matabele were only driven out of the Transvaal at the beginning of 1837, Plaatje has conflated time so that the comet appears immediatley before the Matabele exodus and is heralded by a 'witch-doctor' as presaging disaster:

> Picking up his bones once more, he cast them down in different positions, and repeating the operation a few times, he critically examined the lay of every piece and, having praised his bones again, he said 'Away in the distance I can see a mighty star in the skies with a long white tail stretching almost across the heavens. Wise men have always said that such a star is the harbinger of diseases of men and beasts, wars and the overthrow of governments as well as the death of princes. Within the ray of the tail of this star, I can clearly see streams of tears and rivers of blood.' Having praised his bones once more, the wizard proceeded: 'I can see the mighty throne of Mzilikazi floating across the crimson stream, and reaching a safe landing on the opposite bank. I also perceive clear indications of death and destruction among rulers and commoners but no death seems marked out for Mzilikazi, ruler of the ground and of the clouds.'[39]

Here probably is another reason why Plaatje chose the 1830s. For the next time Halley's comet appeared was in 1910, and it was specifically interpreted by many millenarian movements as heralding the overthrow of the whites (in the quotation above Plaatje uses the phrase 'overthrow of governments'). Not only that, but there were strong millenarian movements of this kind amongst the Barolong, which, as editor of a Sechuana newspaper and living in the area, Plaatje must have known about. *The Rhodesia Herald* newspaper reported events from Kimberley on the 18 April 1910. (Taungs is a town in the very heart of the country of the northern Barolong; it means 'place of the Lion' and is named after the great Barolong chief of the eighteenth century, Tau, mentioned in *Mhudi*. From his sons sprang the various sub-groupings of the tribe)

> There are again rumours of unrest among the natives of Taungs, where it is stated two stores have been burned and a native, who was flogged as a result of the last disturbances, has been arrested for preaching sedition, the natives being told that when the comet appears is the time for wiping out the white man. The available police in Vryberg and Mafeking have been drafted to the district. Inquiry is being made into the truth of the statements going round.[40]

This report tells of the persistence of the disturbance, the scale of it (to require so many police), and the unrepentant quality of its participants. The disturbances, which became known as the 'Bechuana Scare', continued. A report from Kimberley on 25 April went thus:

> *The Advertiser's* Taungs correspondent reports that another native prophet has been arrested at Mogopella by the native headman. There is still one more prophet at large, but the police are vigilant.[41]

In the same paper there is a further report:

> The special correspondent of *The Advertiser* at Taungs, in the course af a review on the position in Bechuanaland says the sentences of five and six-and-a-half years' hard labour on the two natives last October for seditious teaching have evidently not had a salutary effect. To deal with the problem he suggests (1) that the chief and headmen be called together to a meeting at which should be impressed upon them their paramount duty of discouraging by every legitimate means seditious teaching; (2) a meeting should be called of all native missionaries, evangelists, and teachers in the affected area who should be appealed to to counteract the effect of seditious and superstitious teaching; (3) a strong, well-paid and efficient corps of native detectives should be organized and used to the utmost possible extent.

That the effect of Halley's comet was widespread and persistent and was interpreted as presaging the end of the white man is confirmed by events in 1921.

> The second train of events involved the 'Israelites'. Gathered around their religious teachers on Bullhoek commonage near Queenstown, they had been deeply impressed by the appearance of Halley's comet and accepted this as a sign to abandon the New Testament as the invention of the white man. Returning to the Old Testament, they became fanatically indifferent to the threat of modern weapons in the belief that Jehovah was about to liberate his chosen people from the foreign yoke. After repeated warnings to abandon their recently erected huts and return to their various villages, and after leading congressmen had backed this up with a plea that they obey and avoid impending violence from the State, a strong police contingent was despatched to assert government authority. When the Israelites charged with home-made weapons, 171 were shot dead.[42]

This prophetic concern of Plaatje's may also be influenced by the ideas of Marcus Garvey.

The final questions to be asked is what is Plaatje's solution. The revolutionary solution is to be tried as a last resort only, it seems. The prior hope lies in what is symbolised by the women-folk. Plaatje shows himself in his writings to be fully aware of the female emancipation issues, which critics who have condemned his Europeanising of his characters have not taken enough account of. The old life has been partially destroyed in *Mhudi*, a woman is thrown out into the wilderness on her own and she acquires an independence manifested in her ability to face lions and other dangers. Mhudi herself is a symbol of the pride and spirit of her people, and circumstances have forced her into a measure of independence. She is the 'cradle of the race', as sceptical of the Boers as she is of the Matabele. On the individual level she comes to friendship with the women who are symbols of what is virtuous in the other peoples—Umnandi, favourite wife of Mzilikazi (significantly this first lady of the children-slayers is childless) and Annetje, the Boer girl. By splitting the friendship of the individuals from the hostility of the people for one another, Plaatje has been able to give us a glimpse of the possible ideal as well as a view of the real situation. His final warning seems to be contained in an opinion quoted from the *Brotherhood Journal*: 'For Brotherhood is not only between man and man, but between nation and nation, race and race'.[43] In a prize-winning essay written late in 1910 and published in the Johannesburg *Chronicle* (it is otherwise unpublished), Plaatje considered the desirability of the separation of segregation of races and came to the conclusion it was desirable but impossible. The events since the 1830s had led to an 'economic interdependence' (to use a phrase of Peter Walshe's) which was unalterable and irrevocable. In the final passage of the essay he considers first the self-governing black state, then he rejects its possibility and directs his plea to South African liberalism (reflecting something of the naivety of the early Congress leaders), advocating only the banning of the bar and the side-bar.

> They (the blacks) will not pay any taxes unless, as in Basutoland, the money is devoted soley for their use. This will result in a net loss to the Union Treasury of £2,000,000 annually and a large sum to the respective municipalities. Europeans will make the rude discovery that the Kaffir was handy not only as a water carrier, but as the gold mine from which local and general exchequers drew heavily and paid the fancy salaries which helped to educate white children and keep white families in comfort. Millions of money now circulating amongst Europeans will be withdrawn to pay black officials and feed black storekeepers; the effect whereof will be wholesale dismissal of many white men, and then the trouble will begin. Oh, no! earlier still, for I am sure that when you tell the traders of the Transkei to relinquish their holdings and seek fresh pastures in white areas, they are not the Englishmen I took them for if they do not resist the order at the point of a bayonet. The ideal is sound, but how will you attain it? . . . Two things you need to give the native, and two things only must you deny him. Keep him away from liquor and lawyers; give him the franchise and your confidence, and the problem will solve itself to your mutual advantage.

Plaatje's plea is initially to reason, but if reason fails, there is his prediction.

5. David Rabkin: Race and Fiction: *God's Stepchildren* and *Turbott Wolfe**

In *God's Stepchildren*, published in 1924, Sarah Gertrude Millin wrote of the British attitude to the 'colour problem':

> . . . colour was so rare a thing [there] that it was only a matter of casual consequence: the ordinary person did not think of it, or brood over it, or consider it, or understand it.[1]

In *Turbott Wolfe*, published only a year later, William Plomer's eponymous hero, recently arrived in South Africa from Britain, predicts:

> There would be conflict between myself and the white; there would be conflict between myself and the black. There would be the unavoidable question of colour. It is a question to which every man in Africa, black, white, yellow, must provide his own answer.[2]

Plomer and Mrs Millin were to advance radically opposite answers to the question of colour. Their novels, curiously alike, though different in many ways, both reflected the growing importance which the question of colour was assuming in the minds of the South African intelligentsia

* This article was written by Dr David Rabkin as a chapter in an uncompleted study of South African fiction, before he was sentenced to ten years' imprisonment in 1976 under the provisions of the South African 'Terrorism Act'. He is serving his sentence in Pretoria Prison. The chapter has been very slightly edited by Arthur Ravenscroft for publication as an article.

in the 1920s. The problem was not new. It had been present from the time of the first white arrival. Nor was Mrs Millin's novel the first to deal with the 'tragedy of colour', as has often been claimed. J. P. L. Snyman, in his comprehensive study of her work, points out that at least two previous books had dealt with material vey similar to that of *God's Stepchildren*.[3] Certainly, Plomer's novel was an original. No work of fiction had hitherto discussed miscengenation as a possible *solution* to the colour question. Nor had any depicted South African society with Plomer's broad satiric brush and cosmopolitan deftness.

That the decade of the 1920s were a period of exceptional creative upsurge is a commonplace of modern English literary history. The impact of the First World War is often advanced as a cause. It has less often been observed that the period was exceptionally fruitful in South African literature, too, in quality if not in quantity. The years 1924–6 saw the publication of *The Little Karoo, The Beadle, God's Stepchildren* and *Turbott Wolfe*, which together form a very substantial segment of what is valuable in South African prose fiction in English.

As in Europe, it was a period of unrest and upheaval in South Africa. The war had merely interrupted and deferred a tide of rising prices, class conflict, and African resentment. A number of bitter strikes of white miners had been the prelude to the outbreak of war and a warning of what was to come. In 1919 the African National Congress, roused from a period of dormancy, instituted a campaign against the pass laws, which led to armed clashes between white and black on the Rand (it was the whites who were armed).

The general strike and insurrection of 1922 was fought on the basis of the defence and extension of the colour bar in employment, but the militancy of white trade unionists stimulated the growth of black unions too. The twenties witnessed a significant number of strikes by black workers, as well as the remarkable growth of Clement Kadalie's black Industrial and Commercial Workers' Union.

It is the underlying social process, witnessed by these tumultuous events, which is of interest to the literary historian. The basic fabric of South African life was changing, from that of a predominantly rural to a more urbanised nation. It is in this period that the Poor White problem began seriously to concern politicians of all races. The destructive effects of the Anglo-Boer war had dealt a mortal blow to the rural economy, and by 1920 the vast majority of white workers on the Rand were Afrikaans-speaking, recently-arrived, low-skilled whites. In the city they were forced to compete with black labour. And even though protected by discriminatory legislation and custom, the spectre of racial mingling, of 'the white man sinking to the level of the native', became the popular bogey-myth of the time, the watch-word of both the Labour and Nationalist parties, and the basis for their Pact government, which came to power in 1924.

Writing about *Turbott Wolfe*, Michael Wade had commented: 'After such writing the South African novel could scarcely look back, in terms of the racial theme; its period of innocence had ended.'[4] The innocence to which he refers is the perspective of Olive Schreiner, which could leave the question of colour aside, while remaining morally relevant. He puts the cart before the horse, however, because changes in the national life were what put an end to the period of innocence. The colour problem had become acute. Neither the intellectual nor the artist could ignore it. Nor was it any longer possible to accommodate the conflict within the terms of Victorian rational reformism. For that reformism itself had been stricken by the turmoil of war, and mankind's confidence in rationalism had suffered a near-fatal blow.

The appearance, within less than twenty-four months of each other, of *Turbott Wolfe* and *God's Stepchildren*, certainly signalled this new situation. The opposite points of view taken by the two novels ensured a very different reception for them, in South Africa at least. *God's Stepchildren* was immediately popular, recognised by South Africans as the plausible and articulate ejaculation of their racial nightmares. *Turbott Wolfe* was greeted by a furore of protest and vituperation, a national adjectival orgy of denigration, which Laurens van der Post has described amusingly, in his introduction to the 1965 edition of the novel. Mrs Millin's work was immediately successful, running into several editions, and being translated into many languages. *Turbott Wolfe* had to wait thirty years before it was re-issued by Hogarth.

Yet in critical estimation, *Turbott Wolfe* has followed a steadily ascending, *God's Stepchildren* a steadily descending curve. The change reflects changing attitudes towards the question of race in the English-speaking world; a novel which was enthusiastically promoted by the Nazis as a lesson in the evils of racial impurity must today have a serious question mark placed over it. (Ironically, as a Jew, Mrs Millin was an ardent opponent of Nazism.)

Sarah Gertrude Millin was born in 1889, and spent her early years in the Kimberley area, along the banks of the Vaal. One of South Africa's most prolific authors, she wrote sixteen novels, as well as two volumes of autobiography and numerous works of non-fiction and essays. Her early novels recount life along the Vaal river, and the theme of miscegenation is powerfully present from the very beginning. Mrs

Millin has herself identified this pre-occupation with her childhood experience:

> Nothing in my young life has shocked me more than the wickedness of miscegenation: the immediate shame and the way it filled the world with misery.[5]

Nevertheless, it is in *God's Stepchildren* that Mrs Millin first presents this theme in a systematic (one might almost say, schematic) way. *God's Stepchildren* traces the effects, through four generations, of the Rev Andrew Flood's decision to marry a Hottentot woman, Silla. Modelled to some extent on the Dutch missionary van der Kemp, Flood is a 'liberal' whose yearning to sacrifice himself for the betterment of the black races Mrs Millin identifies with a weakness of character. He is an unattractive man with romantic aspirations which he lacks the strength of character to carry out. Mrs Millin contrasts him unfavourably with the Rev Thomas Burtwell, of the nearest mission station, a no-nonsense administrator who teaches the Hottentots practical skills instead of discussing theology with them. The names of the respective mission stations, Canaan and Kadesh (holy) sufficiently indicate the author's attitude towards the rival methods of proselytisation.

The Rev Andrew Flood is already going to the dogs when he decides to marry Silla, and the marriage impells swiftly along the route. The couple have two children, a dark-skinned boy and a lighter girl, Deborah. The boy is absorbed by the Hottentots and passes out of the story. (That Mrs Millin finds his *integration* with the blacks of no interest is significant.) Deborah is sent to Kadesh where she becomes a house servant and a teacher in the mission school. Soon (sooner than a white girl would, it is implied) she looks for a 'mate' and has relations successively with a 'pure-bred' Hottentot and a white trek-boer, Hans Kleinhans. Of this latter union a son is born, whom Deborah names Kleinhans.

Deborah and her child later join a group of Griquas, trekking to establish a new national home in Griqualand East (the original home of the Griquas, a mixed-race tribe, was simply annexed by the British when diamonds were discovered there). In Griqualand East young Kleinhans thrives, being naturally industrious and a good farmer. Light of complexion and with a tawny beard, Kleinhans despises those darker than himself and admires the whites; he is determined to marry a white woman. He sells up his holding, and moves to the diamond fields. Here he is rudely rebuffed by the colour-conscious diggers who will have nothing to do with a 'Bastaard'. He is beaten senseless by a group of white men for trying to speak with them as an equal.

Kleinhans is rescued by an English-speaking farmer, Mr Lindsell, and becomes foreman on Lindsell's farm. He marries a Coloured woman, one of Mr Lindsell's servants. Their first child, a daughter whom they name Elmira, is both very fair and beautiful. She is favoured by the ageing valetudinarian Lindsell, and sent by him to a white school. When her mixed parentage is discovered at the school, Elmira is forced to leave. Not unnaturally she now finds herself wholly alienated from her own family, and suffering from that self-hatred of colour, which, according to Mrs Millin, is the inevitable result of 'mixed blood'. Once more sent off to school in Cape Town, Elmira is again forced to return when the 'secret' of her birth gets out. This time she remains on the farm, becoming an object of attraction to Mr Lindsell after the death of his wife. He marries Elmira, though he is more than twice her age, in the hope that her youth will help to prolong his vigour. The girl accepts the marriage passively, bears Lindsell a son, Barry, and then runs away with a younger white man.

After his father's death, Barry is adopted by his step-sister Edith, and taken to live in Cape Town. Deeply ashamed of the 'stain' on his birth, Barry grows up an introverted and uncertain young man. In this and in the religious fervour which he conceives in adolescence, as well as in physical appearance, he resembles his ancestor, Andrew Flood. Barry goes to England where he is ordained, serves as a chaplain in the First World War (when he shows cowardice, a sign, Mrs Millin tells us, of his Coloured ancestry, as if there were no white cowards), and returns to South Africa, with an English wife. Just when he seems to have achieved happiness, though the impending birth of his child is causing him anxiety, he receives a letter from Lindsell's Farm, informing him that his mother is dangerously ill. Returning to his birthplace, Barry is confronted with the history of his family, which he describes to his wife as:

> . . . my whole story. The natives in their huts. My great-grandmother, old Deborah. Her son, Kleinhans. My mother. Myself. I saw what had come down to me, and what I was handing on to others . . . (p. 306)

Barry decides that, 'for his sin', he will renounce his wife and unborn child, sending them back to England, and go among the brown people as a missionary. He will return to Canaan, where his ancestor, the Rev

Andrew Flood, had first initiated this 'tragedy of colour'.

God's Stepchildren is a frankly racialist novel, of a type common enough in its time, but probably quite rare today. It reflects the general theories of race popularised in the age of Empire, and instilled into the youth of the time by numerous school-boy adventure tales. For Mrs Millin the spectrum of pigmentation, from white to black, is equivalent to the spectrum of mental development, from the fully human to the animal. The browns occupy a rank just above the apes, whom they resemble in many ways. Thus the Hottentots are 'monkey-like people', (p. 8) 'in the main, stupid and indolent', (p. 19) while their Coloured descendants 'often remained to the end of their days gamins by disposition, imitative and monkey-like', (p. 229) as well as being 'too often . . . small and vicious, and craven and degenerate' (p. 228). Small wonder that Barry is ashamed of his ancestry, or that his maternal grandfather, Kleinhans 'despised a man in proportion as he was brown'.[11] But this too, this self-hatred, which, if Mrs Millin's racial theories were accurate, is only a rational view, is interpreted by the author as evidence of her characters' degeneracy.

In other ways, too, Mrs Millin's novel reflects the racial theories of the time. Thus the 'backwardness' of the coloured races is accounted for by a theory of arrested development, according to which the young black person develops more quickly than the white, but reaches a peak of ability sooner and at a lower level. This theory determines the characterisation in the novel, as will be seen below. The early precocity, followed by mental stagnation, is closely linked in the novel with the early sexual maturity supposed to be general among African peoples. In a peculiarly unpleasant way the two notions are thought to bear out the animality of the non-white.

If, in *God's Stepchildren*, all black people are thought of as inherently inferior to whites, nevertheless Mrs Millin reserves a special *frisson* for the person of mixed race. He is thought to combine 'the worst of both races' and to be rejected by both alike: 'Whatever else the black man might be, he was, at least, pure'. (p. 227). That Mrs Millin herself accepts these ideas, and is not merely exhibiting them as typical attitudes is very clearly demonstrated in the section (pp. 228–230) where she steps out of the narrative structure of the novel to discuss race. The following passage generalises the theory in national terms:

In other parts of South Africa, among the Zulus, the Pondos, the Swazis, the Damaras, and other such tribes, the people were big, and black and vigorous—they had their joys and chances; but here, round about Griqualand West, they were nothing but an untidiness on God's earth—a mixture of degenerate brown peoples, rotten with sickness, an affront against Nature. (p. 293)

Here is a fitting argument for selective genocide. It is not surprising that Hitler's ideologues found *God's Stepchildren* a worthy work of literature.

On the evidence of such ideas, it might be expected that Mrs Millin's attitude towards the act of miscegenation itself would be simply negative. It is negative indeed, but a curious duality runs through her attitude, expressed most clearly, perhaps, in a remark quoted from the autobiography.[6] There she refers to two aspects of miscegenation, 'the immediate shame and the way it filled the world with misery'. Thus the white man who has intercourse with a black woman is commiting a shameful, sinful act *whether or not* a child is born as a result. This is the sin, which is to be visited upon even the fifth generation, though Mrs Millin does not tell us which commandment the act violates. Instead she tries to give substance to her shame of sin by depicting the misery it brings to successive generations.

Nowhere does Mrs Millin suggest or imply that the unhappiness felt by the offspring of mixed relationships is caused by the prejudices and racial animosity shown by white South Africa towards its black fellows. On only two occasions does refer to the existence of non-racialist ideas about multi-racial societies. At the very beginning of *God's Stepchildren* she refers to Andrew Flood's British conviction of the 'essential equality of all human beings'. In large measure, the novel itself is intended as a refutation of this proposition. Towards the end of the book, Barry's English wife responds to his confession of 'black blood' with a surprised 'Is that all?' It is very unlikely that Mrs Millin endorses this comment, because some pages earlier Mrs Lindsell's remark is heavily qualified by the reflection that the 'ordinary person' in Britain was unconcerned with colour, 'did not think of it, or brood over it, or consider it, *or understand it*'. (p. 263, my emphasis) Moreover, Mrs Lindsell's *sang-froid* does not survive long, and soon she is demanding that Barry take her back to England, where she 'need not see these brown creatures'. (p. 279) At most there is in Sarah Gertrude Millin a hesitation about endorsing race discrimination *in principle*, i.e. as a universal law, but there is little moderation in her general contempt and distaste for Coloured people, which can be discerned in the tone and imagery of her narrative, as well as in its explicit pronouncements. It is certainly true to say, as the Czech critic

Vladimir Klima remarks, that Mrs Millin was 'too much frightened by miscegenation' to 'present any real analysis' of the phenomenon.[7]

The deficiency of analysis in the novel is supplied to some extent by the strong note of fatalism that runs through the narrative. Mrs Millin's novels in general conform to a fatalistic and often pessimistic outlook on life. *God's Stepchildren*, with its structure based upon the passage of generations, and its great need to compress events and reflection, necessarily moves at a cracking pace. Birth, parturition, and death are viewed in a detached way:

> As, without protest, the stars ran along their endless course, and woman went so many months with child, and seeds burst into life through the earth, and death came swishing along, so, with the same abandoned sense of fatality, Elmira accepted her function as Adam Lindsell's wife . . . (pp. 174–5)

Similarly her comment on the death of the first Mrs Lindsell, after she has catalogued the ways in which the surviving family adjust their attitudes towards the deceased, is a curt 'And life went on'. (p. 139)

Two secondary themes bear out the general fatalism which the novel displays. There is the theme of heredity, which, in addition to the 'attenuated dark stain' (p. 230) borne by successive generations, is expressed in Barry Lindsell's physical and emotional resemblance to his remote ancestor, Andrew Flood. The second is the attack upon liberalism, indeed upon all attempts to reform the world; it is the main content of Part One of the novel, 'The Ancestor', which condemns as futile and mischievous naïevty Flood's attempts to communicate upon equal terms with his aboriginal flock:

> They only knew that the white man was not so much better than themselves, as they had once supposed; and such little respect as they had originally had for him . . . on account of his whiteness, they had gradually lost. They allowed themselves liberties with him . . . (p. 36) [After his marriage to Silla]. The people were all the more friendly to him, too. He told himself that at least he had won them.
>
> They despised him utterly, and his religion. (p. 46) The belief that

any social or political concessions offerd by the whites will be abused by the blacks is, of course, a stock South African response to the liberal proposition. Sarah Gertrude Millin reinforces the 'logic' of this response by making the Rev Andrew Flood a wholly unattractive and inconvincing proponent of liberalism. The emotional life of the character is so shallowly conceived by the author that he appears to the reader as little more than a vague succession of sighs and blushes. Mrs Millin does not give liberalism a chance.

Such are the main features of *God's Stepchildren*, as far as content is concerned. (Consequent deformations in characterisation and style will be examined later, together with a consideration of *Turbott Wolfe*.) In its central theme the novel touches on a concern which is crucial to the South African novel, and became its main pre-occupation in the twenties, largely through the influence of this book. In its obsession with miscegenation, *God's Stepchildren* shares an important concern with William Plomer's first novel, *Turbott Wolfe*. In its treatment of liberalism it touches upon a topic which occupies a more central position and acquires a much greater complexity of conception in the latter work.

William Plomer was born in Pietersburg, in the northern Transvaal in 1903. His father was part of the British administrative apparatus, then engaged in settling claims and restoring administration in the aftermath of war. At an early age, William was sent to boarding-school in England, and only returned to South Africa at the age of fifteen. Owing to the weakness of his eyes, his parents did not send him to a university; instead, he became an apprentice farmer in the Stormberg Mountains of the Eastern Cape. Later, he joined his family in a trading venture in Zululand.

It was the experience of these years which Plomer utilised in the writing of *Turbott Wolfe*, which he completed when he was only nineteen years old. The manuscript was accepted by Leonard and Virginia Woolf at the Hogarth Press. Some time before its publication (delayed by production difficulties) in 1926, Plomer had made the acquaintance of Roy Campbell and Laurens van der Post, then collaborating on the literary magazine, *Voorslag*, in Durban. Plomer joined the magazine, and at this time wrote the stories later published in the collection *I Speak of Africa*. *Voorslag* was short-lived, however, and with Laurens van der Post, Plomer took advantage of a free trip to Japan. He did not return to South Africa, except apparently, for a visit in 1956. In the first volume of his autobiography, *Double Lives*, Plomer disclaims a South African identity, declaring that he 'should be no more justified in pretending to be a South African than in declaring myself a Bantu'.[8] Yet he admits at the same time that he 'must partly belong' to South Africa. It is that part of this particularly cosmopolitan author which resulted in *Turbott Wolfe*. Though Plomer cannot be regarded as a South African novelist, his first novel does belong to the corpus of South African literature and as such it has received increasing critical attention in recent years.

Perhaps the strongest claim on behalf of *Turbott Wolfe* has been made by Laurens van der Post; in his introduction to the 1965 edition, he asserts that *Turbott Wolfe* marks a decisive turning point in the development of the South African novel:

> For the first time in our literature, with *Turbott Wolfe*, a writer takes on the whole of South African life. Suddenly the barriers are down and imagination at last keeps open house in a divided land. The black people of South Africa are no longer just a problem . . . Nor, in *Turbott Wolfe*, are the black people used merely as an incitement to adventure and romance. They take their own place in their own right as individual human beings.[9]

Though van der Post's claims require some qualification, the importance of the appearance of *Turbott Wolfe* is beyond dispute. Merely by its stance in favour of miscegenation it would have been a landmark in South African literature. Yet, despite many deficiencies of thought and construction (of which more below) the work marked a leap forward in its style, its cosmopolitan panache, and its satiric detachment. It is a forerunner of the 'liberal novel' and at the same time a critique of liberalism.

Turbott Wolfe takes the form of a personal narrative told by the eponymous hero to one William Plomer. In shabby lodgings near the sea, Wolfe is dying of 'a fever that he had caught in Africa'. (p. 57) The narrative recounts the events that followed his decision, on medical advice, to leave Britain for Africa and open a trading post in Lembuland. The social conflict into which Wolfe is tossed is identified early in the novel:

> Round us as we talked circulated a crowd of black, white and coloured people: English, Dutch, Portuguese, nondescript were the whites; Bantu, Lembu, Christianized and aboriginal, Mohammedan negroes were the blacks; and the coloured were all colours and all races fused. It came upon me suddenly in that harsh polyglot gaiety that I was living in Africa; that there is a question of colour. (p. 62)

Established as a trader in Lembuland, Wolfe swiftly comes into conflict with the local white farmers represented by Bloodfield and Flesher, broadly drawn specimens of local prejudice and parochial pettiness. They despise Wolfe for his dedication to the arts, and for his apparent determination to treat the Lembus as equals. Wolfe finds an ally of sorts in the Norwegian missionary, Nordalsgaard, described in the typical style of the novel as 'like an immense electric storage battery, full of nervous energy, in secret communication, in secret touch with each individual native soul'. (p. 66)

Wolfe, nicknamed 'Chastity' by the Lembus, has his first brush with the question of colour when he falls in love with a Lembu girl, Nhliziyombi. He lacks the courage (or perhaps the *will*) to declare his love and, at a brief and ambiguous encounter in the forest, gives the girl a gold pin. Later he learns that she is to be married. Wolfe takes consolation in his art, and in long discussions with his Lembu storeman, Caleb Nsomi. But the main plot of the novel only gets under way with the arrival of the Rev Rupert Friston, a young British missionary who comes to replace Nordalsgaard. Friston is highly unconventional and believes that the task of the missionary is more political than religious. Together with Wolfe he visits Francis d'Elvadere, described as a 'voluptuous pioneer', one of the old school of settlers, free of the narrow-minded prejudices of the other whites. At d'Elvadere's the two young Englishmen meet Mabel van der Horst, an Afrikaner with unusual ideas about colour:

'But poof!' the woman exclaimed, 'native question! What the hell *is* the native question? You take away the black man's country, and, shirking the future consequences of your action, you blindly affix a label to what you know (and fear) the black man is thinking of you—"the native question". Native question, indeed! . . . It isn't a question. It's an answer.' (p. 137)

The three whites team up with Wolfe's storeman, Caleb, and his brother Zacchary Msomi, to form a society, Young Africa. The principles of the group are defined by Caleb, in a letter to a local black newspaper:

To put it in a Nutshell, WE BELIEVE:
1. That Africa is not the white man's country.
2. That miscegenation is the only way for Africa to be secured to the Africans.
3. That it is inevitable, right and proper.

4. That if it can be shown to be so, we shall have laid true foundations for the future Coloured World.
5. That we are pioneers. (p. 144)

   Though Young Africa does not itself become very active in the
political sphere, the coming together of the group sets up further
personal conflicts. Both Friston and Zacchary fall in love with Mabel,
and the latter succeeds in winning her. Wolfe takes it upon himself to
warn Mabel against marrying an African, but is rudely rebuffed.
Mabel looks with scorn upon Wolfe's timidity. Friston reacts to the
relationship by taking to a hallucinogenic drug, which brings to the
surface the dichotomy inherent in his position as proponent of miscegenation and lover of Mabel van der Horst.

   Friston recovers from this state, however, and officiates at the
wedding of Mabel and Zacchary. At the ceremony he preaches a long,
rambling sermon which combines a vision of 'Eurafrica' with reference
to Bolshevism. Later Friston goes off on a 'holiday' to 'Swedish East
Africa' where he plans to stay at the kraal of Nhliziyombi. He does not
return. A cable arrives to communicate his death, and among his
papers Wolfe, Mabel and Zacchary find a letter, apparently from a
'Bolshevik Agent'. The letter concludes: 'I have a vague chance of
getting away. If I escape, it will be with the conviction that it will take
more than Moscow to organize Africa'. (p. 197) With the death of
Friston, Young Africa disperses. Wolfe decides to sell his trading post
and return to Europe, where he will lead a frugal, almost hermetic life.
Before he is able to leave, he is summoned by the local authorities and
informed that his trading license has been revoked, as a result of his
general behaviour and especially his political activities.

   After its long period of neglect, *Turbott Wolfe* has been attracting
some critical attention in recent years. Cosmo Pieterse, in his lecture
reproduced in *Protest and Conflict in African Literature*,[10] sees the
novel as a broadly sketched depiction of the germ of conflict in South
Africa. Pointing to the way in which Plomer has introduced a
representative survey of South African social types, he takes the
author's attitude towards miscegenation a bit more simply than
perhaps is justified. There is at least a strong suggestion in *Turbott
Wolfe* that miscegenation, admirable in theory, may prove dangerous,
even cosmically dangerous, in practice:

   I remembered that every civilized man, who considers himself sensitive, in touch with native peoples in his daily life should have in his

heart an image of the failure of Gauguin. Was it a failure? I asked myself: and in the question itself thought I suspected danger. I found myself all at once overwhelmed with a suffocating sensation of universal black darkness. Blackness. I was being sacrificed, a white lamb, to black Africa. (p. 73)

This fear of the unknown is in part a characteristic of Turbott Wolfe's own personality, a shrinking from experience which earns him the nickname of 'Chastity'. As such it is effectively contrasted with the frank impulsiveness of Mabel van der Horst, who at the end of the novel is seen by Wolfe to embody the essential qualities of the new society, Eurafrica. But it is also an independent element in the conception of the novel. Plomer is speculating about the decline of the West, a process which he associates with the rise of the dark races and the triumph of Bolshevism. These ideas were fashionable at the time.

What gives the novel its fresh and surprising quality, however, especially in the South African context, is the jaunty *sang froid* with which the author contemplates the decline. He presents a number of vivid images of corruption and decadence, the most explicit, perhaps, being the drowning of Tyler-Harries, European critic and savant who goes down at sea in the company of a coloured stewardess: 'They were both very far gone in raw cane-spirit, kindly supplied by the lady'. (p. 62) The image of Tyler-Harries's death recurs as a part of Friston's hallucinations. The decadence of present-day Europe, as exhibited by its representatives in Ovuzane (the bloodless aestheticism of Wolfe on the one hand, and the coarse brutalism of Bloodfield on the other) is contrasted with the energy and integrity of the nineteenth century. Klodquist, Nordalsgaard and d'Elvadere represent the latter, men not tortured by doubts and retaining the open-minded rationalism which shows Europe at its best.

What it all amounts to is something larger and less well-defined than the indictment of liberalism, which Michael Wade sees as the main content of the novel.[11] Though Wolfe's attitude is clearly shown to be inadequate by the end of the novel, there is no indication that Friston, who has turned to activism, will fare any better. Indeed, his expedition to the Tugela river has obviously ended in disaster at the hands of the local tribesmen. The letter sent to him by the 'Bolshevik agent' also hints at inadequacy and confusion. In truth, *Turbott Wolfe* does not end in any clear way, as Cosmo Pieterse points out. The fragments of verse and prose appended to the narrative are intended to be gnomic and ambivalent.

In this context, it is helpful to look at William Plomer's own assessment of the novel. In *Double Lives*, Plomer writes:

> . . . in the matter of writing a novel, I was attempting to reach by a short cut what can only become visible by taking an arduous road . . . the whole proceeding is crude and immature, and disfigured by an unpleasant superficial smartness or vulgar cleverness.[12]

Of course, the author is too harsh. His novel's wit and cleverness are far from unpleasant. Nevertheless, Plomer obviously had a sense of some lacuna in the work, which makes him refer to a short cut. The lacuna can be described, at the level of content, as an inability (rather than an unwillingness) to consider fully the implication of the situation which the novel presents. Thus for instance, the character of Zacchary Msomi is scarcely developed, though in the nature of things he might be expected to be leading voice in Young Africa.

Where Zacchary remains a purely visible image (Plomer describes him, physically, with some care), the whites remain voices, rather than beings. Indeed the novel as a whole has a kind of radio-theatre quality: the voice of 'William Plomer' retelling the narrative of Turbott Wolfe who in turn mimics and satirises the speaking tones of the other characters. Plomer himself describes it as 'an ejaculation, a protest . . .'[12] Here, if not in the nature of the protest, it resembles *God's Stepchildren*.

Indeed, the two novels have a number of common features, apart from their general concern with miscegenation and their embryonic treatment of the problem of liberalism. Both are schematic in their conception, though in *God's Stepchildren* the scheme is based on plot, in *Turbott Wolfe* on character. Both employ a style which is abbreviated, suggestive, brittle, rather than ample, exhaustive and controlled.

Plot in *God's Stepchildren* is the enactment, through four generations, of a proposition which is fully developed in the first section of the novel ('The Ancestor'). The sequence of events is determined by the need to change the historical backdrop periodically, from the trek of Adam Kok's Griqueas to the Diamond Fields and on to suburban Cape Town. Fundamentally, the options open to the descendants of Andrew Flood do not change or develop. Actual mechanical development of the plot is therefore necessarily a matter of chance, as is the discovery of Kleinhans by Adam Lindsell. Yet for all her fatalism, Mrs Millin is unable to imbue the twists of her plot with the sense of an inevitable

Hardyesque tragedy (something she would perhaps like to do), for the essence of her proposition about miscegenation is that it is a *voluntary* act of evil, all the consequences of which are implicit in what she herself called the 'immediate shame'. The narrative developed by Mrs Millin is thus full of incident but barren of events. That is why she is able to develop an essentially irrevelant interest in the circumstances of the Lindsell family, without any distraction from the main topic. Indeed the main topic, since it is quite static, must needs be defined by contrast with the surrounding scene. Many things happen, in *God's Stepchildren*, but little changes.

By contrast, William Plomer has called the plot of *Turbott Wolfe* 'exiguous and somewhat absurd . . . There was not much of a story, but the story was not the point'.[14] What plot there is involves simply an unfolding of character. What happens to the characters is implicit in the author's initial conception of them. Even the development of Friston from debating society politics to some kind of activism is an unfolding of a latent extremism, conceived of as a trait of character. The only true event in the novel is the departure of the Norwegian missionary Nordalsgaard, the representative of nineteenth-century energy, who vacates the stage in order that the decadence of his spiritual successors may be exhibited. That *Turbott Wolfe* succeeds in its intention of portraying a violent society on the brink of extreme change, despite this absence of a plot, is to a large extent due to the very dynamic conception and execution of character. The author is highly aware of the source of contradiction, unbalance and confusion in the individual, and, by developing them, gives the narrative energy and impetus. Moreover, he exploits the dislocations between manner and substance efficiently, his characters combining in unlikely and therefore interesting ways self-confidence and confusion (Friston), aggression in manner and diffidence in action (Wolfe) and nonchalance with deep concern (Mabel).

Of this approach to characterisation in the novel, Plomer has written:

> I had no intention of drawing a self-portrait or of giving a naturalistic account of African life. Somebody called the book 'expressionist', and like many first books it exaggerated the literary faults and excesses of its period . . . it was a violent ejaculation, a protest, a nightmare, a phantasmagoria—which the dictionary defines as 'a shifting of real or imagined figures'.[15]

The expressionistic quality of the characterisation can best be seen in

the minor figures, who are drawn larger than life and with undisguised-
ly satirical intent. Plomer's disavowal of naturalism liberated him from
social documentation of the type which he attempted so disastrously in
his long short story, 'Ula Masondo'. He thus overcomes by sheer
bravado the artistic problems involved in depicting an alien people from
the outside, paying for this sleight-of-hand solution to the point-of-
view problem by a certain distancing and precocity.

That this broad depiction of character (concentration on the typical
rather than the socially average) does not become wholly arbitrary, and
therefore without interest, is due largely to the young novelist's grasp
of the historical moment which his novel arrests. Thus his portrait of
the Rev Justinian Fotheringhay and his wife is not merely absurd, but
also a meaningful portrayal of a certain dead-end in Victorian Imperial
culture, one contrasted with integrity of Francis d'Elvadere. That this
historicism is deliberate is clearly shown by the fragment of prose,
purportedly by Friston, appended to the end of the novel. This analysis
of the 'politico-aesthete' refers to the ideological turmoil of the years
entre deux guerre:

> He staggers, poor man, under the weight of the past; and he
> struggles, poor man, under the load of the future. He has not got over
> the French Revolution when he is faced with the Russian. He has not
> digested the Renaissance when he is confronted with Cubism.
> Dadaism he finds easier . . . 'Post-War', murmurs the Politico-
> Aesthete . . .[15]

This connection between the events of the novel and the deepest
undercurrents of the metropolitan historical process is an awareness
rare in South African writing, one found previously only in Olive
Schreiner.

Where character is the major form of the revelation of content in
Turbott Wolfe, it is largely incidental to the purposes of *God's
Stepchildren*. Mrs Millin attributes immutable qualities to the races
and, with minor distinguishing variations, applies them to her
variously coloured characters. The method is, of course, more
noticeable in the black characters, who are developed only to the extent
that they are required to embody the author's thesis. Kleinhans, who
according to the plot of the novel must have been a man of some force of
character, makes virtually no impression on the reader. In contrast
Adam Lindsell, whose character is developed with some care (at least
we are told a lot about it) plays no significant part on the action which is

either the product of his unique personality or a stimulus to its further development.

Mrs Millin's technique illustrates clearly the weaknesses of naturalistic character depiction. Her representative figures are designedly average, 'ordinary people' whose portrayal involves no revelation of principles moral or social, but merely fills in outlines laid down by the author by other means. They are therefore of little interest.

Sarah Gertrude Millin did not 'discover' the problem of colour. Nor was William Plomer the first to satirise South African racial attitudes. The importance of these writers in the development of the South African novel lies rather in their identification of the colour question as the central moral issue of South African society. Thus, both Olive Schreiner and Pauline Smith, while not excluding the question of colour from their range of discussion, saw it as an area where the moral issues which they were concerned with should be brought to apply. It was not for them the testing ground of morality that it constitutes, for the first time, in the writings of Mrs Millin and William Plomer.

Another way of putting it is that the awareness of colour is the dominant imaginative process at work in these novels. From their opposed points of view, both Mrs Millin and Plomer are writing from an impulse that originates in the awareness of colour. The segregated imagination has as its *starting point* the division of the races.

Such an awareness has been a dominant trend in South African fiction in English ever since the twenties. It characterises the work of Laurens van der Post, Alan Paton and Nadine Gordimer. Michael Wade has argued that 'Plomer's achievement . . . was essentially extraneous to the growth of an indigenous fictive tradition in South African literature in English'.[17] English liberalism, which Wade identifies as the universe of discourse in Plomer's novel, has nevertheless implanted itself very firmly in the awareness of English-speaking writers, and has in most cases been their point of departure for advancing a critique of racism. That the outlook has its limitations in dealing with the South African experience is possible. But it is premature to speak of it as 'extraneous'. We have yet to see the growth of any self-sustaining alternative tradition, though the work of black writers, and especially of La Guma in the novel, has held out some promise in this area.

In her essay, 'The Novel and the Nation in South Africa', Miss Gordimer remarks of the colour question:

. . . it still is *the* question. It's far more than a matter of prejudice or discrimination of conflict of loyalties—all things you can take or leave alone: we have built a morality on it. We have gone even deeper: we have created our own sense of sin and our own form of tragedy.[18]

If, as Miss Gordimer implies, the tragedy is a bogus one, then the whole course of the South African novel since *God's Stepchildren* may well be a diversion. But writers cannot choose the ground of their creativity. The segregated imagination will become an anachronism, some time in the South African future. For the white South African novelist writing in English it has, since the twenties, been an unavoidable path. For the critic the criterion has therefore been similarly predetermined. How honestly has the writer charted the path? How far has he been able to see beyond it?

6. Michael Wade: South Africa's First Proletarian Writer*

Mine Boy must be considered Peter Abrahams' first substantial novel. It was published in 1946 under the imprint of Dorothy Crisp; it was reissued in 1954 by Faber, after the double success of *Return to Goli* and *Tell Freedom*; and it made its inevitable appearance in Heinemann's African Writers Series in 1964. It contains an element of the inevitable also in its constitution, in relation to Abrahams' development. His need to express exhaustively the various meanings held for him by the experience of life in Johannesburg had been manifested clearly and frequently in his short stories and in *Song of the City*, and for the South African writer rendering the unusual point of view of the black man in white society, the urban situation presented the archetypal challenge.

Mine Boy represents, perhaps, a more disciplined and less diffuse attempt to meet this challenge than *Song of the City*, and yet in overall terms it is arguably less successful. By selecting two aspects of urban life, each of them a matter of economic necessity, and sticking to them, Abrahams is able to present a more easily graspable pattern of experience within an ideological framework that is relatively clearly defined while avoiding the diversity of episode and resultant weaknesses of plot that mar *Song of the City*. On the other hand, the worlds of the African mineworker and the shebeen queen possess relatively little elasticity, and the temptation to reduce character to wooden stereotype within a predictable plot structure is often overwhelming.

*From: *Peter Abrahams* (London: Evans, 1972).

To say that the ideological framework that encompasses the novel is a limiting factor would not necessarily imply an adverse criticism, since the canons of social realism make no allowance for the criteria of bourgeois aesthetics. This is to say that *Mine Boy* is a proletarion novel whose plot displays a Marxist perspective on life. It is proletarian in the sense that it is about members of the working class and consciously stresses the idea that. the conflicts and difficulties of the Africans in town life in South Africa have their basis in the class struggle. It contends that the problems of white workers are fundamentally similar. The two groups share a common interest: when they recognise this and act together they will overcome their problems.

This was the party line on South Africa for a long time, and Abrahams' acceptance of it is unsurprising in relation to his political development. The book was written during the war, at a time when his association with communists in England was close, and direct experience of South Africa fresh in his mind.

William Empson's well-known essay suggests that proletarian equals modern pastoral,[1] and certainly elements of Empson's argument are borne out by Abrahams' performance in *Mine Boy*. The hero, Xuma, is a highly representative figure, coming raw from the country to seek work on the goldmines in the big city. He undergoes a transformation in the course of the novel, from being the embodiment of everything that is rural in location and traditional in morals, to the new man, hero and leader of the new class: but his successful growth depends on the health of his former roots.

Xuma as a character is defined by his experiences in the city. These are intimately connected with the inhabitants of a house in Malay Camp (an old, slum area of Johannesburg once populated by Africans, Coloureds and Indians) which doubles as a shebeen (a sort of saloon bar where liquor is sold under illegal conditions). Until 1962 it was a criminal offence in South Africa to sell alcoholic beverages of almost any kind—except traditionally prepared beers, and those only under rigorously specified monopolistic circumstances—to non-whites. As a result the practice of illicit liquor selling flourished, especially in the towns, where it became institutionalised in various forms. The inhabitants of the house include Leah, the shebeen-keeper; Daddy, an elderly and incontinent drunkard; Ma Plank, Leah's older assistant; Eliza, Leah's adopted foundling who has become a school-teacher; and Maisy, a winsome urban lass. The household revolves around Leah, predictably enough, since she is perhaps the archetypal Abrahams dominant female, motherly, powerful, decisive, fearless, protective, sexual and wise. She is frequently imitated, if never surpassed, in the later novels. She takes in the helpless Xuma, who is lost, hungry and cold on the night of his arrival in the city from the north.

If Xuma represents the rural life at the beginning of the book, Leah embodies all the learning that the city has to teach, and the polarity that quickly emerges between town and country is first manifested through their relationship. She is soon telling him (in order to avoid misunderstandings):

I am here you see, I come from my people, but I am no longer of my people. It is so in this city and I have been here many years. And the city makes you strange to the ways of your people, you see? (p. 23)[2]

But he doesn't really understand and the more extended, allegorical explanation given by Daddy at Leah's behest similarly fails:

The custom and the city,' he murmured, then his eyes lighted up and he smiled. 'The custom and the city, ah. very funny. Just you listen . . .'

He got up and walked up and down the room. He rubbed his hands, smiled knowingly and smacked his lips. He lifted first one shoulder then the other.

'Very funny,' he said. 'One day the city came to visit the custom, Xuma. And the custom was kind. It gave the city food and it gave the city beer and it gave the city beautiful young women . . .'

'No, Daddy,' Leah interrupted.

'Quiet, woman!' Daddy said very firmly.

Leah smiled.

'. . . As I was saying, it gave the city beautiful young women. And then what do you think? Unbelievable. The city didn't say a word. It didn't say "No thank you" and it didn't say "thank you." And the people said, "Ah, everything will be all right now, the custom and the city are friends". Hmmmm . . . They did say that and they went out into the fields to look after their crops. And when the sun was going down they came back and looked for their beer but their beer was gone. And then they looked for the custom but he had gone too. And the city was there laughing at them. And now they go to jail if they drink beer. That's why I like beer . . . Very funny, heh, Xuma? Well, that is it and I want to go to sleep . . .' (pp. 24–5)

This passage is intended to give the reader a wider view of the situation rather than to influence the raw young Xuma. He is soon at moral odds with Leah over her refusal to share the information she buys about the liquor squad's interest in the doings of the shebeen queens with any of her colleagues in the trade:

> 'You will not tell the others,' (the policeman) said.
> 'I look after myself,' she replied and turned away.
> The policeman rode away.
> 'Come,' Leah said and led the way back to the house.
> Xuma caught up with her and took her arm.
> 'Will you tell the others?'
> 'What is it to you?' she said pulling away.
> 'You are a strange woman.'
> 'You are a fool! . . . Come! I have much to do.'
> . . . Leah went out and shut the door behind her.
> Then she pushed her head back into the room again. 'Xuma, I'm not angry with you but don't be such a fool. If I tell the others the police will know we have been warned and that will be no good . . .'
> (pp. 39–40)

It is clear that Xuma's country code is meant to embody, in however naive a manner, virtues like loyalty whose application may seem universal but which are rejected by even the kindly and good in the city. The relevance of his values has to be proved afresh, but this can only happen after they have developed and been modified through participation in urban life.

This plan of action is rigorously executed by the author, within the limits of his ability. It follows from these requirements that every episode Xuma encounters, every relationship he makes, must in some way exemplify an aspect of the city life, so that he will be able to accumulate experience by contact with it. The plot is exceedingly episodic, but far from the liveliness and vigour of the picaresque. Most of the small episodes, cameos encapsulated in the texture, thrust in by the brutal syringe of coincidence, have to do with violence, and Xuma's response to violence establishes the purity of his moral sense. His friends find his reactions inappropriate and embarrassing. This separates him from their passive if resentful acceptance of the exigencies life presents for the black townsman.

On the first of these occasions, during his first afternoon in the town, he goes for a walk in the streets of Malay Camp under the direction of Joseph, the brother of Leah's man. This is an opportunity for Abrahams to attempt to present a vision of the city through Xuma's unaccustomed eyes, but the result is rather confused. It is heavily authorial, saturated with information that Xuma could not have had time to acquire, and decidedly weak through its very lack of specificity in the evocation of atmosphere. But the standard description of the African working class disporting itself on a Saturday afternoon comes to an abrupt and significant climax.

A Coloured man and a very pale woman passed Xuma and Joseph.
'Look at those black fools.' the woman said.
The man laughed.
Xuma felt a pang of shame and turned to Joseph.
'They are the fashion makers,' Joseph said.
'But it is foolish.'
Joseph looked at him and said nothing.
Suddenly a Pick-up Van swerved round a corner. Policemen jumped out and ran down the street. The crowd scattered.
'Come!' Joseph said.
People ran in all directions. The gamblers made a grab for the stakes and ran . . . Only the Coloured people did not run.
'Come!' Joseph urged again.
'But we have done nothing.'
'They will not ask you,' Joseph said in disgust and dashed down the street.
A policeman was only ten yards away and he was coming straight at Xuma. Xuma waited. He had done nothing. He had just stood there watching. The policeman came nearer. He raised his stick and brought it down with force. It missed Xuma's head and struck his left shoulder. Pain shot through his body.
'I have done nothing.' he said and grabbed the policeman's arm before he could hit again.
'Let go! Bastard!' the policeman shouted and kicked out. Xuma felt pain shooting up his leg.
'Dog!' he whispered and struck the policeman in the face. A look of strange surprise crept into the policeman's eyes. Xuma trembled with anger. He bunched his great fist and struck again. Hard. The policeman groaned and collapsed in a heap and lay still.
Xuma looked around. The van was still a distance away but two policemen were closing in on him.
'Now I will run,' he said and ran down the street.
'Stop that man,' one of the police shouted.

A Coloured man stepped into the road and held up his hands. Xuma braced himself. His heart was pounding but he ran easily. He must be careful or this yellow bastard would deliver him to the police.

Another Coloured man stepped into the road. Xuma felt afraid. To run and knock down two men at the same time was impossible. They would catch him. He could hear the feet of the policemen behind him. He hated the Coloureds. He would hurt one of them before they got him. These half-castes!

An unbelievable thing happened. The second Coloured man knocked the first one down and ran down the street waving to Xuma. Xuma smiled and increased his pace.

'Thank you, brown man,' Xuma said.

'This way.' the man said and swerved into a passage, 'we will lose them.'

Xuma followed him. (pp. 30–32)

Whatever the deficiencies of narrative technique, the implausible convenience of the episode's position in time, one cannot deny a certain skill of economy that evidences itself in the actual presentation. Every little internal event or perception tells: it has its weight in the rhetorical structure; and this fits precisely with Abrahams' strategy. He is, after all, concerned with a kind of propaganda—information conducive to the establishment of particular conclusions. And in this he is success-ful. Xuma's resistance to the policeman occasions surprise in the latter. The point is taken that resistance is an unusual response in the circumstances. The divided behaviour of the two Coloured men illus-trates the contradictory situation of their entire community, and Xuma's reactions to them suggest his greenness as well as the black stereotype of the Coloured people. Xuma's closeness to the rural tradition is suggested by the simplicity of his thoughts and words, and the ceremonious courtesy with which he thanks his deliverer. The most important underlying rhetorical point it also conveyed strongly: the necessity and effectiveness of concerted action and solidarity between all oppressed people in the face of the oppressor. The level at which this is effective is allegorical rather than symbollic: at this stage Xuma is the innocent hero, natural man in his unfallen state. But he is so little related to his new reality that after his escape from the policeman he cannot find his way home again:

Xuma had found the street without trouble. But it was difficult to find the house. The houses all looked the same in the gathering twilight.

The same verandahs. The same yard gates. The same corrugated iron walls leaning drunkenly backwards. And all the same dirty colour. (p. 34)

As well as Xuma's fundamental displacement the passage suggests that depersonalisation and lack of individuality are a condition of non-white urban life. This suggestion is taken up and elaborated into a full-scale dramatisation of the Marxist theory of alienation in the description of Xuma's work on the mines. The passage stands in its own right and is convincing and horrifying.

With another he had pushed the loaded truck up the incline. The path was narrow on which they had to walk and it was difficult to balance well. And the white man had shouted, 'Hurry up!' And the induna had taken up the shout. And one little truck after another, loaded with fine wet white sand, was pushed up the incline to where a new mine-dump was being born.

But as fast as they would move the sand, so fast did the pile grow. A truck load would go and another would come from the bowels of the earth. And another would go and another would come. And another. And yet another. So it went on all day long. On and on and on and on.

And men gasped for breath and their eyes turned red and beads of sweat stood on their foreheads and the muscles in their arms hardened with pain as they fought the pile of fine wet sand. But the sand remained the same. A truck would come from the heart of the earth. A truck would go up to build the mine-dump. Another would come. Another would go . . . All day long . . .

And for all their sweating and hard breathing and for the redness of their eyes and the emptiness of their stare there would be nothing to show. In the morning the pile had been so big. Now it was the same. And the mine-dump did not seem to grow either.

It was this that frightened Xuma. This seeing of nothing for a man's work. This mocking of a man by the sand that was always wet and warm; by the mine-dump that would not grow; by the hard eyes of the white man who told them to hurry up.

It made him feel desperate and anxious. He worked feverishly. Straining his strength behind the loaded truck and running behind the empty truck and looking careful to see if the dump had grown any bigger, and watching the sand from the earth to see if it had grown any less. But it was the same. The same all the time. No change.

Only the startling and terrifying noises around. And the whistles blowing. And the hissing and the explosions from the bowels of the earth. And these things beat against his brain till his eyes reddened like the eyes of the other men! (pp. 65–6)

The analysis of the psychological consequences of this degrading form of work is expressed through Xuma's own reaction, and his implied frame of reference is again his rural background, where one worked for direct benefits, both tangible and intangible. Depersonal-isation and reduction of the individual to a unit in the managers' calculations come into this, but the virtue of Abrahams' description lies in convincing us of the effects of the experience on Xuma in terms of neurotic behaviour. Because the reduction of a human being to the level of a 'sheep' (Xuma says the eyes of the other miners 'are like the eyes of a sheep') is a process; it begins with the realisation of how pointless one's work is. This realisation is stronger and more demoralising in the long run if a point of contrast exists. For Xuma (and presumably the other mineworkers) this lies in their own rural experience. Other obvious aspects of the mine-workers' lives, such as racial prejudice, exploitation, an irresponsible attitude towards safety on the part of the managerial group, are all touched upon. Abrahams' initial emphasis on alienation is not only his most original and profound contribution to an outsider's understanding of the experience, it is also the most effective. The evocation of Xuma's growing sense of anxiety and psychic unrest as the nature of his work fails to compensate for the battering his senses undergo from the continual noise, explosions and whistle-blasts of his strange new environment amounts to a fine piece of psychological realism.

One reason why this passage stands out is the predictable nature of the remaining treatment of Xuma's work. Xuma becomes a boss boy, working underground, endowed with considerable responsibility for the safety and work performance of the gangers under him. Together with Paddy, his white foreman, he elicits compensation from the reluctant management for one of the miners who has been stricken with pneumoconiosis (miners' phthisis), which used to be the scourge of South African mineworkers: he draws attention to a fault in the wooden struts in one section of the mine, and disagrees with the engineer's diagnosis of its safety. Later, the collapse of these supports leads to the book's climax.

The political aim of this book is realised through standardised events of this kind, in which the relationship between characters who represent larger and conflicting interests are confined within a pre-determining ideological framework. But the description of the effect of the work on Xuma's sensibilities succeeds on a different and more meaningful level because in it Xuma exists simultaneously and convincingly as an individual as well as a representative of a class. He is not merely the stock hero of stock goldmining situations but a man in a universal situation whose reactions to specific aspects of it acquire universal significance.

The theme of alienation is broadened by embracing victims whose symptoms are not directly related to work, but to the general racial set-up. Three of these stand out: Daddy, a nameless African doctor, and Eliza, Xuma's teacher girlfriend. Daddy, as has been mentioned, is a hopeless alcoholic wreck of a man who lives at Leah's house: yet he embodies, with an effort, the version of wisdom which narrates for Xuma the parable of the custom and the city. Even at critical moments, such as the solemn council Leah holds to try to find out who is betraying her liquor-selling activities to the police, Daddy is able to do no more than lean 'against Ma Plank, his mouth half-open, a drunken film over his eyes'. (p. 186) In general Abrahams' treatment of him is gauche to the extent of patronage. Daddy is a rigid stereotype, a scarcely credible character, a jerky puppet laden with the idea of folk wisdom corrupted by urban degradation. This makes his life story even more difficult to accept, the contrast falling short of the grotesque when we learn that:

'. . . when he first came to the city he was a man. Such a man! He was strong and he was feared and he was respected. And now you scorn him. You may think I am an old woman but I tell you, Xuma, he was a man such as I have never seen.' (pp. 115–6)

The narrator is Ma Plank, who goes on to tell how

'. . . when there was trouble about the passes he stood at the head of the people and he spoke to hundreds of them and the police feared him.

'He understood and he fought for his people but he understood too much and it made him unhappy and he became like Eliza. Only he fought. And listen, Xuma, that one lying there in his own piss is wiser than Eliza. He can read and write even better than she can. He found Leah in the street and looked after her . . .' (p. 116)

Daddy dies because he has been knocked down by a car. After an intensely melodramatic deathbed scene, when he describes the funeral, Abrahams penetrates the layer of sentimentality that covers too much of the surface of the novel.

> At the head of Daddy's grave they put a little cross with a number. And under the number they wrote his name. Daddy was called Francis Ndabula . . .
>
> For a time people would mourn Daddy, and then they would forget him and the mention of his name would grow rare. Another old man would ultimately become the drunk old man of the street. Maybe they would call him Daddy too. And the Daddy who was Francis Ndabula would be forgotten. Only those of his own house would remember him. And even for them the memory would grow faint and misty. Life is so . . . (p. 200)

In this way the contrast between the two Daddies is given perspective and significance. Understanding dawns with clarity to the extent to which urban life for the African in South Africa is fundamentally a process of depersonalisation, of stripping the individual of his identity and reducing him to membership of a menial group. Even within the confines of this group, personal identity is problematical—even for his closest companions Daddy's real name has disappeared. The suggestion seems to be that there is no escape for the black man from the crippling virus of racist exploitation that pervades the urban environment. At first there is a retreat from the complete and depersonalised slavery of the work world into the meagre protection of a group of fellow-oppressed, within which a sort of half-man may be permitted to emerge. The fullness of being is suggested only in death, which is too late.

Thus this passage is closely linked with the earlier description of work alienation, and both have their structural origin in the description of city life—'the custom and the city'—Daddy gives Xuma at the beginning of the book. It is ironically fitting that the cause of Daddy's death—the motor accident—is peculiarly urban.

The final comment 'Life is so . . .' is meant to convey a sense of defeat, a fatalistic attitude induced in the mourners by the unremitting hostility of their environment and their living conditions and experiences. It is thus not intended to suggest a fundamental acceptance of basic processes or conditions of reality that are intrinsically inescapable, such as the rhythm of birth and death. Abrahams' lack of deftness in merging his point of view with that of the group of mourners gives rise to the possibility of confusion.

This quality of fatalistic acceptance of defeat is also prominent in Xuma's first encounter with the black doctor. They meet one evening in a crowd of people watching police in a rooftop chase after a man who has been playing dice in the street. The man falls, and the doctor intervenes.

Then the man moved. The crowd became individuals again. The doctor ran forward and knelt beside the man. The crowd pressed close around.

'Give him air,' the doctor said.

Xuma pushed the crowd back. 'Give him air,' he repeated.

The doctor felt the man's body all over.

'It's all right, only his arm is broken.'

The doctor looked at Xuma.

'Help me get away,' the man whispered.

Suddenly the crowd pushed and moved back. Policemen pushed through.

'Stand back,' the foremost shouted.

Xuma moved back with the crowd. Only the doctor remained.

'You!' the policeman said to the doctor. 'Didn't you hear?' The doctor got up and looked at the policeman.

'I'm Doctor Mini.'

The policeman laughed. Another behind him pushed forward and smacked the doctor in the face. Xuma bunched his fist and took a deep breath.

'You'll hear about this,' the doctor said.

The second policeman raised his hand.

'You'd better not,' another policeman said and stepped forward.

'He is a doctor.'

The other two looked at the older policeman. There was disbelief in their eyes.

'It's true,' the older policeman said.

'I want to take this man with me,' the doctor said, looking at the older policeman. 'His arm is badly broken and he's got to be looked after.'

'No bloody fear,' the first policeman said. 'He's going where he belongs, in jail.'

The doctor took out a card and gave it to the older policeman.

'I'm attached to the General Hospital, and this is my home address if you want me. I'm taking this man with me. You can come and get

him in an hour's time. And when you come I want to lodge a charge
against this man for assaulting me!' (pp. 104–5)

Xuma helps the injured man to the doctor's car, and goes with them
to his home, where he finds the same sort of middle class domestic
comfort he has just seen in the flat of his white overseer, whom he had
met by coincidence in the central part of the town earlier during the
evening. Dr Mini and his wife receive him kindly and understand his
bewilderment. He feels ill at ease, as he had felt in his foreman's
apartment: 'As though he did not belong there and it was wrong for him
to be there.' But the doctor explains:

'. . . You are not copying the white man when you live in a place like
this. This is the sort of place a man should live in because it is good for
him. Whether he is white or black does not matter. A place like this is
good for him. It is the other places that are the white people's. The
places they make you live in.' (p. 109)

Just then the doctor's nurse comes in excitedly to tell him that the
patient has escaped through the window.

Xuma watched the doctor's face. For a minute there was sadness and
hopelessness in it. Like the faces of the men who had worked on the
pile of fine, wet, white sand that would not grow less. It was there for
a minute, then it was gone, and his face was again cold and calm and
hard to make out. (p. 110)

The doctor dismisses Xuma brusquely, and he feels hurt: but his wife
behaves more graciously:

He turned abruptly and walked to the door. The doctor's wife
followed him. She held out her hand and smiled at him.
    'Thank you very much,' she said.
    Xuma took her hand. It was soft and small like the white woman's.
(p. 110)

The white woman in question is Di, the girlfriend of Paddy, Xuma's
Irish foreman. Xuma has met them earlier in the same evening during a
lively stroll through Johannesburg streets, savouring from afar the
forbidden delights of the white man's existence. They had invited him
to Paddy's apartment, where he had eaten with them, ill at ease: she

had tried to persuade Xuma of the irrelevance of colour as a barrier between human beings, but the going is hard. Afterwards she holds a colloquy with her boy-friend, who is significantly named 'Red', not only because of the colour of his hair, on the subject of Xuma: it is remarkable mainly for its confusion. Di contends that Xuma is 'not a human being yet' because, unlike Eliza, he has not reached the stage of resentment: 'She's a social animal; he's not'. Paddy exhorts her to 'for God's sake have faith in human beings. It is not enough to destroy, you must build as well. Build up a stock of faith in your breast in native Xuma, mine boy, who has no social conscience, who cannot read or write and cannot understand his girl wanting what you want.' (p. 101)

Doctor Mini makes one more appearance, when he stands helplessly at Daddy's deathbed. Abrahams' view of him carries a trace of doctrine: the doctor mirrors, and embodies, the impotence and guilt of the middle class African, politically isolated from the mass of the oppressed workers, and yet a part of them by virtue of his colour and his rejection at the hands of the white community. In relation to his own group it is scarcely surprising that his response to his work resembles that of the black miners: and this identity of response to work is the author's way of showing that Doctor Mini and Johannes the miner are in the same political boat.

The most complex and least successful study in alienation is Eliza, the teacher with whom Xuma falls in love. Her portrayal is mainly unsuccessful because of the very peculiar and consistent manner in which Abrahams falls victim to a version of feminine mystique in all his attempts at female characters. Thus Eliza's idiosyncrasies—her veering moods, fits of guilt and remorse, alternating bouts of acceptance and rejection of Xuma, culminating in her sudden and secret departure from the scene—*may* all be the effects of the corruption of her potential. This corruption is caused by the resentment thrust upon her by her racial position as an educated African woman in South African society. As she puts it after rejecting Xuma in bed:

'I am no good and I cannot help myself. It will be right if you hate me. You should beat me. But inside me there is something wrong. And it is because I want the things of the white people. I want to be like the white people and go where they go and do the things they do and I am black. I cannot help it. Inside I am not black and I do not want to be a black person. I want to be like they are, you understand, Xuma. It is no good but I cannot help it. It is just so. And it is that that makes me hurt you . . . Please understand.' (p. 89)

Her alienation takes the form of a crisis of identity. She cannot allow her attraction for Xuma to reach whatever degree of fulfilment is attainable precisely because of the unnatural limitations on this fulfilment that exist. She cannot identify her destiny with Xuma's obvious traditional virtues of strength, honesty and purity of mind because she has been seduced into seeing them as relative to the equally obvious virtues of the achievements of the white society which surrounded her but are denied to her.

Unfortunately all this is somewhat vitiated by the fact that almost all Abrahams' female characters behave in the same 'typically feminine' way as Eliza, being capricious, indecisive, moody, dangling their men on a string. All they lack is the intellectual awareness Eliza has of her problem of identity.

Still, she is a phase in the process of Xuma's personal development. An inner conflict takes places between his passion for Eliza and his liking for Maisy; he only grows out of the one and brings the other to realisation at the very end of the book. Both are, of course, representative figures within the propaganda framework. Maisy, whose hand, unlike Eliza's, Di's or Mrs Mini's is work-hardened, stands for the real quality of black city life, without fundamental convictions and without pretensions; whereas Eliza is a torn product of the unborn future, a destructive half-born child, yearning for the inevitable reality to come.

After Xuma and Eliza consummate their bliss and enter on their brief and remarkably conventional domestic idyll, the plot, such as it has been, becomes alarmingly episodic. In very short order the reader is presented with the murder of Dladla, a violent friend of Leah's who has been betraying her business activities to the police: Leah's subsequent arrest on suspicion and release, Daddy's fatal accident and death (after which Xuma is entirely surrounded by women—Leah, Eliza, Maisy, Ma Plank, Lena—a characteristic situation for one of Abrahams' heroes), Eliza's sudden departure, Leah's capture in the act of concealing liquor and her sentence of nine months' imprisonment. As she is taken away by the police, she makes an almost authorial apology, to the reader as much as to Xuma: '. . . I am sorry everything happens together . . . Life is so always'. (p. 229)

Leah's arrest brings Xuma's psychic crisis to a head; the urban conditions of life seem to triumph over the purity of his spirit, and he constitutes a classic case of severe alienation:

Since that Saturday night when Leah had walked down the street with policemen flanking her, all feeling had left Xuma. Only a tiredness remained. A tiredness and many questions that were a strain on his brain for he could find no answer to them. And sleeping, too, was hard, for the tiredness of the body had to fight the restlessness of the mind. It was as though the real Xuma was dead and only a shell remained. There was feeling, but it was like the feeling of a stranger, for it did not hurt. He did not feel pain any more. There was no lump in his throat. His heart did not beat violently. He could smile easily. He did all the ordinary things he had learnt to do since he came to the city. Everything seemed just as it had been. But it was though another person looked at them and did them and thought about them. Something was lost. Something that had been there all the time, inside him. It was not there now. (p. 229)

Ma Plank and Maisy came to see him, to housekeep and to try to 'cheer' him.

He had wished they would not come to his room but it had been too much trouble to ask them, so he left them and they had come. They had tried to speak but there was nothing to say. Then, after a time, they had stopped coming. The last time Maisy had been to his room she stood at the door and said, 'When you want me, come to my work place. Ma Plank is there with me. We will be happy to see you.' Then she had gone. Many days ago that had been . . . (pp. 236–7)

By this time Xuma has 'become a citizen of Malay Camp'. He is recognised and greeted in the street by his fellow inhabitants, who know of his troubles, 'for in a strange manner that no one knows, the people of Vrededorp and Malay Camp get to know about everybody else'.

He goes to visit the house in which he had slept his first night in the city, Leah's house, and finds strangers living in it. He imagines he sees it filled with his old companions, but 'suddenly the illusion had faded'. The reader is presented with the realisation that for Xuma, Leah's house and her circle had been a transitional stage between rural tradition and urban barbarity. Leah and Daddy had their roots in the past, too. The blow had been cushioned for him by the false security afforded by the house and its inhabitants; he is now at last face to face with the complete grim truth of city life.

It is at moments like this one (there are not enough of them, however) that the novel really functions in the way a proletarian novel should. The central character (who unavoidably belongs to a different class from that of the reader) is presented to the reader as possessing an inner reality much like his own, as feeling and suffering in the same ways for reasons which emerge to attain concrete and specific substance in relation to the genuineness of the hero's emotional life. The hero becomes an individual, shedding the grey garb of 'the worker' or 'the miner' or 'the black man', and his circumstances become real in proportion to his individuality, instead of the mere evocation, however powerful or tiresome, of a propaganda litany. The reader is made to understand that a working man's working life *is* harsh and dull and unpleasant, that his home circumstances aggravate rather than alleviate the overall effect of depression this has, and that the *results* in terms of feeling, of emotion, of psychological state, are recognisable to the reader because he has, for whatever reasons, experienced them himself, if not to the same degree. In short, the main propaganda function of the proletarian novel is to transform the worker into a suffering (in the broadest sense) human being; and this is where it coincides with its purpose as a work of literature.

Perhaps it is true that the nature of such a work makes moments like these rare and elusive: it is certainly the case that this level is not maintained through the climax of the book, which comes immediately after. It begins with a lengthy conversation between Paddy and Xuma early one morning as they go off night shift. Paddy tries to urge Xuma out of his depression, telling him he must fight against it: not, as Xuma objects, with bare hands against guns:

> '. . . There is another way.'
> 'What is it?'
> 'You must find it, Xuma. Out of your feeling and out of your pain it must come. Others have found it. You can too. But first you must think and not be afraid of your thoughts. And if you have questions and you look around you will find those who will answer them. But first you must know what you are going to fight and why and what you want.'
> 'Why do you, a white man, talk to me like this?'
> 'Because first, Xuma, I am a man like you, and afterwards I am a white man. I have seen the sickness of your mind. I work with you every day and I saw your sickness and I understood.' (p. 235)

This provokes Xuma into being unusually articulate:

> 'You say you understand.' Xuma said, 'but how can you? You are a

white man. You do not carry a pass. You do not know how it feels to be stopped by a policeman in the street. You go where you like. You do not know how it feels when they say 'Get out! White people only'. Did your woman leave you because she is mad with wanting the same things the white man has? Did you know Leah? Did you love her? Do you know how it feels to see her go to jail for nine months? Do you know Leah's house? Did Leah take you in in the middle of the night?' Xuma's voice rose. 'Did Leah talk to you and laugh with you from the side of her mouth? You say you understand. Did you *feel* these things like I do? How can you understand, white man! You understand with your head. I understand with pain. With the pain of my heart. That is understanding. The understanding of the heart and the pain of understanding, not just the head and lips. I feel things! You want me to be your friend. How can I be your friend when your people do this to me and my people?' (pp. 236–7)

And he concludes: 'I am a black man. My people are black. I love them'. But Paddy , the Red One, is equal to Xuma's outburst:

'That is good. It is good to love one's people and not to be ashamed of what one is. But it is not good to think only as a black man or only as a white man. The white people in this country think only as white people and that is why they do this harm to your people.'
    'Then I must think as a black man.'
    'No. You must think as a man first. You must be a man first and then a black man. And if it is so you will understand as a black man and also as a white man. That is the right way, Xuma. When you understand that you will be a man with freedom inside your breast. It is only those who are free inside who can help free those around them.' (p. 237)

Xuma's outburst to Paddy has the effect of getting rid of the immature egocentricity that has clouded his perceptions (though of course to be fair, the mechanics of the plot do seem to conspire to produce the feeling that everything happens to *him*), and leaves a clear field for new impressions and ideas. Paddy seizes the chance of making Xuma see himself as a social being, part of a broader social organism whose functions can be explained, understood and altered. But Xuma does not have much time to ponder the implications of his new vision. The following night he arrives at work to find that there has been a collapse in the underground workings, and his friend Johannes is trapped with Chris, his white foreman, Paddy's friend. Xuma and Paddy go down, against the manager's advice, and come up bearing the bodies of their friends. The engineers arrive and find that the props had collapsed at a place where Xuma had previously warned of danger: The manager and engineers conclude that Chris and Johannes, foreman and boss boy,

> '. . . lost their lives through panic.'
> Paddy grabbed the man and felled him with one blow.
> 'They looked after their men,' he said. 'We warned you about that thing a long time ago.'

Xuma emerges as an individual and refuses to take his men down on shift until the supports are repaired. Paddy is caught indecisively in the middle. The manager calls the police; striking is prohibited for non-white workers in South Africa:

> 'Come on, Paddy!' a white man called. 'It's all very well to play with them sometimes but we must show these kaffirs where they belong. Come on!'
> This is what I argued with Di about, Paddy thought. This is the test of all my beliefs. Xuma has taken the leadership, I must follow. Di was wrong about him. He's a man. In the distance they could hear the siren of the police cars. Soon now the police would be here. Paddy walked over to Xuma and took his hand.
> 'I am a man first, Xuma,' he said.

He goes on to call on the black miners to refuse to go down, and Xuma smiled. Now he understood. He understood many things. One can be a person first. A man first and then a black man or a white man . . . (p. 249)

The police arrive to arrest Xuma and Paddy. A melee breaks out and Xuma, after knocking two policemen down, makes his escape, somewhat improbably, on foot to the house in the suburbs to tell Maisy that he loves her. His emergence to full manhood has at the same time resolved the Eliza-Maisy conflict: his love for Maisy is a reflection of his maturity. Then Maisy accompanies him on his way back to give himself up to the police, because he says he cannot forsake 'the Red One', and:

> '. . . there are many things I want to say too. I want to tell them how I

feel, and how the black people feel . . . It is good that a black man should tell the white people how we feel. And also, a black man must tell the black people how they feel and what they want. These things I must do, then I will feel like a man. You understand?' He looked at Maisy. (p. 251)

Maisy understands.

Perhaps the obvious comparison for *Mine Boy* is William Plomer's *Ula Masondo*, his short novel (or long story) about a Zulu tribesman who goes to work on the mines in Johannesburg.[3] *Mine Boy* displays nothing of Plomer's elegance, economy or wit, and in some respects Plomer seems closer to an adequate awareness of urban African life than Abrahams. But there are two important distinctions to be made: first, significantly, in Plomer's story the final word is left to an outsider, a white storekeeper who once sold the hero a blanket. Abrahams uses no such technique of letting letting the facts and the mistaken judgments speak for themselves, whether ironically or directly. His purpose differs from Plomer's being more directly political, and he attempts to remain steadfastly within the black world with all its inarticulacies and bewilderments when it comes to making judgments. Secondly, and the two points are connected, Plomer's work belongs to that large genre which charts the corruption of the innocent tribesman by the city's wiles and temptations. It is not relevant to object that Plomer's sympathy is clearly with the victim. Abrahams refuses to accept the stereotype of the black man as a victim, and Xuma differs from Ula and all his literary fellow-fallen in that he finds his true strength and being in the city. Thus he is in the end conscious of the price he had paid and must go on paying, simply to retain his integrity as a black man and a worker in a white bourgeois world. This consciousness is an important extension of the realm of possibility for the newly-urbanised African.

After the woodenness of characterisation, the improbability of diction, the failure to create a convincing matrix of work experience (a serious drawback in a novel of this kind) and unevenness of plot have all been duly noted and condemned, *Mine Boy* remains an important novel, even in some ways a powerful one. Its power is derived from the imaginativeness of the undertaking and the originality and scope of the underlying idea, which turns the literary stereotype of the inevitable corruption of the innocent black man by the white city on its head.

7. Kenneth Parker: Nadine Gordimer and the Pitfalls of Liberalism

In a lecture delivered at a National Union of South African Students Winter School, Nadine Gordimer noted that:

> Conflict, they say, has kicked us into print. Well, I cannot deny that
> . . . Conflict can provide a deep and powerful stimulus, but a culture
> as a whole cannot be made out of the groans and sparks that fly. And
> it is out of a culture, from which man's inner being is enriched as the
> substance in an integrated community grows fuller, that a literature
> draws its real substance in the long run. The thirst that comes from
> the salt of conflict will need some quenching.[1]

A little later on in the same article she shows how the existence of conflict, in a special sense, affects the creative artist:

> The greatest single factor in the making of our mores in South Africa
> [she observes] was and is and will be the colour question. Whether it
> is the old question about what the whites are going to do about the
> blacks, or the new question of what the blacks are going to do about
> the whites, or the hopeful question of how to set about letting the
> whole thing go and living together, is still THE question. It's far
> more than a matter of prejudice or discrimination or conflict of
> loyalties—we have built a morality on it. We have gone even deeper,
> we have created our own sense of sin and our own form of tragedy.
> We have added hazards of our own to man's fate, and to save his soul

he must wrestle not only with the usual lust, greed and pride but also with a set of demons marked 'made in South Africa'.[2]

A few years later, in an interview with Alan Ross, Miss Gordimer explained how she functioned as a writer. While she felt that she had no allegiance to South Africa *as a writer* (my italics), she did, *as a person* (my italics) have a responsibility toward the situation to which she was born, which she characterised as being:

> a white South African, brought up on the soft side of the colour-bar . . . whether I like it or not, this has been the crucial experience of my life . . . I have no religion, no political dogma — only plenty of doubts about everything except my conviction that the colour-bar is wrong and utterly indefensible. Thus I have found the basis of a moral code that is valid for me. Reason and emotion meet in it: and perhaps that is as near to faith as I shall ever get.

Consequently, she told Ross, when she writes about people, about their private selves, she is aware that:

> . . . they are what they are because their lives are regulated and their mores formed by the political situation. You see, in South Africa, society is the political situation. To paraphrase, one might say (too often), politics is character in South Africa. I am not politically-minded person by nature . . . I have come to the abstractions of politics through the flesh and blood of individual behaviour. I didn't know what politics was about until I saw it all *happening to people*.[3]

I have quoted the novelist at some length in order to indicate, from the outset, the extent of her conscious awareness of and pronouncements on the position of the writer in South Africa.[4] It is a popularly held view in 'liberal' South African circles that conflict is the single most important influence upon the writer: it is reputed to be both a source of inspiration and the supply of raw material. Whether this is valid view or not, Miss Gordimer is, I believe, correct in her assertion that mere flying sparks are inadequate; they fall on the terrain essentially hostile to the lighting of a creative fire. While she recognises that the conditions which give rise to and entrench conflict must be eliminated, she also recognises that the amelioration of conflict will not, by itself, automatically inaugurate the integrated community from which she asserts literature draws its sustenance. And it is crucial, here, to have an indication of what she means by 'culture' and by 'community'. In the lecture at the NUSAS Winter School from which I quoted earlier, she noted that 'culture is the whole life of the human spirit in communities; it is the means, and also, perhaps, the end of civilised living'. In other words, the concept of culture cannot be separated from the notion of community; it is the two in conjunction which enable the life of the spirit to function. Conversely, one must deduce that neither culture nor the life of the human spirit can flourish in South Africa because of the absence of community. Miss Gordimer has gone on to spell out quite explicitly what the implications are for the writer in South Africa:

> Our literature that a few years ago was being hailed with some justification as remarkably living and questing is in danger of degenerating into accepting the role of art as an embellishment of leisure. Any piece of writing that thrusts deep into life, here, will find itself not in the bookshops and libraries, but in the desk drawer, waiting, as the work of many writers did in Germany and Russia, for times to change, and for the dialogue in which truth begins, to be heard again. Only then shall we be able to speak of a South African literature.[5]

Two fundamental implications would seem to arise from the statement: firstly, the rejection of the notion of art as embellishment of leisure (and thus, presumably, of art which is the privilege of the privileged); secondly, that a truly 'South African' literature will not emerge unless the writers are prepared, despite known risks—and she means risks to their art, not political risks—to probe deep into the whole life of the society.

It is the delicate balance between these relationships—between her concept of culture, her notion of community, her criteria for creativity—which provide the intellectual focus for Miss Gordimer's first major successful novel, *A World of Strangers* (1958).[6] It begins as the story of Toby Hood, the young scion of English upper-class people with well intentioned leftish tendencies, who is sent to manage the Johannesburg branch of the publishing firm which enables the family to live well while indulging their (quite genuine) interest in anticolonial causes. Toby is quite keen to escape but the family's determined concern with public issues frustrates his own desire to explore personal relationships.

His first significant experience of South African society is provided by a visit to The High House, the mansion of the wealthy mining

magnate Hamish Alexander. It is here that he meets the first of three
people who will loom large in his life: Cecil Rowe, the disorganised,
pleasure-loving divorcee, who becomes his mistress. But it is Anna
Louw, the Afrikaner woman (another divorcee—this time from
marriage with a South African Indian) who introduces him to the world
of people engaged in the struggle for black political emancipation. Most
important, it is at a party to which Anna takes him, that he meets
Steven Sitole, the man who will have the most profound effect upon his
life.

Toby is an excellent choice as narrator. The fact that he is a foreigner
enables Miss Gordimer to make us see, thorugh him, situations
without misconceptions, predispositions. The fact that Toby is self-
aware, articulate, and self-critical, sometimes disarmingly awkward,
assists the process. He establishes his credo quite early on in the novel:

> The atmosphere of ideological flux which I had breathed all my life
> sometimes terrifyingly thin, a rare air in which one must gasp for the
> want of the oxygen of certainty, of an established way of life.
> Paradoxically, there had been bred into me a horror of the freedom
> that is freedom only to be free; I wanted to be free to cling to what I
> should break from, if I wished. I did not think that a man should have
> to lose himself, in Gide's sense, in order to find himself. Something in
> me clung strongly to the need for mediating powers—tradition,
> religion, perhaps; a world where you might, if you wished, grow up
> to what was expected of you. My mother and my father gave up a
> great many small, unworthy things that together, constituted a
> workable framework of living, but what did they have to offer in their
> place? Freedom; an empty international plain where a wind turns
> over torn newspapers printed in languages you don't understand.
> (p. 32)

If this passage reveals nothing else, it reveals one aspect of Miss
Gordimer's work—that she is not afraid to tackle problems which her
more deliberately political counterparts have tended to eschew. After
all, there is a deep and abiding sense in which Toby is quite right—why
should an individual be required to live in the rarified atmosphere of
ideological flux? We will encounter the problem in all its ramifications
with Steven, but for the moment it is necessary to draw attention to it,
and to point out that in the case of Toby, the answer would seem to be
clear: while one can theoretically defend the general principle of the
kind of freedom Toby espouses, it can only with difficulty be justified in

the case of the particular protagonist. Recall the contexts––Britain emerging from the aftermath of a World War. Even more important, we had been told that Toby's father had fought in the Spanish Civil War. Thus, Toby does not at this early stage comprehend that he can despise 'freedom'—particularly the freedom 'only to be free'—precisely because he has not merely the freedom, but particularly the privileged means to do so. Even more, what Miss Gordimer alludes to at the end is the notion that 'freedom' is not the empty international plan of Toby's rhetoric, but it is precisely the torn newspapers printed in languages you don't understand which points to its indivisibility. One could forgive Toby, at this stage, if his remarks could be construed as being cynical. But they are not; they are genuinely-felt sub-Fosterian rumblings. The fact that they are felt with such fervour amplifies their oddness.

One of the first lessons that Toby thus has to learn is that the world of personal relationships to which he wishes to cling has a particular South African slant. One of the ideal relationships would have been the bringing-together of Cecil and Steven; after all, in his view they both have the same zest for life that he values so highly. But he quickly understands that the two will never meet, and so begins to make the kind of compromise that earlier on he had gound so remiss in his parents. The decision comes at a critical moment—Cecil had shortly before observed to him that her child would not reveal that he had seen Toby in the passage of the flat in the early hours of the morning. He begins to recognise that just as she has another life, so he, too, has one which revolves around Steven. He recalls that:

Each tacitly forwent inquiry into that [the life] of the other, because each suspected that the discovery of his own life by the other would make the parenthetic shared relationship impossible. I heard her say, to some people with whom we were having coffee after a cinema, 'Toby does a lot of work among the natives'. Later, when we were alone, I asked her, 'What made you tell the Howards that I did a lot of "work" among the natives?' 'Well, don't you' she said, yawning. 'I never have,' I said. She let it drop; she assumed that anyone who had anything to do with Africans was concerned with charity or uplift, and that was that—she wasn't going to quibble over what she satisfied herself could only be a matter of definition. And I, I left it at that, too. I had my little flirt with danger by questioning her at all; thankfully, I hadn't had to take it any further.

For I knew that if I told Cecil that my closest friends in Johannesburg were black men, and that I ate with them and slept in their houses, I would lose her. That was the fact of the matter. And I was damned if I was going to lose her. (p. 155)

Now, at this stage, it would be quite easy to succumb to the desire to lambast Toby for 'dishonesty', for political and personal cowardice. What I think Miss Gordimer tries to show is that to do that would be too easy an option. Toby's problem is that his sacrifice will have to be even greater—in order to keep Cecil—and in order to keep Cecil and Steven apart, he has to begin to sacrifice his beliefs. At this stage he is a greater victim than either of them because he believes that he can have the best of both worlds. From this desire follows the error of judgment which culminates in his moral offence—the desire for personal relationships leads to personal betrayal. The magnitude of the act becomes clear only after Steven's death. And the point to recall is that it is done wittingly. We have seen that Toby consciously decides not to lose Cecil. It is also important to realise that he is clearly aware of the nature of the society he lives in, of how it operates, and of his own reactions to it. His peregrinations make him realise that:

all these people lived together in one country, anyway; all their lives were entangled by propinquity. (p. 79)

But he also realises that propinquity has to concede pride of place to power. All the elements of the society's codes are designed to keep people apart, and he comes to a stunning realisation—stunning, because it is so simple:

I passed from one world to another—but neither was real to me. For in each, what sign was there that the other existed? (p. 186)

I think that what the novelist is saying is something rather more profound than the usual observation that 'never the twain shall meet'. To say that is, to some extent, to accept the mutual recognition of two worlds. What she is saying is that, in their different ways, neither The High House nor the townships gave any real indication that they were aware of each other's existence. Thus, if at The High House blacks are the everpresent, uniformed, but silent servants, then in the townships the world of the white man is reflected only in its outward appearances such as Coca-Cola advertisements. And to attempt to ape this life is fruitless, if one takes the case of Steven's friend Sam, the quiet composer, whose attempt to collaborate with a white 'patron' leads to disaster. His music ends up as a pretentious mishmash of sounds which emphasise for Steven the sterility of 'European' models when compared with the vibrancy of the life of the townships. But Sam is important in one other way: Sam is involved in politics, and this sets him at the opposite pole to Steven. But let us be clear why he is committed in this way. Miss Gordimer emphasises the point that Sam is politically involved not only because he desires freedom for blacks, but—and this is the critical point—because he has accepted the white man's standards and methods of living. But Sam is accepting the white man's world, as he sees it, at a time when the white South African is constantly apologetic about it. The paradox is not merely that this position proves Toby's contention that both sides were essentially ignorant of each other's existence; it also gives quite savage insights into the fragile veneer which passes for culture. Two instances will suffice: the first is at The High House, where Marion Alexander is showing off her new 'find', a small and rather dingy painting by Courbet, set in an even more unpleasing frame. More than that, the new find is in a room which the novelist categorises as being in the Table Bay genre, the characteristic of which is that it did not contain one single discomforting brushstroke. Not only is the Courbet out of place in this room because of the other 'pictures', but also because of the programmed responses of the admiring women. Thus, for Miss Gordimer, the world of The High House is not just a world where money rules, but a world where money and privilege evoke insincere responses. The second instance occurs when Toby is taken to a recently-opened Italian coffee bar. His friend apologises for the slow service and then explained the popularity of the place:

'It's pathetic,' he said. 'They've got so little to hold them together, they'll rush to any new rallying point you offer them like dogs tearing after a bitch. Specially if they can pretend they're somewhere else; Italy, for example,' he waved a hand at the abstract mosaics, the black, bitter brew in the cups. 'Anyway it does give one the illusion one's in a civilised country', he added, for himself. (p. 64)

And so Toby slowly begins to learn that:

. . . to have a 'life out there', a real life in Johannesburg, you'd have to belong to one or the other, for keeps. You couldn't really reconcile one with the other, the way people were, the way the laws were, and make a whole. The only way to do that was to do what Anna Louw had done—make for the frontier between the two, that hard and lonely place as yet sparsely populated. (p. 193)

This is one of the central codes that come out of the novel. We are not given a great deal of information about how Anna Louw arrived at the frontier, except that she came to it from another one—that of an Afrikaner background in a small town. That she should be a political radical, as well as someone who is intensely humane, doggedly persistent and infinitely patient neither surprises the reader nor gives the impression that she is somehow extraordinary. In fact, it is her 'ordinariness' which strikes us. When she sleeps with Toby, she does it as 'an extension of conversation'. More importantly, her views on the dilemma of white South Africans are clear:

We always feel apologetic about it, she smiled. 'You get used to hearing people from England and Europe telling you that there's *nothing* here—rolling their eyes and throwing up their hands . . . You don't know exactly what they mean, but you feel they're right . . . I used to think that it was because everything in town life here relates to another world—the plays are the plays of Europe, the cabaret jokes are those of London or New York . . . you know what I mean? Johannesburg seems to have no *genre* of its own . . .? That's what people feel. Partly. But now I think there's something else. Loneliness; of a special kind. Our loneliness. The lack of a common human identity. The loneliness of a powerful minority. (p. 75)

Equally clearly she explains to Toby her views about Steven's choices. She insists that Steven's choice is 'romantic':

. . . and I am down on it. I understand the need to be romantic in some way, but I'm down on this way. It's a waste of energy. You won't catch Steven working with Congress or any other African movement, for that matter . . . The only defiance he's interested in is not paying his bills, or buying drink. He's got this picture of himself as the embittered, devil-may-care African, and believe me, he's making a career of it. He doesn't care a damn about his people; he's only concerned with his own misfortune in being born one of them . . . (p. 115)

When Toby protest that Steven should not be forced to give up to political action whatever small part of his life he can call his own, the reply is quite uncompromising:

> He wants the results of that political action, doesn't he? . . . He wants to be free of the pass laws and the colour bar and the whole caboodle? — Well, let him fight for it. (p. 116)

The general principle of the obligation to fight for freedom is thus clearly enunciated. But it is not something which can be left at the level of a slogan, an exhortation, particularly when we are confronted with a character as original as Steven Sitole, who is the real hero of the novel. With him, Miss Gordimer begins to break out of the bonds of South African liberalism. Steven's views are not particularly palatable for the liberal or radical conscience of whites. The kind of conscience that can take a Sam in its stride, because he is a known phenomenon; or even learn to accommodate a La Guma's Beukes, finds it hard to credit a Steven Sitole. Even for his fellow Africans he is:

> . . . a new kind of man, not a white man, but not quite a black man either; a kind of flash — flash-in-the-pan — produced by the surface of the two societies in friction. (p. 126)

Even his close friend, Sam, has to concede that Steven is different, a white man in black man's skin. But he is wrong in a most essential sense: Steven is not at all concerned with the trappings and appurtenances of acquisition which all the other whites, and, indeed Sam, feel they need to encircle themselves with. Sam does, however, point out a major difference about how to see Steven: while Anna Louw sees Steven's behaviour as a loss to the African people, Sam sees it as a loss to Steven himself. Finally, it is Toby who reflects that:

> On the side, he's got a private revolution of his own; it's waged for himself, but quite a lot of other people may benefit. I think that about Steven. He won't troop along with your Congress, or get himself arrested in the public library, but, in spite of everything the white man does to knock the spirit out of him, he remains very much alive — getting drunk, getting in debt, running his insurance racket. Learning all the shady tricks, so that in the end, he can beat dear old white civilisation at its own games. He's muscling in: who's to say that he won't get there first? While the Congress chaps are pounding fiercely on the front door, he's slipped in through a back window.

But, most important of all, he's alive, isn't he? He's alive, in defiance of everything that would attempt to make him half-alive. (pp. 116–7)

But Toby is quite wrong. From Anna Louw he recognises that the only way forward is to move into the barren no man's land between the two worlds in friction—not to take up a middle ground, but to present a realistic alternative to both worlds, from which real community might arise. After Steven's death he is to learn from Sam, and from the 'Congress' people whom he meets at Sam's place, the need for a patient, principled action. The notion of the back door as an alternative is untenable: for it to have any meaning (and then perhaps only in the case of the exceptional individual, but never in the case of whole groups of people), it would be essential to know that Steven could, as a black man, make the same kinds of choices, and in the same kinds of ways, as Toby, the white man, can. Thus, having stripped Toby slowly of his illusions about personal relationships (his world remains one of 'strangers' because the gaps exceed the points of cohesion), and by implication of a 'European solution', Miss Gordimer proceeds to probe the alternatives. Whether she quite convinces us that to be a black is to be committed, that the notion of a 'private life' is not possible until freedom is achieved, is doubtful. But I do not think that her interests in the novel are in that direction. It would seem that the main intention was to make an initial statement about how white South Africans can operate in South Africa: Cecil Rowe by embracing her Guy Patterson, and in so doing, indulging her despair; Anna Louw by being arrested for her political activities; Toby himself, with his letter written to Faunce to say that he will stay on in South Africa. And yet . . . his last contact in the book is with Sam, who shows us that while he looks forward to Toby's return to Johannesburg in time for the christening of the new baby, he really does not hold out much hope for that kind of well-meaning humanism. It is a doubt, on Sam's part, which throws into sharp relief the whole notion of the extent to which whites may be expected to partake of the freedom struggle side by side with blacks.

Before we proceed to look at Miss Gordimer's attempted answer to this central problem of what role whites may play in the South African liberation struggle, it is necessary to look briefly at her next novel, *Occasion for Loving* (1963)[7] in which she begins to explore, in some depth, the dilemma of the white South African liberal. In a paradoxical sense, the formulation answers the question: if you are a victim of the liberal dilemma (particularly the South African variety), what can you contribute to the liberation struggle? Conversely, since you are held at arms length as a participant, your dilemmas are made even more manifest. In this regard, Jessie Stilwell is one of the author's most important characters. Indeed, Jessie is the expression of the author's aphorism that '. . . one might say (too often), Politics is character in South Africa'.[8]

Jessie Stilwell is carefully characterised. She is the daughter of a mine official who died when she was eighteen months old. By the time she was three, her mother had married again—to Bruno Fuecht, the family's best friend and an upholder of European values (as distinct from South African 'European' ones). Jessie's pampered home life is interrupted by marriage, which is itself cut short by her husband's death in action. When she re-marries some years later, one of her problems is her son by the first marriage. He cannot adapt, particularly to the environment of the large, rambling seedy but alive house of his step-father, a historian who is collecting material to write a new book about how the white west had invaded the African subcontinent and exploited its human and natural resources. His single-minded research makes him only marginally aware that his own university was, at that very moment being told by the Government to discontinue its admission of black students, except by prior permission. But, for him, the past was both safer and more exciting than the present. In keeping with this honouring of the past (as well as an easy and genuinely hospitable nature) Tom Stilwell readily agrees that his old friend Boaz Davis, a Jewish South African, who was returning from England to continue his researches (into African music) should stay with them. Boaz has to go on frequent and extended field trips and is unaware that his wife Ann (who was Rhodesian-born but had spent most of her life in England) had in the meantime developed a rather tempestuous love affair with Gideon Shibalo, a black artist whose other claim to fame was that he had to forfeit a scholarship because his application for a passport had been rejected by the Government. Inevitably, the affair has to end. After a harrowing, yet often humorous, odyssey by Ann and Gideon through hostile country in a small car, in which they end up at Jessie's Natal Coast shack, Ann returns to Boaz. They leave immediately for Europe. Gideon is left behind.

But all this is essential context for what is effectively Jessie's personal quest: how to live as wife and mother within the context of South Africa. It is the same problem which confronts La Guma's outcasts, or Jacobson's country folk. How to strike a balance between the impositions of the 'law' and the demands of integrity is not the exclusive preserve of either a particular class or colour. But the problems are different. It is not so much that Jessie was brought up and continues to live in comparative wealth and privilege: her problem is that she cannot, with ease, reverse the direction of her whole past, a past in which it is the white who is pampered and the black who ministers. This everyday awareness of different roles based upon the criterion of colour becomes the psychological shackle that cannot easily be shed. Just as Tom Stilwell wants to rewrite African history, or as Boaz Davis wants to rediscover African musicology, so Jessie has to jettison all the values learned in childhood, to recognise not the separateness but the interdependence of the groups, the irrelevance of the artificial categories by which the State continues to control both culture and community.

The effects of this process are driven home quite sharply in one of the many discussions in the interlude in the beach cottage. The cottage itself is part of the estate of Jessie's stepfather Fuecht, who had died a week or so after his return to Europe—but not before he had confided, obliquely, to Tom Stilwell, at the airport, that he Fuecht, was Jessie's real father. Another example of European deceit? Or of the difference between Europe and its white South African version? At any rate, Gideon finds himself behaving like Ann and Jessie: lying for hours, as if he, too, had been washed up on this shore, like the fish or the dead seagull—the symbol of freedom of spirit finding death on the inhospitable Natal coast:

If he [Gideon] sat about doing nothing it was always a marking time, an hiatus between two activities or desires. It was a matter of despair, exhaustion or frustration. You lay on your bed in your room and drank because you could not do what you wanted to do.

And even when he worked, those empty landscapes for which he was particularly noted were:

Just fooling around. Seeing the sort of thing some painter has done and trying it out. (pp. 220–1)

The abandonment to leisure, the experimentation with form in painting—these are unrealities for Gideon. What is real for him are two inter-related facts: the life of the black township totally dedicated to the business of making a living to stay alive, and the frustration of the life of the spirit in these surroundings. That is why, despite his bouts of drunkenness, Gideon will, as Tom Stilwell observes, '. . . be all right. He'll go back and fight; there's nothing else.' (p. 288) It is Tom Stilwell, again, who earlier sees the essential inadequacy of the liberal vision, and of the Stilwell code as an example of that vision. It was 'a . . . failure, in danger of humbug. Tom began to think that there would be more sense in blowing up a power station, but it would be Jessie who would help to do it, perhaps?' (p. 279) We are not told why it might be more sensible (than what?) to blow up a power station, although the liberal need for symbolic acts must be a powerful pointer. The important part of the reflection is, however, the recognition that Jessie would be capable of such an act. And she can do this because she finally comes to terms with her condition, her attitude to Gideon and to the Gidéon–Ann affair, during another talk in the beach cottage. She is rather shocked to find that Gideon had a wife and child, and that his defence for his refusal to dwell on this comes down to 'what's gone is gone'.

> He saw that this frightened her in some way, but there was no room in him for curiosity about others. There was no part of his apprehension that was not cut off by concentration of forces that had brought him there; by what he shared with the girl, and what he could not share with her. He could not answer the woman, either, with the rush of affirmation for the present that suddenly came to him; but *this* is my life! Yet she spoke as if he had: 'You can't pick and choose', she said. 'You have either to accept everything you've been and done, or nothing. If the past is going to be past, finished, this will be as lost as the things you want to lose.'
>
> 'Those must be things that are over and done with,' he said. 'You must know how it is.' (p. 244)

To this Jessie readily agrees; to continue to shed one's skin, like a snake, in order to live, but in the end, 'I am what I was then[before her marriage to Tom Stilwell] as well as what I am now; or I'm nothing.' (p. 245) It is because of her acquisition of her possible role in the scheme of things, of her recollection of the lessons of the past, of her articulation of values which transcend the simply political, that she might, perhaps, be in at the time of the throwing of the bombs. Where Gideon will be acting from a quite legitimate, but rather limited, definition of the notion of freedom, Jennie's as yet unformulated vision will be based upon three important foundations: firstly, the awareness of the uselessness of Europe (whether in the form of Fuecht or of the seagull) and, secondly, of the recognition of the complementarity between Gideon and herself; finally, that it is Gideon who, because he has nothing else left to do but fight, holds all the aces.

Miss Gordimer's next novel, *The Late Bourgeois World* (1966)[9] can be considered as the culmination (perhaps even an attempt at a fusion) of the issues treated in the earlier novels. At its simplest level, the fictive present, it is the story of reactions to an event. Elizabeth van der Sandt is at breakfast with her solicitor lover when she receives a telegram which informs her that her husband, Max, from whom she is separated, had committed suicide by driving his car into Table Bay harbour. He was the son of a respected United Party politician (as a member of the 'opposition' party, when he spoke of 'unity' he meant between English and Afrikaner). Max had shocked his parents by going into left-wing politics, had become more and more alienated from his chosen political colleagues and finally found himself engaged in lone political activity—a sort of Tom Stilwell throwing a bomb as a sign of desperation rather than belief in its efficacy. Arrested and convicted, Max eventually becomes a prosecution witness in trials against several of his erstwhile colleagues.

From the moment Elizabeth receives the telegram she is involved at three levels: the immediate present of driving out to a boarding school to tell her son Bobo of his father's suicide before he can find out from someone else; the future, in her relations with Graham Mill (who, incidentally, specialises in defending political prisoners) and Luke Fokase, the resistance fighter; but, above all, the past, of how Max ended up the way he did. And what makes for the great strength of the novel is the way in which (particularly) past and present are interfused.

Max ended up dead in a car in Table Bay harbour because of obvious and clear political choices he had made. He cannot in any sense of the word be described as being innocent. But he also ended up in the harbour because of the mindless arrogance of his parents. The Van der Sandt's are characterised as representative of the white English-speaking bourgeoisie, who grasp power unto themselves, wield it without either pity or favour, and yet claim that they are 'innocent' because they 'did not know'. Miss Gordimer is at her deadliest when she pinpoints the essential evilness of the representatives of South African bourgeois morality. Elizabeth reflects that 'their son was dead for them the day he was arrested on a charge of sabotage'. Theo van der Sandt resigned his seat in Parliament, and he never came to court, though he made money available for Max's defence. She (his mother) came several times:

We sat there on the white side of the public gallery, but not together. One day when her hair was freshly done, she wore a fancy lace mantilla instead of a hat that would disturb the coiffure. Her shoes and gloves were perfectly matched and I saw with fascination that some part of her mind would attend to these things as long as she lived, *no matter what happened.* (p. 36)

It is this world that Max attacks with his little bomb. The paradox is that in one sense it is already dead from its own inelasticity, yet contrives to retain its prodigious power to punish those who challenge it simply because it has constructed a whole panoply of devices for its protection.

How each of her three main characters—Elizabeth, Max, and Luke Fokase—respond to their situations constitutes the core of Miss Gordimer's portrayal of the late bourgeois world. To start with Max. Because he is the son of an 'English' politician, Max continues to be enmeshed in his past. Even when he has broken away, has become involved in revolutionary politics, there is an abiding sense in which he feels that he is 'breaking the rules'. Whether his moral confusion is a function of his political confusion, or vice versa, may well be a matter for dispute, but what would not seem to be at issue is that breaking away from the parental and social codes of his past left him incapable and unprepared to cope with his new role. His sexual inconstancy, his emotional instability—indeed, his gravitation from one white radical political organisation to another—are all eloquent pointers to his search for some kind of order. His mother describes his behaviour as a 'horrible selfishness', and in a sense in which she could not have meant it, comes close to the truth. That Max betrays his colleagues in order to escape a lengthy prison sentence is, for his mother, final proof of the extent to which he has betrayed the European code of stiff upper lip, of playing the game according to the rules. Max's father, it must be recalled, had resigned his Parliamentary seat when his son was arrested—because he felt somehow responsible for his son's 'transgressions'. But this is precisely the code of playing according to certain rules that Max has rejected. He cannot be expected to both reject and subscribe to them at the same time. Yet he knew that to betray his colleagues in order to gain personal benefit was, in the end, cowardly—but this knowledge was based on a code of honour much deeper than his parents could comprehend. His death is both a symbol and a pointer to the way in which European solutions to the problems of South Africa are, for Miss Gordimer, not tenable: they end up, like the dead seagull, on the Natal coast, being fed upon by ants.

For Elizabeth, the woman whose 'normal' life is as a laboratory technician, Max's death is freedom of a different kind. She cannot talk of him as her 'first husband' because at thirty she cannot be too sure about what she may still do. And what she may still do, is, in a sense, to take over where Jessie Stilwell left off: to agree to do some work for Luke Fokase of the Pan-Africanist Congress.

Unlike Jessie, who presented us with only fugitive glimpses of latent potential, Elizabeth demonstrates actual choices. The two most important are in relation to her lover Graham Mills, and to one of her dead husband's former political associates, Luke Fokase. Without wishing to labour the symbol, it could be argued that Graham stands for Elizabeth's present, while Luke represents the future. She continues to live with Graham, but refuses to marry him, and agrees to help Luke by acting as the conduit for money his organisation receives from abroad. The two decisions, when placed side by side, can only be interpreted as a recognition on Elizabeth's part that there is a future, and that the present must somehow be subservient to that future. And the process by which Elizabeth arrives at her conclusion is of no less importance. Miss Gordimer subjects her protagonist to a relentless self-scrutiny, until Elizabeth has to admit, at last, that the notion of building bridges between the races, of the European liberal humanist code of cricket across the colour bar, is a chimera. She is forced to admit that '. . . friendship for its own sake is something only whites can afford'. (p. 119)

This recognition is a measure of the extent to which Elizabeth breaks with a code from which Max was never prepared to free himself totally. For Max the future would somehow be an uneasy and unpredictable mixture: not of black and white separately, but of black-and-white. What Elizabeth learns thorugh her contact with Luke is that the future will be black, but not exclusively so. Luke is the representative of the new politics. He rejects white involvement, except for specific purposes; he is less concerned with ideology than with action. Miss Gordimer makes him a figure of great precision (she describes him in some detail) yet he remains somehow enigmatic, mysterious. Elizabeth thus recognises something unique—that if she wants to take part in the game, she will have to play according to rules over which she will have no control, and which may even change while the game is in process. Whether this open-ended commitment to an unknowable future, based upon trust in the makers of the rules is a realistic choice, particularly where the only seeming criterion is one of action rather than an ideology or a political programme, is another matter. In the end, I suspect that Miss Gordimer has proved the first part of her epigraph from Kafka: 'There are possibilities for me, certainly'—but the rest of the epigraph: 'but under what stone do they lie?'—would seem to continue to elude her. But she does, at times, come very close indeed to an answer.

8. Michael Wade: Nadine Gordimer and Europe-in-Africa*

It is perhaps early to pronounce on the significance of *A Guest of Honour*[1] in relation to Miss Gordimer's oeuvre. It is her longest and most ambitious novel; it is about politics and personal relationships; its broad outlines are bold and make a recognisable shape, but in detail its design is close and intricate. Caution over making uninhibited judgments at such close quarters in time need not prevent one from stating two obvious parallels: if the book is the African novel's *Nostromo*, it is also Miss Gordimer's personal *Middlemarch*. In it she triumphantly routs the problems characteristic of South African novelists with which she has always had to grapple, such as the unself-conscious rendition of black characters, and allows herself a much more confident and explicit statement of the values she regards as permanent against a background of bewilderment and instability.

Although almost all the action of this book takes place in a fictitious African country, the book is as much—and even more—about Europe than it is about Africa. It is about that weird historic experience of Europe-in-Africa, the casual transplantation of ideas and values into a foreign organism, and the forcible suppression of any of the signs of natural rejection that occurred. It examines the relationship between Europe and Africa, what Europe did, and the results for both; and the summation of its 'message' is, incompromisingly, aimed at the Western world, the world of European and especially liberal values. The

* An abridged version of a section of the author's doctoral thesis for the University of Sussex.

book may be said to embody some African lessons in the history of Europe.

The hero—and for once Miss Gordimer is unequivocal about this; his proportions, physical and intellectual, *are* heroic—is Colonel Evelyn James Bray, retired colonial civil servant, who had been deported from the country in which he was serving ten years before the action of the book begins, at the demand of the local white settlers, when as District Commissioner he had sided with and encouraged the leaders of the embryonic African nationalist movement as the struggle for independence from Britain was initiated. When the book opens, independence is about to be granted, and Bray, who has been living in semi-retirement with his wife Olivia in a house they have renovated—and in a sense revived—in a dead village in Wiltshire, is invited back to Africa by the man who is to be the country's first president, Adamson Mweta, whom Bray has helped and guided both in Africa and England, through the stages of nationalist agitation and, later, negotiations at Lancaster House. Mweta sees Bray as returning to fulfil a task which he had been interrupted by his deportation ten years before. Bray himself is sceptical about this, but accepts the invitation to be present as an official guest at the country's independence celebrations.

Once there, he finds it difficult to extricate himself: although he has booked himself onto a flight home, he significantly fails to include this information in a letter to his wife, and when Mweta finds him a task to perform as special education adviser in Gala, he accepts it. Gala is the province where Bray has served as District Commissioner, and whose local white settler community had produced the successful agitation to have him deported. Thus his return is a more complete cycle of fortune than he had anticipated.

One of the most convincing indications of the mastery of Miss Gordimer's maturity as a novelist is the enormously skilful creation of a secondary network of relationships which serves as an entirely convincing backdrop to the main action of the plot. The tone of daily life in both the capital and Gala is precisely and unfalteringly rendered: the expatriate and indigenous intelligentsia of the capital—administrators, junior ministers, university personnel—mostly young, all at least superficially committed, for the time being, to their shared objective situation, generate a generalised feeling of tension, though not unnaturally, the current flows mainly in the form of gossip. The individual characters (especially the whites) constitute a marvellously characteristic cross-section of those who stayed on or came to do their bit with the advent of independence in any of the former British territories of Central Africa in the 'sixties'. Neil and Vivian Bayley are young, attractive, upper-class, radical: he is the registrar of the new university, she, coincidentally, niece to the outgoing Governor's wife. Bray, in the capital, stays with Roly Dando, the illusion-free Welsh lawyer who had supported the nationalists from the outset and has 'stayed on' to become attorney-general in Mweta's government. Hjalmar and Margo Wentz are exiles first from Nazi Germany, and then, a generation later, from South Africa, this time with two almost grown children and the corresponding necessity to make a living: they are trying their hand at running a hotel.

These people constitute a kind of entity, an objective correlative called Europe-in-Africa; and they variously embody aspects of the recent and contemporary European experience. Some scarcely touch Africa, and are in turn unmarked by it: others have deeper emotional investments than they suspect. What emerges from them as a group is again a contradiction of their confident, elitist appearance; the clear impression is that they know neither where they are nor what time it is. They take sensible precautions of various kinds: Margo Wentz has her daughter Emmanuelle 'fitted up' with a birth-control device, Vivian Bayley keeps her 'riot bag' packed. This sense of dislocation is borne out fairly conclusively by what Rebecca Edwards, who is one of them and yet essentially different in one crucial respect, says to Bray of the men of this circle, later in the book when she and Bray are living—and having an affair—in the remote provincial town of Gala:

'. . . I got into a bad way down there. They didn't trust Gordon [her husband], any of them . . . I knew they were sorry for me. They persisted in being sorry for me. It made me behave funnily; I can't explain, but when they made passes at me—Neil, the others—I saw that they felt they could do it because *to me* they could risk showing that things weren't so good for them, either. I felt sorry for them. I felt what did it matter . . . (pp. 462–3)

The weakness in the European men is a matter of some significance, in terms of what the book expresses about the relationship between Europe and Africa: it is a question of a crisis of confidence permeating an entire culture, from within.

Bray is at the centre of this. He is created to satisfy the historic requirements of Western culture: a courageous man, intellectually and physically (a colonel in the Second World War, decorated for bravery), upper-class, liberal in politics, firmly wedded to the code of behaviour in personal relations that most clearly characterises English liberalism. The basis of his decision to return to Africa at Mweta's request is rendered in terms of this code:

> 'He naturally assumes you'll come out of exile.' They laughed. But they were talking of Mweta; the strange shyness of twenty-two years of marriage made it possible for her to say: Do you want to go? The passionate beginning, the long openness and understanding between them should have meant that she would know what he wanted. And in a way she did know: because for them it was a code so deeply accepted that it had never been discussed—one was available wherever one was of use. What else was there to live by? (p. 6)

His wife Olivia's conflict lies in her Englishness, in the feeling that she has become one with her rightful heritage, that:

> . . . this life in Wiltshire, this life—at last—seemed . . . the definitive one, in the end . . . She was, after all (in the true sense of after all that had gone before) an Englishwoman. (p. 7)

She nonetheless, or because of this, recognises the code as possessing the kind of fundamental validity that might threaten the security of her patrimony.

The similarity of this starting-point to the position of the Stilwells in *Occasion for Loving* is clear and meaningful—and even more so are the differences:

> The Stilwells' code of behaviour was definitive, like their marriage; they could not change it. But they saw that it was a failure, in danger of humbug. (*Occasion for Loving*, p. 279)

> . . . One must be open to one's friends. You've got to get away from the tight little bourgeois family unit. In a country like this, people like us must stick together—we live by the sanctions of our own kind. We haven't any anonymous, impersonal code because the South African 'way of life' isn't for us. But what happens to you, yourself . . . I don't know. The original impulse towards decency hardens round you and you can't get out. It becomes another convention. (*Occasion for Loving*, p. 243)

Jessie makes explicit the dilemma of Europe for the South African liberal, which is linked, of course, to the form the same dilemma takes for the South African novelist: the creative impulse, like the original impulse towards decency, needs precisely what it lacks—space among the rabbit-warrens of tradition to develop its individual shape and style, to take refuge or simply to rest without necessarily atrophying from exposure to a shrivelling climate that demands its continuous exercise. Bray inherits such a tradition, and in him the 'original impulse towards decency', though its statement is modified to an almost perilous simplicity—'one was available wherever one was of use'—is elaborated and sensitised into a finely-wrought but robust instrument of life. Another way of putting it would be that Bray's uncertainties begin at a much more complex level of experience than the Stilwells'. On the other hand, this very quality of almost inborn confidence of sensibility carries its peculiar dangers, especially in the situation the authoress creates for her hero. The character-structure of the book is such that Bray, as hero, as quintessential European (the word is doing heavy duty here) is surrounded by a spider's web, wherever he goes, of alternative possibilities; and from time to time the filaments make contact with a full-elaborated version of one of these potential Brays. On some levels Bray's lecherous old friend Roly Dando is one of these: on others, more significantly, it is the defeated Hjalmar Wentz who fulfils an image of what Bray might have been. But there are chance encounters, too, like the momentary aberration of the perceptions when one mistakes a stranger for a friend—and the experience possesses disturbing qualities. At an early stage in the plot, during the independence celebrations, Bray and Dando are in the bar of the capital's largest hotel, and Bray is confronted by one of those might-have-beens, an absorbed doppel-gänger of himself.

 . . . a tall, blond young man from out of town to whom they all listened with the bright show of attention accorded to wits or experts. He was what is recognised as a Guards officer type, perhaps a little to typical ever to have been one. Not so young as all that, either; his small, handsome, straight-backed head on broad shoulders had longish, silky hair thinning on the pate, and when he smiled his teeth were bony-looking. He had a way of bearing down with his nostrils and drawing air audibly through them to express exasperation or raise a laugh. Certainly his friends found this irresistible. His diction was something no longer heard, in England, anyway. Most likely explanation was that he must have taken part in amateur theatricals,

under the direction of someone old enough to have modelled himself
on Noel Coward . . .

'. . . O Lord yes. Her father's getting right out too. *Right* out. The
place at Kabendi Hills has gone. Carol's broken-hearted about the
horses . . . to Jersey, I think . . . Chief Aborowa said to me last week,
there's going to be trouble over the culling—some of these chap's
had that bloody great government stud bull the department's spent a
fortune on—and I said, my dear chap, that's *your* worry, I hope
there'll be a couple of billion gallons of sea between me and your cows
and your wives and the whole damned caboodle . . . I don't want
Pezele near my stool. I said don't be a damned fool, Aborowa—as
soon as I get him alone there's no nonsense, I talk to him like a Dutch
uncle, we were drinking brandy together . . .

. . . Priceless! One of the women was so overcome she had to put
down her glass.

. . . Heavens, that's nothing—Carol buys old Aborowa's wife's
corsets for her.' (pp. 45–6)

The encounter reveals that this level on Europe is also part of Bray's
being: and its failure to develop in his case, by whatever counter-
tropistic combination of historic light and shadow, is obviously in one
sense fortuitous: the fatuous colonial civil servant belongs to his class,
follows the same occupation as he himself once chose. Nor is the
difference easily accounted for by the passage of time, because this
analogue of Bray mouths the accepted wisdom of Bray's own earlier
contemporaries.

Thus the possession of a tradition is one of those pleasant-seeming
things that is in itself quite neutral, in the sense that the manner of its
influence on a given individual cannot be predicted. It cannot be simply
asserted that Bray is in this respect more fortunate than Tom Stilwell or
Elizabeth van den Sandt. Also, he operates in a different world from
them.

Since this fact is one of some importance in understanding the
combination of choices the author has made at a crucial stage in her
development, it may be as well to examine its implications without
delay, as these will in any event bear on our conclusions about Bray.
The movement from South Africa as locale to this fictive version of a
newly-independent African state, formerly a British colony in Central
Africa, is as much a movement in time as it is in place. Miss Gordimer,
as a novelist (as we have seen) is much preoccupied by time, by the
interaction of historic process and human experience. Having taken for

her material the matter of Southern Africa, and having reached a stage in her account of reality where to go forward would be objectively impossible without resorting to the dubious techniques of science fiction or the extravagance of fantasy (in other words, since *The Late Bourgeois World* is the last stop before the revolution in South Africa, and as that hasn't come yet) Miss Gordimer finds a new state of being to explore; and this state of being represents in a sense, according to one kind of view of history, a 'step forward', 'progress' from the pre-revolutionary stage which she sees South Africa as having reached. 'Independence' is not really the same thing as 'freedom', even political freedom; nonetheless, a black majority enjoying political rights and ruling over a white minority is a potential extension of the South African experience—and it also constitutes the kind of base in reality from which Miss Gordimer, as novelist, likes to write.

In terms of time, then, Bray's return, matched by the independence celebrations and the departure of types like the colonial civil servant in the bar, seems like a rebirth. The literary triteness of this idea is belied by the thoroughness which deserves to be called unsparing, with which it is worked out in the novel. Indeed, a whole cluster of verbal and concrete images accumulate around it: a new state is born, Bray's eldest daughter gives birth to her first child, Rebecca initiates Bray into a new experience of love within which he begins, figuratively, virginally; Edward Shinza, Mweta's one-time mentor and present opponent, and Bray's contemporary in years, fathers a child; as the plot develops and Bray is forced to shed illusions and make basic choices, he chides himself for behaving like a virgin in terms of the moral decisions that are forced on him by political events (pp. 128–9, 197, 214, etc.): and through all this Bray is changing, as it were, into himself. The process is one whereby his code is jerked into use by a series of unexpected, random blows, and suddenly the finely-balanced mechanism, so apparently robust in overall design, has to perform against the bursting-forth of a new kind of reality—which may resemble the turmoil that surrounded the beginnings of the vestigial accretions that came to form the code itself. On this historic scale, the geographic provenance of the code is of little importance: what is called in question is the possibility of permanent validity:

> The house in Wiltshire with all its comfortable beauty and order, its incenses of fresh flowers and good cooking, its libations of carefully discussed and chosen wine came to Bray in all the calm detail of an interesting death cult; to wake up there again would be to find oneself

acquiescently buried alive. At the same time, he felt a stony sense of betrayal. (pp. 129–30)

This emotional process takes place as he drives back towards Gala after his first reunion with Edward Shinza, in the remote Bashi area. There he has discovered that Shinza, his contemporary, has fathered a child, but he has made other discoveries as well. The uncommunicative young man he had given a lift to part of the way turns out to be a trade unionist who has been detained without trial for two months and seventeen days at the prison in Gala itself, and interrogated and beaten because the authorities have viewed him as a troublemaker. Shinza displays the boy's weals to Bray, as a symbol of the estrangement between himself and Mweta.

In a sense Shinza is a centre of life from whose immediacy of feeling Bray derives an enhancement of his own sensibility. The completeness of Shinza's experience at this point is contrasted with the plain fact of Bray's innocence, or ignorance; working at the boma, on intimate terms with Aleka, the provincial officer of Gala, Bray has had no idea of the possibility of occurrences like the detention and torture of Shinza's young man.

The construction of the book takes the form of a pattern of polarities radiating outward from Bray. Polarity implies continuation between extremes, which requires movement; thus this is not at any stage a fixed pattern. The polarities operate on the levels both of character and experience; thus, when Bray first meets Shinza, the former stands for the contribution age makes to youth, wisdom of experience to the energy of innocence, while Shinza is a man in his prime, who has just fathered a child and entered a new phase of political life, a man who is beginning again both physically and intellectually, planning for the future. Bray sees his contribution to the future as coming from the accumulation of past experience—his own and that of others: Shinza reckons himself a potent force, alive in the present with ideas about his own participation in a future he himself intends to help to create. This is a polarity that at least begins to operate on the level of character:

Rough, dark-flanked mountains enclosed the road and himself. Shinza had another kind of confidence, one that Bray was provoked by, not just in the mind, but in the body, in the senses; Shinza moved in his immediate consciousness, in images so vivid that he felt a queer alarm. A restlessness stirred resentfully in the tamped-down ground of his being, put out a touch on some nerve that (of course) had

atrophied long ago, as the vagus nerve is made obsolete by maturity
and the pituitary gland ceases to function when growth is complete.
Shinza's bare strong feet, misshapen by shoes, tramped the mud
floor—the flourish of a stage Othello before Cyprus. He was smoking cigarettes smuggled from over the border; friends across the
border: those who had cigarettes probably had money and arms as
well. And the baby; why did the baby keep cropping up?—Shinza
held it out in his hand as casually as he had fathered it on that girl. He
did not even boast of having a new young wife, it was nothing to him,
nothing was put behind him . . . (p. 129)

The images make it clear that Bray is reached, physically, by
Shinza's physical being. The phrase 'misshapen by shoes' carries
connotations similar to Achebe's use of the Ibo characterisation of the
first white men in that area as 'men without toes'. It is also reminiscent
of a conversation in *Occasion for Loving*, where the campaign of a
Rhodesian nationalist party to get its members to discard their shoes as
a particular instance of political protest, is discussed. The shoes
suggest the limitations on life and the human spirit imposed by the
forms of European culture or 'civilisation': Shinza's vigour, opposing
these restrictions, is expressed in 'bare strong feet'. The peculiar
masculinity of this vigour is stressed in the conventionally male
connotations of smuggled cigarettes, 'money and arms'; and at the end
of the passage the implied contrast with Bray emerges significantly, on
the dimension of time: '. . . nothing was put behind him . . .':

Shinza might as well have been thirty as fifty-four. No, it wasn't that
he was an ageing man who was like a young man—something quite
different—that he was driven quite naturally, acceptedly, to go on
living so long as he was alive. You would have to drop him dead, to
stop him.
   The house in Wiltshire with all its comfortable beauty and order,
its incenses of fresh flowers and good cooking, its libations of
carefully discussed flowers and chosen wine came to Bray in all the
calm detail of an interesting death cult: to wake up there again would
be to find oneself acquiescently buried alive. (pp. 129–30)

The personal polarity radiates various other levels of contrast:
between Europe and Africa, between two senses, or ideas, of time,
between the rigid separation of flesh and spirit and their natural
coalition—between two visions of the present political realities. As the

moving parts in the structure begin to roll, the polarity between Bray and Shinza tends towards self-abolition. In a sense, in the end, in death Bray *becomes* Shinza; and in the process he undergoes a remarkable reversal of roles.

One of the major ways of identifying the relationship between Africa and Europe—a conventional identification, within whose frame of reference Bray was arguably working even at the time of his recall from the colony—is to see Europe as mentor, Africa as pupil. Of course, such a definition begs a great many questions, historically and economically, and yet Bray, in the beginning, seems prepared to accept its validity—in fact, its stifling inevitability. After Bray discovers the illegal detentions and beatings, at his first meeting with Shinza, he feels that he must confront Mweta with his knowledge: but he is—partly—aware of the complexities such a decision must involve:

> He ought not, he was perhaps wrong to question Mweta about anything. He had made it clear from the beginning that he would not presume on any bond arising out of their association because he saw from the beginning that there was always the danger—to his personal relationship with Mweta—that this bond might become confused with some lingering assumption of authority from the colonial past. I mustn't forget that I'm a white man. A white man in Africa doesn't know what to see himself as, but mentor. He looks in the mirror, and there is the fatal fascination of the old reflection, doesn't matter much, now, whether it's the civil servant under a topi or the white liberal who turned his back on the settlers and went along with the Africans to Lancaster House. If I don't like what Mweta does, I'd better get out and go home to Wiltshire. Write an article for the *New Statesman*, from there. (p. 130)

Full self-awareness is clearly ruled out, as Bray acknowledges. When he sees Mweta, he has a further realisation:

> I have hurt him. I have hurt him by so much as acknowledging the other one's existence. They couldn't change the relationship in which they have stood to each other, he—Bray—and Mweta; he must have endorsement from me, that is my old role. (pp. 164–5)

The mentor-pupil bond obviously constitutes a polarity, but just as obviously it is not of a kind which lasts forever. Pupils learn, and cease to be pupils. Bray appreciates the objective changes that have taken place, destroying the colonial structure within which the relationship had operated—and whose abolition was the symbolic ending of whatever was held back automatically, by definition, in the relationship between white and black; but if he is to live up to his private contention that he has returned to Africa as an individual rather than a 'European' he has to understand the implications of this change on the personal level as well. Miss Gordimer is interested in illustrating the difficulty of this, and how Bray's position is all the more delicate because he is among the few Europeans who have, in the past, *understood* that the nature of their official relationship with Africa possessed within it the seeds of its own decay. He explains to Rebecca, later, in an attempt to sort out his own reaction to his discovery that Shinza is associating across the border with Somshetsi, a militant exiled guerilla leader whom Mweta has expelled from the country for endangering relationships with the leader of Somshetsi's homeland:

I understand perfectly what I was doing . . . when Shinza and Mweta started PIP it was something I believed in. The apparent contradiction between my position as a colonial civil servant and this belief wasn't really a contradiction at all, because to me it was the contradiction inherent in the colonial system—the contradiction that was the live thing in it, dialectically speaking, its transcendent element, that would split it open by opposing it, and let the future out—the future of colonialism *was* its own overthrow and the emergence of Africans into their own responsibility. I simply anticipated the end of my job. I . . . sort of spilled my energies over into what was needed after it, since—leaving aside how good or bad it had been—it was already an institution outgrown. Stagnant. *Boma* messengers, tax-collecting tours—we were a lot of ants milling around *rigor mortis* with the Union Jack flying over it . . . But now I think I ought to leave them alone. (pp. 246–7)

This awkwardly abstract apologia reflects his personal conflict, which amounts to a crisis, at finding himself, in a sense, caught on the Mweta-Shinza polarity, one on which the opposing forces are moving very quickly in opposite directions, with the snapping of the thin thread of continuity that still holds between them becoming imminent. But it also indicates the ground of his difficulties, since clearly his position on this continuum is personal as much as political in its nature. In this respect (as well as others) Bray's apologia is, to say the least, incomplete. There is a momentous level which he has left out, or ignored, on which he transgressed the official structure of his role, apart from the historic level to which he turns his attention; and the embarrassingly lifeless text-book phraseology of his self-justification is enough of an indication where the ommission lies. In colonial times, for obvious reasons, broad though the interpretation of the instructive relationship may have been, one element of conduct was strictly excluded from it: the crucial element as far as the English liberal morality was concerned—that of personal relations. Bray's transgression in this respect may have been unconscious, unintentional, inevitable, but its consequences were more complete, more final, than he perceives. At this stage the weakness in his position is largely that he is persistently unable to come to terms with this. On a previous occasion, not much before the one already quoted, he tries to express to Rebecca his unease at the way in which his relationship with Mweta is, he thinks, being misinterpreted. Lebaliso, Gala's chief of police, has been transferred, obviously as a result of Brays' having confronted Mweta with the fact of the illegal detention of Shinza's young protégé.

> 'I was a sort of symbol of something that never happened in Africa: a voluntary relinquishment in friendship and light all round, of white intransigence that can only be met with black intransigence. I represented something that all Africans yearned for—even while they were talking about driving all white people into the sea—a situation where they wouldn't have had to base the dynamic of *their* power on bitterness. People like me stood for that historically unattainable state—that's all.' He thought, am I making this up as I go along? Did I always think it? . . . 'But the idea persists . . . Aleke thinks, now, Lebaliso's been removed at my pleasure. I can see that. He tells me this morning about Labaliso being given the boot as if remarking on something I already know.' (pp. 220–1)

It is not very surprising therefore that Bray's relationship with Mweta, his entire position, in fact, is seen by others solely in terms of power and influence, when Bray himself is sufficiently a victim of his code to be able to admit the personal level as a factor. He fears to be seen as mentor, knows (and tries to exploit the knowledge) that Mweta seeks his approval; but never admits to his consciousness for the same kind of analysis the presence of the entirely different demands of personal friendship that in fact constitute the basic fabric of the situation. In this respect both of the above attempts at self-clarification and analysis of his situation fall short of being adequate because both

Mweta and Shinza had been personal friends; Bray's 'work' with them was outside, in his own terms, the historic framework he uses for self-analysis. He falls short of recognising his relationship with Mweta for what it is, and thus miscalculates his own situation. He is aware only of the dangers and complexities of being 'the European in Africa': he has yet to learn those of being Mweta's friend but Shinza's ally.

Such a position is impossible in terms of the framework of English liberalism within which Bray's actions are located, and Miss Gordimer takes the reader through a sequence of events that gradually make this plain to Bray, producing the interesting structural effect of the integration of the Shinza-Mweta polarity into Bray's own psychic economy. The events include the annual party congress—an episode which evokes unrestricted admiration for the technical skill with which Miss Gordimer presents it—during which Bray uses the credit he had accumulated in his colonial past to persuade an old chief to get 'his' delegates to support the Shinza line. As a result of this 'service rendered', he is accepted, not without reluctance, by Shinza's lieutenants into their policy-making group. But Bray also has his customary tête-a-tête dinner with Mweta straight after the Congress, after Mweta's symbolic (and charisma-based) defeat of Shinza (the ostensible issue is whether the Secretary-General of the trade union movement should continue to be elected by the unions or become a presidential appointee).

The build-up of stress within Bray is illustrated at the Party rally at the end of the Congress:

Shinza had gone back to the Bashi—had left the capital, anyway: '–I'll see you at home, then,' presumably meaning Gala. Without him, it was almost as if nothing had happened. All these people before Mweta, old men in leopard skins with seed-bracelets rattling on their ankles as they mimed an old battle-stride in flat-footed leaps that made the young people giggle, church choirs with folded hands, marching cadets, pennants, bands, dancers, ululating women, babies sucking breasts or chewing roasted corn cobs, men parading under home-made Party banners—the white-hot sun, dust, smell of maize-beer, boiling pluck and high dried fish: the headiness of life. Bray felt it drench him with his own sweat. If he could have spoken to Mweta then (a gleaming beaming face, refusing the respite of the palanquin, taking full glory of sun and roaring crowd) he would have wanted to tell him, this is theirs always, it's an affirmation of life. They would give it to another if, like a flag, you were hauled down tomorrow and another put up in your place. It's not what should matter to you now. And he wondered if he would ever tell him anything again, anything that he believed himself. The other night was so easy; how was it possible that such things could be so easy. Suddenly, in the blotch of substituted images, dark and light, that came with the slight dizziness of heat and noise, there was Olivia, an image of a split second. It was easy with her, too. She did not ask; he did not broach. It made him uneasy, though, that she and Mweta should be linked at some level in his mind. Of course, there was an obvious link; the past. But a line between the solid walk down the carpark to lobby for Shinza ('Semstu, my old friend'), and the presence of the girl—always on him, the impress of a touch that doesn't wash off—could only be guilt-traced. And guilty of what? I have gone on living; I don't desire Olivia: something over which one hasn't any control; and the things I believe in were there in me before I knew Mweta and remain alive in me if he turns away from them.

He felt, with the friendly Hjalmar at his side and the amiable crowd around him, absolutely alone. He did not know how long it lasted; momentary, perhaps, but so intense it was timeless. Everything retreated from him; the crowd was deep water. A breeze dried the sweat in a stiff varnish on his neck. (pp. 377–8)

This frozen moment is the first symptom of what is going to lead to Bray's brief but fatal disintegration, and it is significant that Hjalmar, who is to be his inheritor, in a sense is his only companion. The pendulum of their relationship is drawing towards the edge of its swing, and its return journey is swifter and more comprehensively catastrophic than could have been expected. There are, after all, two sides to Bray's background, and in a way their existence—the tension and continuity between them—constitutes the basis of the wider series of polarities that characterise the structure of the book. The side that tends to dominate at this stage may also be the forme in which Bray's character is cast. It is part of a tradition, a European (or at least English) aristocratic cultural tradition which goes back historically to the age of chivalry. Bray feels guilty because he has betrayed love and friendship, his wife and his man friend, thus going against this very basic element in his makeup. He is 'uneasy' that Olivia and Mweta—or rather, his behaviour towards each of them—'should be linked . . . in his mind'. This unease is a manifestation of what he has distastefully called in himself 'the virginal drawing away of skirts from the dirt'. (p. 214) It functions as a physical premonition of death, and is associated, structurally, with what Bray himself has seen as an 'interesting death cult'—the house in Wiltshire, which is the end product of this tradition, this process of historic evolution, from feudal chivalry through imperial 'justice' to modern liberalism. The house in Wiltshire is a pole of contrast with the house at Gala: at this moment, this polarity seems to work as an allegory of life and death. The whole of the European experience is in a way summed up and ended, a line drawn underneath, by the house in Wiltshire; the house at Gala sees the new beginning, the obstinacy of the will to live and change, the desire to be involved in life. By a paradox that is only apparent, Bray associates his 'betrayals' not with change but continuity, an internal consistency. He has no control over his lost desire for Olivia because one can never control the direction of desire—which is the direction that life takes—and 'the things I believe in were there in me before I knew Mweta and remain alive in me if he turns away from them'.

Thus it may be suggested that Miss Gordimer has abandoned one of her fundamental positions in relation to the treatment of time in her novels. In its conventional form in modern fiction, the individual experience of 'fulfilment' in the cant literary sense takes place 'out of time': its duration is not immediately recognisable as such. Examples crowd to mind from the works of Lawrence, Forster, Virginia Woolf and Joyce; and in Miss Gordimer's work we find many characteristic incidents of the kind, from Joel's revelation of love for Helen in *The Lying Days*, to Elizabeth's transcendent linking of the space walkers to the drowned men at the end of *The Late Bourgeois World*.

The orthodox presentation of the interplay of time and human character in the English novel is carried, it seems to me, on the same wave of radical optimism that bore the novel genre to the commanding heights of literary expression in English. That is, whatever tragic individual events may occur, the main tendency of development in human relations is ameliorative. Thus the possibility of fulfilment, on the individual or social level, is always present and usually in the process of enlargement, as a result of the pervasive if unrecognised underlying belief that people are capable of learning the lessons of experience. It is in Conrad's work that the most powerful negation of this melioristic mythos occurs; and the instance relevant to our purpose is, of course, *Nostromo*.

And it is in the massive surface confusion of chronology, of the 'linear' approach, that the essential clue to what I hope we are getting at, appears. Enough has been written about the Tolstoyan scale of the work—it treats of politics and human beings as the subjects of history,

and history as the subjects of Eternity—and it aims at totality. The
result, as far as human cognition of time goes, is on one level, an
intentional, controlled jumble. Through this maze no individual
character is able to find openings into possibilities of greater freedom,
let alone any kind of fulfilment. The aims of *A Guest of Honour* are in
many ways parallel to those of *Nostromo*. The topography of Miss
Gordimer's African state is disjoined in rather similar manner to that of
Costaguana. The heroes of both books are liberals faced with the
problem, on the personal level as well as the political, of action, in order
to secure the possibility of amelioration, of fulfilment. There is a
remote, but recognisable connection between the relationships of
Charles Gould and *Nostromo*, in the one book, and Mweta and Shinza
in the other, particularly in the manner in which good and pure
intentions are affected in both cases by the necessity of action. And,
even (though from a strictly structural point of view) the massively
disjunctive endings of the two works have parallel functions.

For Conrad, then, a rejection of the common, optimistic metaphysic
of the English novel is related through a confusion of the way in which
human beings perceive and deal with time.

Miss Gordimer rejects the view of history that underlies conventional
linear time-perception as narrative method, and comes up with
resultant rejection of the connected melioristic metaphysic, though she
sees it as irrelevant rather than fundamentally erroneous, and thus her
irony is of a different and less tragically portentous kind than
Conrad's.

What is the notion of history that she hypostatises, then? The clue to
its nature springs from two courses: two meditations on death on pages
385 and 465 of *A Guest of Honour*, in which it is seen both as a
continuation and as 'interruption'; and the circumstantial parallel
between Bray's death and that of Steven Sitole in *A World of Strangers*.
Something that appears from this (very clearly) is that in Miss
Gordimer's developed work the only experience that really transcends
time is death, and either it is arbitrary and without significance or its
significance is a barren enigma. History has no human consolation in
this novel.

Its shape, however, is defined; the major movement is remorselessly
cyclical, and human antics resemble those of Tom Thumbs caught in
the drum of a tumbler dryer. The dialectic, shall we say, is not absent
from this idea—but it may be an illusion. As Mweta's 'pragmatism'
becomes more pronounced—by allowing, for instance, the big mining
company to arm its own private army to put down strikes—and

Shinza's ideological commitment more fervent, and closer to expression in action, Bray finds that decision has ineluctably taken place within him, rather than been made by him. If it is political freedom he is interested in, circumstances rather than an act of free will commit him to action on behalf of his interest. His last meeting with Shinza, in a servant's room in riot-torn Gala, expresses the dilemma in terms of the shape of Bray's participation in history.

'. . . look, James, I want you to go for us. Now.'
   'To Switzerland.'
   'Anywhere. Everywhere.'
   Bray looked at him.
   'Oh that ILO thing—well it's too late. There's a chance now that may never come again. You know what I'm talking about. This mine wasn't my doing, I don't have to tell you that—but now that it's going this way, I'll have to move if I'm ever going to move at all. We must make use of it, you understand. It may still go a long time, and if it becomes a general strike . . . if the whole country—James, what I want is you to go and get money for us. Quickly. Now. You know the right people in England. There are a few contacts of mine . . . There's Sweden, East Germany. We must take money where we can, at this stage. I've got some, already, I've had some, of course. Somshetsi must have money if he's going to help us and I need him. I need him, James. He's got trained people . . . you know. With a small force of trained people in the right places at the right time, you take over your radio station and telecommunications . . . airport . . . you can bring it off without . . . almost without a scratch. If Mweta can't hold this country together and we hang back, what're you going to get? You're going to get Tola Tola [a right-wing former cabinet minister arrested on charges of attempting a coup]. You see that. Tola Tola or somebody like him. That's what you'll get. And the bribes'll be bigger in the capital and the prisons will be fuller, and when the rains are late, like now, people will have to scratch for roots to make a bit of porridge, just the way it's always been here.'
   Bray thought, he's saying all the right things to me; but then Shinza paused, and in this room that enclosed them as closely as a call there was the feeling, as often happened between them, that Shinza knew what he was thinking: was thinking the same of himself, and said, 'I never thought I would ever do it. Now I have to.'
   He said, 'What will I say to you? I'll think it over?'
   Shinza gave a sympathetic snort.

'When I've "thought it over" I'll only know what I know already: that I didn't think it would ever be expected of me. Not only by you. By myself.'

Shinza smiled at him almost paternally. 'I suppose we didn't know how lucky we were to get away without guns so far. Considering what we want. You don't expect to get that for nothing.'

It will be such a very little token violence, Bray; and you won't feel a thing. It will happen to other people, just as the tear gas and the baton charges do.

'But do you expect it of yourself?' Shinza was saying, detachedly interested.

'Yes.'

'Good God, James, remember the old days when we used to come to your place starving hungry after meetings? After riding a bicycle fifteen miles in the rain from Mologushi Mission? And when the order came from the secretariat that I was to be 'apprehended' and you decided it didn't say arrested so you could 'apprehend' me to tell me about it —?'

They laughed. (pp.429–30)

The two decisions are one—either that, or the first contained the seeds of the last. In either event, time has described a cycle, and Bray is back at the beginning—or is it a new beginning? The question is not answered with finality, but the reader is invited to scan the evidence, or at least hunt for clues.

These may be found in differences, rather than similarities; the whole passage stands in wry juxtaposition to Bray's earlier explanation (to Rebecca) of how he had come to take his stand in colonial times. This is intellectualised and rather pompous, suggestive of post facto self-justification, a distortion—no doubt unwilling and unconscious—of reality. It even contains specific reference to the 'dialectic', the significance of which as a clue to real meaning only becomes clear at this much later stage. Now the moment of decision is seen as already past, as never having existed, as perpetually deferred to infinity: 'When I've "thought it over" I'll only know what I know already: that I didn't think it would ever be expected of me'. Already the post facto self-justification has begun: 'It will be such a very little token violence, Bray—but again the grammar of differences supervenes: 'and you won't feel a thing. It will happen to other people, just as the tear gas and the baton charges do.' At this point Bray at least begins with more self-knowledge; but he is beginning the same kind of thing, a future which is merely an intensification of the past. And this tells us the meaning of his earlier meditation, already mentioned, on page 385:

> But human affairs didn't come to clear cut conclusions, a line drawn and a total added up. They appeared to resolve, dissolve, while they were only reforming, coming together in another combination. Even when we are dead, what we did goes on making these new combinations (he saw clouds, saw molecules); that's true for private history as well as the other kind. (p. 385)

He thinks in these terms just before he leaves the Capital for the last time, after the party congress, and immediately after having arranged for the illegal transfer of Rebecca's funds to a Swiss bank account. The Presidential motorcade sweeps past, and the sight of 'the black profile of Mweta's face rushing away from his focus' provokes him to these considerations, which conclude:

> Next time we meet—yes, Mweta may even have to deport me. And even that would be a form of meeting. (p. 385)

But there is to be no further meeting. What Bray has experienced is a prefiguration, or an intellectual intuition, of his own death.

There is another link in this chain of events; since there are three altogether, perhaps the illusion of the dialectic hovers. The second, which reinforces the speculation of the first and links it with the third, and climactic one, which is the actuality of Bray's death, takes place on the final journey, after order has broken down in Gala and Bray is taking Rebecca away, to an unknown destination. He, at least, is on his way to fulfil what Shinza has required of him'

> His mind was calm. It was not that he had no doubts about what he was doing, going to do; it seemed to him he had come to understand that one could never be free of doubt, of contradictions within, that this was the state in which one lived—the state of life itself—and no action could be free of it. There was no finality, while one lived, and when one died it would always be, in a sense, an interruption. (pp. 464–5)

This is a clearly-defined acceptance of the stage beyond the classic liberal problems of action. It is an intellectual advance for Bray, but it is also an acknowledgement of what is already real and actual, a state of affairs he has helped to bring about before having intellectually resolved the conflict. It leads swiftly to the mystery of death itself.

Bray's death is arbitrary and shocking. As they drive towards the capital, he and Rebecca are stopped by a roadblock, a huge tree-trunk across the road. They get out to try to shift it, and as Bray takes the car jack from under the back seat, he is set upon and beaten to death by a band of men.

> Then he was below them, he was looking up at them and he saw the faces, he saw the sticks and stones and bits of farm implements, the sun behind. Something fell on him again and again and he knew himself convulsed, going in and out of pitch black, of black nausea, heaving to bend double where the blows were, where the breath had gone, and he thought he rose again, he thought he heard himself screaming, he wanted to speak to them in Gala but he did not know a word, not a word of it, and then something burst in his eyes, some wet flower covered them, and he thought he knew: I've been interrupted, then— (p. 469)

Afterwards Rebecca crawls out of the ditch where she has been hiding, and tries to clean his face, taking the shattered frames of his glasses out of his cheek. Then they are found:

> Some people came down the road. An old man with safety-pins in his earholes and a loin-cloth under an old jacket stopped short, saying the same half-syllable over and over. There were little children watching and no-one sent them away. All she could do before the old man was to shake her head, again, again, again, at what they both saw. The women sent up a great sigh . Bray lay there in the middle of them all. They brought an old grey blanket of the kind she had seen all her life drying outside their huts, and an old door and they lifted him up and carried him away. They seemed to know him; he belonged to them. The old man with the safety-pins said to her in revelation, 'It is the Colonel! It is the Colonel!' (p. 475)

Bray finds synthesis in death; he belongs to Africa, to Africa; he is recognised there. His final echo of the intellectual conclusion towards which he had been working for a long time, from the time of his re-awakening, confirms the idea in reality: the shape of his life is different from the orthodox notion governed by the concepts of European liberalism. The demonstration is incomplete, however, for one or two revelations have still to be made, even though the central affirmation—'It is the Colonel! It is the Colonel!' has taken place.

Up to now all the narration has been from Bray's point of view, and he has been the sole centre of consciousness. (His development has been a progression from false to real, in terms of what his consciousness has constituted, and it is never presented as infallible.) With his death the narration passes to Rebecca, and a sense of continuity is successfully evoked.

> After a little while she went and sat on the white-washed milestone at the side of the road . . . She watched him all the time. She became aware of a strange and terrifying curiosity rising in her; it was somehow connected with his body. She got up and went over to his body again and looked at it; this was the same body that she had caressed last night, that she had had inside her when she fell asleep.
>
> The basket and his briefcase had been flung out of the car and so were not burned. She picked them up and balanced the briefcase across the basket beside him, to keep the sun off his face.
>
> And more time went by. She sat on the road. Her shirt was wet with sweat and she could smell it. Sometimes she opened her mouth and panted a little until she heard the sound and stopped. She was beginning to feel something. She didn't know what it was, but it was some sort of physical inkling. And then she thought very clearly that the flask was still in the basket and got up firmly and fetched it and poured what was left of the coffee into the plastic cup. As she saw the liquid there, it all came back with a rush, to the glands of her mouth, to her nerves, to her senses, to her flesh and bones—she was thirsty. She drank it down in one breath. Then for the first time she began to weep. She was thirsty, and had drunk, and so it happened: she had left him. She had begun to live on. (pp. 474–5)

What is being described here is a rebirth. Rebecca emerges unformed, in some respects, but in possession of formidable knowledge—a sort of new genetic package, a second chance to realise a different potential from that which she started her first life. The point of this effect is important. Throughout the novel the reader has been carried on a whole body of assumptions about the significant aspects of both the political and the personal life—Bray's assumptions, the assumptions of the upper class English liberal. Sometimes they have worked, at others proved inadequate. But the reader either shares them

or he doesn't, and there is no scope for examining the validity of their
origins. Rebecca's rebirth takes her almost immediately out of
Africa—for the first time—and into Bray's other world, the world that
formed him—Europe (and subtle emphasis has been placed on the idea
that Bray is a natural cosmopolitan within the European context, not
'just' an Englishman). So she faces, without preconceptions, the
ground of his assumptions. This most meaningful 'knowledge' she
confirms in the few dreamlike days spent in the capital with her old
friends; it concerns the bald facts of Bray's death:

> With the brandy glasses in their hands they talked about what had
> happened. Out of that day—yesterday, the day before yesterday,
> the day before that: slowly the succeeding days changed position
> round it—another version came into double exposure over what she
> knew. The men who had attacked were a roving gang made up of a
> remnant from the terrible riots that had gone on for a week centred
> round the asbestos mine. A Company riot squad led by white
> strangers—'*You see.*' Vivien interrupted her husband, 'I knew
> they'd get round to using those men from the Congo and Mweta
> wouldn't be able to stop them. I knew it would happen'—had opened
> machine-gun fire on strikers armed with sticks and stones. The white
> man dealt with them out of long experience of country people who
> needed a lesson in the name of whoever was paying—they burned
> down the village. The villagers and the strikers had made an unsuc-
> cessful raid on the old Pilchey's Hotel, where the mercenaries had
> quartered themselves. Someone had put up those road-blocks, prob-
> ably with the idea of ambushing the white men (hopeless, they had
> left already, anyway) . . . It was said that the one who started the
> hut-burnings was a big German who didn't travel in the troop
> transports but in his own car.
>   Vivien said, 'But this was a little Volkswagen, and there was a
> woman in it.'
>   'To asbestos miners an army staff car's the same as any other kind.
> A car's a car.' Neil spoke coldly to her.
>   'Nobody knows anything, any more, when things get to the stage
> they are now. I don't suppose Mweta knew they would machine-gun
> people. Burn their houses over their heads. He just put it into the
> hands of the Company army, left it to their good sense . . . That's
> quite enough.'
>   She offered the information, 'The people who helped us knew
> Bray. An old man with safety-pins in the holes in his ears. He knew

him from before.' (pp. 477–8)

That this is a two-pronged movement towards the completion of Bray's dialectic of life and death is made obvious by the use of the image of 'double exposure'. This suggests confusion, two competing versions of what is true, and is, of course, related to the principle of polarity that permeates the structure. Only here there is a superimposition, so that the conflicting elements—the elements themselves—tend to coalesce. Thus there is, on one level, no comprehensible or significant difference between Shinza and Mweta, or Rebecca and Olivia, Bray's wife in Wiltshire—or Bray and the German mercenary. But the key word that marks the author's control over the way the passage develops is 'know'. It is about knowledge, without arriving at it: the strikers did not *know* who Bray was, that he was their man; Neil does not know anything except that some things were probably not *knowable* in advance, or in the particular circumstances—and this kind of knowledge is shown to be academic, explanatory and irrelevant. Rebecca's contribution is more pointed, based on a clear memory of real knowledge: 'The people who helped us *knew* Bray'. In the end, Bray knew something, too: that he had been interrupted. Such knowledge is meant to imply wisdom: tasks are only begun when they seem fulfilled, no man dwells in his promised land, but the ongoing quality of life demands continuous participation until the moment of interruption comes. Withdrawal is betrayal. Neil's academic, historicist, empirical, European-style 'knowledge' comes to nothing, in Africa at any event: and if that is true of Africa, may it not be the case elsewhere?

In other words, what has been at issue in Bray's second life in Africa has been the validation or otherwise of Europe's historic presence in Africa. And as Bray's control over himself and his situation had gradually broken down, so the code of values and the historic experience on which it had been based is discredited, because that code and that experience have been responsible for creating the situation itself. But Bray has in the meanwhile begun to live again. Uninhibited, this time, by the accumulation of irrelevant tradition, he is also protected by it.

The polarity that emerges to prominence in the penultimate section of the book bears out this interpretation. Hjalmar Wentz, the survivor of Europe, who smuggled his wife out of the shadow of the gas chambers, confronts Bray in Gala on the latter's return from a meeting with Shinza in the bush. His daughter, the sexy Emmanuelle, has fled the country with Ras Asahe, the arrogant young broadcaster whose father had been a supporter of Shinza years before: but it is the failure of a coup from the right that has led to his flight. Hjalmar is having a nervous breakdown; the final straw has an interesting consistency. (pp. 418–9)

Hjalmar and his experience are quintessentially European, like Bray and *his*—and they simultaneously undergo the same kind of breakdown: the long-established marital cycle has come off the rails. Of course, in Brays' case this is much more low-keyed, heavily modulated but the ironic purpose of the coincidence is manifest. Breakdown takes different forms, but in a chaotic age all its forms have one meaning. The objective fact of coincidence itself bears on this meaning. Why is the same moment in time employed for the two identical revelations (and it may be noted that what actually takes place in this charged instant is only, in each case, a report of what has already happened) in a long novel with plenty of space in it for manoeuvre—and with very little dependence on coincidence as a technical device? Surely the answer is that the novelist wants to suggest the notion of a particular shape possessed by time, a shape whose nature is external to and independent of human experience and perceptions?

It is, in fact, all very Yeatsian. Bray's active life has undergone what seemed like a cycle of return, reawakening—but the circle was actually a gyre, and points of resemblance between the first and second revolutions were simply the mockery implicit in this shape of historical experience. The second time round coincides with, is in fact a part, a very insignificant part of, a great cusp of time, a decisive lurch toward the abyss on the part of European civilisation. This was the conclusion towards which Miss Gordimer was moving in *The Late Bourgeois World*, a book in which the moral certainties of the characters, and the gestures and affirmations based on them concealed (it seems to me) a profound authorial uncertainty, almost confusion; the surface is very brittle. In *A Guest of Honour*, on the other hand, the uncertainties and moral groping, the sense of inadequacy, of inability to grasp and deal with the complexity of events, constitute the uneven surface of a new underlying certainty, a sense of the shape and direction of things. Miss Gordimer succeeds in realising this new certainty not through an experiment in form but in a fairly rigorously orthodox traditional novel, which perhaps emphasises the degree of her success. She works in an area of uncertainty with 'the instruments at our disposal' and produces a carefully-shaped and unwavering result. European history is plunged into a period of uneasy transcience, and the polarity between the two men representing the stage immediately past stretches tighter and tighter until it snaps. Hjalmar, invited as a matter of course by Bray to accompany him and Rebecca on their last journey together out of the localised chaos of Gala, surprisingly declines.

Bray has once remarked that Hjalmar had a talent for survival, and later he adds the rider that the precocious Emmanuelle has inherited this. But here the price of survival is revealed, and Hjalmar is shown as an essentially 'linear' character, withdrawing from the complexities of reality into an obsessive concentration on small, single, self-imposed tasks of the imposition of a meaningless and miniscule order: as a cultural symbol he possesses frightening implications. The civilisation of the West lives on, but with inner life (and connections with vital forces) banked down, drained to the lowest embers, while the external manifestation goes on tirelessly, mechanistically and without relevance repeating its little technical tricks and expertises—not even substituting for the living relationship with the core of reality it once possessed. Both Hjalmar and Bray, the Europeans, are drawn to the tree, the magnificent, ancient, carelessly fertile, parasite-rotten but vigorous symbol of Africa underneath which Bray has chosen to work in Gala. Thus while Bray, who cannot survive, shows some sort of sympathetic understanding of the tree's meaning, the response of Hjalmar, the survivor, is an etiolated repetition of the empty European habit of tidying up, imposing a meaningless formal order. This final comment applies not only to the history of the white man in Africa.

Thus they part, Bray, involved with history, and therefore with life, to go to his death, Hjalmar, withdrawn from the meaningful structure of time, to go on smoothing down the ripples of his mind.

What we know about Bray and Europe is placed in perspective by Rebecca. She flies to Switzerland and goes into a bank fitted out with plush solemnity, like a comfortable temple, where Bray had sent the money. In her hotel that evening she finds herself in the lounge together with a honeymoon couple.

A young couple were sitting there, stirring the cream on their coffee and slowly finishing bowls of berries sprinkled with sugar. They murmured to each other in German something like, 'Good . . .?' 'Oh very good'—and went on dreamily licking the spoons. The girl wore trousers and a sweater with a string of pearls, she was tall and narrow-footed and remote. The man, shorter than she, looked not quite at home in rather smart casual clothes and had a worried little double chin already beginning beneath his soft face. The girl yawned and he smiled. It was the stalemate of conversation, the listlessness of a newly married couple who have never previously been lovers. 'Very good,' he said again, putting his bowl on the tray.

The wine rose to her head in a singing sensation and she thought of them sitting on politely round a coffee table for ever, he slipping down into fatness and greyness, she never released from her remoteness, while their children grew, waiting to take their places there. She became aware of an ornamental clock ticking away the silence in the room between herself and the couple. (p. 495)

The last image is perhaps crucial. Measured time, reduced to an ordered precision, divides her experience from the life of Europe. The Swiss clock in a Swiss hotel lounge and the bourgeois Swiss couple, motionless and apparently 'sunken into hebetude', are analogues for Hjalmar in Gala; or rather, both are analogues for what has happened to Europe, while Rebecca is on the outside, where the life is, but cut off from it, with a different history, separated by the clock from the experience of Europe.

England, as Bray's birthplace, is the centre, however, and further confirmation of Bray's speculation about life in time is afforded through Rebecca's perceptions of London.

. . . She went unrecognised here; she was the figure with the scythe.

Yet this was where Bray came from: there were faces in which she could trace him. An elderly man in a taxi outside a restaurant; even a young actor with sideburns and locks. He might once have been or become, any of these who were living so differently from the way she did. It was as if she forayed into a past that he had left long ago and a future that he would never inhabit. She wandered the bypasses of his life that he had not taken, meeting the possibility of his presence. (p. 497)

Bray is, however, a particular case, and the matter of his 'belonging' is still unsettled. Two clues are given, which are suggestive of the full irony of his fate. There is the chance meeting with Emmanuelle (pp. 501–2) and the revelation that Hjalmar's daughter has inherited a yawning intellectual emptiness from Europe, besides the useless trick of survival. She is quite unaware that in her second-hand rhetoric she has stumbled upon the crucial question, while at the same time enunciating the grounds of one possible answer. These have been hinted at, already; Hitler has been mentioned twice in the book, the first time by Emmanuelle's father, at a party at independence time, in a discussion with an African doctor, the country's first medical graduate:

> Odara laughed. 'But it always comes down to the same thing: you Europeans talk very reasonably about that sort of suffering because you don't know . . . you may have thought it was terrible, but there's nothing like that in your lives.'
>
> Bray saw Margot Wentz put up her head with a quick grimace-smile, as if someone had told an old joke she couldn't raise a laugh for.
>
> 'Well, here you're mistaken,' her husband said, rather grandly, 'we lived under Mr Hitler. And you must know all about that.'
>
> 'I'm not interested in Hitler.' Timothy Odara's fine teeth were bared in impatient pleasantness. 'My friend, white men have killed more people in Africa than Hitler ever did in Europe.'
>
> 'But you're crazy,' said Wentz gently.
>
> 'Europe's wars, white men's killing among themselves. What's that to me? You've just said one shouldn't burden oneself with suffering. I don't have any feelings about Hitler.'
>
> 'Oh but you should,' Mrs Wentz said, almost dreamily.
>
> 'No more and no less than you do about what happened to Africans. It's all the same thing. A slave in the hold of a ship in the eighteenth century and a Jew or a gipsy in a concentration camp in the nineteen-forties.'
>
> 'Well, I had my seventeenth and eighteenth birthdays in the detention camps at Fort Howard, the guest of Her Majesty's governor,' said Odara, 'that I know.'
>
> 'Her two brothers died at Auschwitz,' Hjalmar Wentz said; but his wife was talking to Jo-Ann Pettigrew, who offered blobs of toasted marshmallows on the end of a long fork. (pp. 33–4)

The image in the last sentence is macabre; but it is the moral significance of recent European history in Africa, as understood by most 'Europeans', as they call themselves, who live there. Odara, the doctor's, point is mere political affectation, tinged with a danger the presence, let alone the magnitude, of which he is unaware. The comparison he draws, between his own detention prior to independence and Margot Wentz's 'slave in the hold of a ship in the eighteenth century and a Jew or gipsy in a concentration camp in the nineteen-forties', has just enough surface validity to make its absurdity clear.

The level of validity is the continuity of cruelty—European, 'civilised' cruelty—that links Odara's experience with those evoked by Margot Wentz: but this is swamped in the depths of Timothy Odara's historical egocentrism.

Perhaps there is this link, then, between Odara, a minor character of no intrinsic significance—or, rather, between this episode and the other brief mention of Hitler, later in the novel: on Bray's first return from Gala to the capital, after he has seen Shinza and encountered the young trade unionist who had been illegally arrested and beaten, he has dinner with Neil and Vivien Bayley. (pp. 154–5)

The link is between Odara's wilful ignorance of history and Mweta's pragmatic brand of ahistoricism: and this illuminates the polarity between Mweta and Shinza, who quotes Fanon and brings to bear the history, at least , of liberation movements elsewhere on the continent on to his political action, while the former is getting the best deals he is likely to be offered by the same businessman in whose interests the colonial power had ruled and plundered his country. (p. 164)

Mweta is ultimately condemned on the grounds of historical confusion, for in the end he has to call in British troops to restore order—and a degree of security in his own tenure of power. But then, if the shape of history is the inexorable Yeatsian corkscrew, Mweta has no more chance of escaping his own little spiral than Shinza his—and at the end of the book they are thoroughly 'separated out' from each other, as it were, with Shinza in exile in Algiers.

Emmanuelle suffers from the same ahistorical affliction, but in her it is a disease amounting to grotesque deformity. She is in herself an end product, a fusion, combining all the best of what Europe had to offer: her maternal grandfather an emancipated, Germanised professor of physics, her father once courageous enough to risk his life for love and for what he knew to be good in the face of prevailing evil. But all she is left with, in Africa, is a facility for music and the instinct for survival. It is the tragic end of the European liberal line: a pretty and vacuous performing monkey, adept at imitating her lovers' phrases, and agile enough to duck under the blows of Fate. She is in a polar relationship with Rebecca, also born in Africa but without any such burden of cultural inheritance, who is learning all the time, not only receptive but able to discern and to develop what she accepts, to integrate it with the basic qualities of her being. So Rebecca, neither European nor African, unbound and unconfined by any moral and political frame of reference, is able to absorb (in more senses than one), and even embody the most shattering discovery of Miss Gordimer's novel: the non-existence of Europe, or of that idea of Europe in terms of historical and cultural and moral-significance that has stood sometimes as a consciously-sought goal, sometimes as objective correlative, but always there, always just outside the reach of her heroes and heroines, just beyond the imaginative frameworks of the lives they lead, the matrix of African reality their creator provides for them. In *The Lying Days*, Europe's meaning has to be discovered from scratch. In *A World of Strangers* and *Occasion for Loving*, it is Europe that possesses the solidity of moral reference from which the leading characters strive to derive their impulse to action. In *The Late Bourgeois World* the new perspectives that emerge from an awareness of European decay are, like the very awareness, themselves European. In all these works the solid bedrock of what I have called moral reference is the Europe of renaissance humanism and romantic liberalism, the Europe of the centrality of the individual in relation to nature and the community; the Europe where the idea of love was apotheosised, the value of the communication between man and man formed into discovery, the meaning of tragedy understood. It was an idea, and it informed the very pattern of Miss Gordimer's novels, though always from the outside. Bray is a conscious embodiment of this idea, and this is the magnificent justification of saddling him with the burden of narration almost throughout the book. His ambiguities, uncertainties, responses to pressure, and eventual decisiveness in the midst of breakdown, both inner and outer, reflect the growing discovery that he has to make but is spared from absorbing, that the objective meaningfulness of this idea is ephemeral: its elaborate and ornate structures have turned to mist, dispelled by the African sun.

But Rebecca has known Bray as a man (hence the emphasis on physical detail in their relationship) and not as the embodiment of idea or ideal, has been influenced by him, received, as it were, a kind of imprint, so that it has become a matter of instinct for her to seek the real and the healthy in relationships and objects. She encounters no meaning corresponding to Bray's in London, and her meeting with Emmanuelle, like her confessional session with the Swiss banker, is a confrontation with nothingness, a void where the structure behind the idea might have been anticipated to exist. The only thing that is left is the 'house in Wiltshire':

She thought of Olivia as an empty perfume bottle in which a scent still faintly remains. She had found one on one of the shelves in the wardrobe of her hotel room: left there by some anonymous English woman, an Olivia. She knew nobody in the city of eight millions. She had nothing in common with anyone: except his wife.

At times she was strongly attracted by the idea of going to see Olivia and his daughters. But the thought that they would receive her, accept her in their supremely civilised tolerance—*his* tolerance—this filled her with resentment. She wanted to bare her suffering, to live it and thrust it, disgusting, torn life from her under their noses, not to make it 'acceptable' to others. (p. 498)

In other words, the strictly personal continuity that exists between Bray and herself has nothing to do with Europe or England. The hours at Wiltshire might provide a structure of values that would 'tolerate' her suffering, but not one that would validate it in any permanent moral or human sense. Thus again, where continuity, or at least contact with a mighty and potent scheme of values, might have been expected, none can exist because the scheme no longer does.

Of course it is possible that Miss Gordimer has never quite understood, herself, what she boils down to the 'house in Wiltshire'. She doesn't really come to grips with it, and quickly turns it into a symbol of things past. Rebecca, the new person, reborn into the old society, is unlike her predecessors, Helen Shaw and Jessie Stilwell, in Miss Gordimer's fiction. She shows little curiosity, to discover the nature of what they would have regarded as a rightful part of their heritage from which they had been unfairly excluded. So Wiltshire, Bray's past, what made him, remain mysterious, readable only in what became of him.

The final ironic twist occurs in the closing paragraph of the book, and bears full blast on the nagging question of knowledge that underpins the presence of the European in Africa:

Hjalmar Wentz also put together Bray's box of papers and gave them over to Dando, who might know what to do with them. Eventually they must have reached the hands of Mweta. He apparently, chose to believe that Bray was a conciliator; a year later he published a blueprint for the country's new education scheme, the Bray Report. (pp. 503–4)

This links the structure together in important ways and places. First, it comments on the passage quoted earlier in which Vivien and Neil and Rebecca talk about Bray's death (pp. 477–8) and for all the bright knowingness that the young Bayleys possess, they are unable to achieve true knowledge, or come near to an understanding of the nature of knowledge—which has so much to do with their presence in Africa.

It also seals the limits of possibility on this level of knowledge, deadening the echoes set off by Dando.

> He was talking of Bray. 'The thing is, of course, all our dear friends abroad will say he was killed by the people he loved and what else can you expect of them, and how ungrateful they are, and all that punishment-and-reward two-and-two-makes-four that passes for intelligent interpretation of events. That's part of it that would rile him. Or maybe amuse him. I don't know.'
>
> Vivien's beautiful controlled voice came out of the dark. 'I wish we could know that James himself knew it wasn't that, when it happened,'
>
> 'Of course he knew!' Roly spoke with the unchallengeable authority of friendship on a plane none of the others had shared. 'He's got nothing to do with that lot of spiritual bed-wetters finding a surrogate for their fears in death! He knew what's meant by the forces of history, he knew how risky the energies released by social change are. But what's the good. They'll say 'his blacks' murdered him. They'll go one further: they'll come up with their guilts to be expiated and say, yes, he certainly died with Christian forgiveness for the people who killed him, into the bargain. Christ almighty. We'll never get it straight. They'll paw over everything with their sticky misconceptions.' (p. 479)

Dando 'knows' more than he admits: he has made Rebecca aware that he knows of Bray's illicit transfer of her money to Switzerland, for instance. And perhaps he has a hand in Mweta's final gesture, since Hjalmar handed Bray's papers on to him. But even his admission of inadequacy, his unconscious invocation of the source of the kind of knowledge his culture is supposed to possess par excellence—'Christ almighty. We'll never get it straight'—even this falls short of what Bray had really learnt, and what is confirmed, not only structurally, by the ending:

> . . . human affairs didn't come to clear-cut conclusions, a line drawn and a total added up. They appeared to resolve, dissolve, while they were only forming, coming together in another combination. Even when we are dead, what we did goes on making these new combinations (he saw clouds, saw molecules); that's true for private history as well as the other kind. (p. 385)

True of Africa and Europe—or Europe-in-Africa—too; but also a formulation distinctly out of the main stream of the European novelistic view of time, linked as it almost invariably is with particularist, individualistic, liberal—'meliorist' ideas. The whirling of the molecules cancel out, rather ruthlessly, the liberal European universe, the reality that Jessie and Helen hungered after so keenly: and it utterly confirmed beyond doubt, in the last lines of the book, in 'The Bray Report'.

There is a chance of knowledge but to attain it the individual must kick away from the firm ground of culture stability that enables him to learn in the first place: then he must endure the agony of free floating in the space of experience, and hope to discern direction.

So in a rather subtle manner, in perhaps her most important novel, Miss Gordimer not only kicks the burden of the great myth of the metropolitan culture that has always been a problem in her work: she also digs away at the foundations of the fictive monument that myth has erected to it, and undermines one of the major struts of the structure of the English realistic novel. Of course, this is not the same thing as saying she has found her African feet, or given the novel in Africa an indigenous foundation: but she has written something big that contains the seeds of a conscious rejection of those aspects of Europe and the West in general that the West itself considers most central to its tradition, and an essential cultural export—or neo-imperialist imposition. An idea of history radically removed from the conventional Western one at least opens the possibilities of a new interpretation of African experience, of the imaginative realisation of Tom Stilwell's project in *Occasion for Loving*—a new history of Africa that is not a history of colonisation, but of life. It may be significant that South American writers of fiction have also chosen the sensitive territory of time as prime target for attacking an imperialist past; the relationship of Borges or Gabriel Garcia Marquez to European culture is just as tortuous and ambivalent as Miss Gordimer's, and perhaps they have a common starting point.

In any event, Miss Gordimer has developed through her novelistic career to a point which has eluded both her nearest South African contemporaries, Abrahams and Jacobson. But Abrahams and Jacobson both live in exile, are both, perhaps with increasing reluctance, Europeans, citizens of the western world. Miss Gordimer is the only one of the three to have realised an autonomous creative self, perhaps as free as she would desire to be of a culture and a tradition whose relevance she sees as severely limited and in any event distorted and impotent; and she has done it with both feet on South African soil. This is one compelling reason why she is the most important of the three as a South African, or an African writer.

9. Michael Wade: Art and morality in Alex La Guma's *A Walk in the Night**

In 1962 Mbari Publications of Ibadan secured something of a coup in publishing Alex La Guma's novel *A Walk in the Night*;[1] against the background of what London-based publishers were bringing out at the time in their scramble for the African market, this work stood out for its sense of the concrete and its integrity of purpose. La Guma's next two novels, *And a Threefold Cord*[2] and *The Stone Country*,[3] were also published outside Britain, by Seven Seas Publishers in East Berlin. It was not until 1967 that Heinemann's took him into the London-based canon of 'African writers' by issuing *A Walk in the Night* together with a selection of his short stories in a single volume.[4]

La Guma's situation as a writer is made complex by three factors: the first is the directness of his involvement in South African politics, which led directly to the second—the fact of his exile; but it is the third that will be our starting point. It is an unfortunate atmosphere of tedentiousness that surrounds his work, without any kind of necessary or organic relationship to it, manifested largely by what others have written about it. Brian Bunting's foreword to *And a Threefold Cord* begins:

> It is difficult to propound the cult of 'art for art's sake' in South Africa. Life presents problems with an insistence which cannot be ignored, and there can be few countries in the world where the

---

* An abridged version of a section of the author's doctoral thesis for the University of Sussex.

peoples, of all races and classes, are more deeply preoccupied with matters falling generally under the heading of 'political' . . . If art is to have any significance at all, it must reflect something of this national obsession, this passion which consumes and sometimes corrodes the soul of the South African people.[5]

Bunting's literary conclusion follows a page and a half later:

It is in the lives of the Non-white people that the South African drama is played out with the greatest intensity. Their joy and sorrow, happiness and hardship are experienced with a depth of emotion which is quite beyond the range of experience of most whites. For this reason it is most likely that when the 'South African Tragedy' comes to be written, its author will be a Non-white. To say this is not racialism but realism.[6]

This is headily prescriptive stuff, echoed in the blurb to La Guma's third novel, *The Stone Country*:

There is no Art for Art's sake in a book based upon the truth about apartheid, or for an author who chooses this shameful and vicious oppression of people as his theme . . .

While it is not altogether clear who is being 'got at' in this way, the inescapable implication is that there is a right kind of literary response to the South African reality, and a wrong kind, and that La Guma's, by virtue of its freedom from arty fripperies and frivolities, is the right kind. Bunting's conclusion is rather more dangerous: the rightness of La Guma's literary response is somehow bound up with the colour of his skin.

A superficial reading of the novels themselves, while not entirely dispelling the clouds of tendentiousness, at least demonstrates the inaccuracy of the basic premise. While one cannot be sure what Bunting means by the cult of 'art for art's sake' (something which no one has 'propounded' as appropriate to the South African situation), one may conclude that certain kinds of fictive response, probably in view of his conclusions about the likely authorship of the 'South African Tragedy', by white authors, are indicated. But one finds in La Guma's writing a concern for artistic method and technique every bit as obsessional as, say, that which characterises the early fiction of Nadine Gordimer; 'reality' is no mirror-image photograph in his novels. This is not meant to be a qualitive judgment: in fact, it is frequently La Guma's failures in technique that mark him out most clearly as the conscious artist. Nonetheless, he is very far from standing at the opposite pole to a (highly putative) outgrowth of extreme aestheticism. Our purpose will be to demonstrate something of the complexity and integrity of his aesthetic through a close analysis of his first full-lenght work of fiction, the novella *A Walk in the Night*.

The critical tendentiousness is intensified, alas, by commentators whose ideological commitment is different from that of Brian Bunting. In an otherwise reasoned assessment of *A Walk in the Night*, Lewis Nkosi writes:

> This impressive short work has distinct Dostoevskian undertones, which, I hope, is not too large a claim to make for it.[7]

This over-reaction may owe something to the depressed state of South African fiction which upsets Nkosi in the rest of the article; but the claim, nonetheless, is too large.

But it would be mistaken to assume that La Guma himself is entirely the passive victim of these unusually extreme forms of critical misrepresentation. He is associated with social realism, and with a doctrinaire interpretation of South Africa's political reality; there is no doubt in *my* mind that this influences the critical response to his work. Is there any significant way in which he may be said to fulfil through his fiction the implied claims made on his behalf by Brian Bunting? Perhaps the question may be phrased differently: since he is a contemporary writer, facing the problems of South African novel-writing in a current form, does his work amount to an idiosyncratic response to those problems? Different from that of, say, Nadine Gordimer? If so, what is the nature of the solutions he propounds?

Having made this association it may sound wilful to suggest that on a certain level the South African writer whose work La Guma's novels resemble most closely is Sarah Gertrude Millin. Perhaps the most obvious area of relationship is the problematic one of the hero. Like Mrs Millin's, La Guma's characters occupy a narrow range of experience. They are drawn from the urban Cape Coloured proletariat in and near Cape Town. No great range of individuality is presented, within the monochrome world of their existence, in terms, say, of motives or aspirations, though the behaviour of the characters may sometimes be bizarre or extreme. Mrs Millin's devotion to the lower middle and working class among the whites, and the rigid constrictions she placed on the quality of her characters' sensibilities, provoke an effectual resemblance that conceals fundamental differences of outlook. For, if Mrs Millin is in some respects the Celine of the South African novel, La Guma is its Graham Greene. While Mrs Millin is convinced of the inherent narrowness of human potential, seeing her characters' limitations as an iron grid generated from within the psyche, La Guma's attitude is that man's capacities may be restricted, frustrated or distorted by a hostile environment, but that essential divinity, the spark of the Godhead, within his character will somehow persist to flourish, occasionally, however modestly, in the most surprising of circumstances. This may sound paradoxical in a Marxist novelist, but La Guma's Marxism (in his fiction, at any rate) is a paradoxical animal—and in any event, Marxists are not debarred from feeling reverence for humanity. Mrs Millin, on the other hand, revered nothing human except, possibly, the accumulation of great wealth and the exercise of power (as distinct from the mere desire to achieve these ends).

Perhaps the definitive distinction between La Guma and Mrs Millin arises out of their respective treatments of the great Romantic novelistic goal, individual fulfilment. Mrs Millin writes of fulfilment as the great illusion, afflicting men's imaginations with tantalising visions and thus contributing to the twin processes of rationalisation and self-deceit that she sees as underlying nearly all human behaviour. This paradigm pervades her novels, but it emerges in starkly abstract clarity in *What Hath a Man?*,[8] her story of the Catholic intellectual whose emigration to Northern Rhodesia and liberal attitude to black people issue inevitably in the death of his son, the only person he has ever been able to love.

La Guma sees fulfilment, however, not as a product of man's inherent self-deceit, but as, for *his* characters, the great impossibility. It never enters their minds except as a fleeting day-dream, and when it does, the form it takes is interesting:

You ought to get yourself a goose, he thought. You've been messing around too long. You ought to get married and have a family. Maybe you ought to try that goose you met downstairs. Her? *Bedonerd.* When I take a girl she's got to be nice. Pretty nice. With soft hair you can run your hands through and skin so you can feel how soft her cheeks are and you'd come home every night mos and she's have your diet ready and Friday nights you'd hand over your pay packet and she's give you your pocket money and you'd go down to the canteen and have a couple of drinks and if you got too fired up she's take care of you. Funny how some rookers are always squealing about having to hand over their pay Friday nights. Jesus, if I had a wife I'd hand over my ching without any sighs. But she's got to be one of them nice geese, not too much nagging and willing to give a man his pleasure.

Then he sat bolt upright as a woman screamed in the corridor outside and the thought that jumped into his mind was, Oh God, they found that old bastard. (p. 44)

The old bastard who has been found is the corpse of an old, down-and-out white actor, almost paralysed by alcohol and senility, whom Michael Adonis, the narrator of the above internal monologue, has a short while before killed, in a moment of what almost amounts to drunken whimsy. He had not intended to kill the old man; but his control over the events that shape his fate is, like that of all the characters around him, meagre. Indeed, given the social and economic context of Michael Adonis's day-dream, its content is fascinating and ironic. For *A Walk in the Night* is a novel about coloured slum-dwellers in Cape Town's notorious District Six, an area of depression and hopelessness, whose inhabitants are continually on the receiving end of the varied brutalities built into the South African political system. At the beginning of the novel Michael Adonis has lost his job, having been sacked for exchanging words with the white foreman who objected to his going to the lavatory. By the end, six hours later, he has been co-opted into a gang of minor criminals, and is going out with them on his first 'job' in another sense of the word. And the structural situation of his day-dreams of respectability, of 'fulfilment', is characteristic of the ironic detachment of La Guma's treatment of most of the characters within his fictive framework. The actual content of the vision is in any event beyond the furthest reach of probability of realisation, but that it comes to him immediately after he has committed a murder is equalled in ironic appropriateness only by its interruption through the discovery of that murder.

But Michael Adonis's modestly impossible vision of fulfilment does not proceed out of self-deceit or rationalisation. As I hope to show, it is the other side of the coin of awareness — awareness of the fundamental injustice of a life where to be coloured is to commit a crime against oneself. Michael Adonis knows, for instance, that the law exists 'To kick us poor brown bastards around'; a much more direct, and concretely-expressed, sort of awareness than the mythical intimacy with the white man's character that William Plomer's criminal character is saddled with in 'Ula Masondo'. Almost all of Michael's experience takes place on this level of concrete immediacy; his day-dream vision is the nearest he comes to abstract thought. It arises out of the tension between the limitations imposed on his vision by the quality of his experience and what La Guma perceives as, perhaps, the grace inherent in the very precise existence of that vision.

Thus La Guma is much closer to the main stream of the Western novel than Mrs Millin. If, for the most part, he writes about deprivation, and successfully conveys the experience of it, this is because he is setting up a concept which exists in a state of dialectical opposition to its implied counterpart, the traditional goal in the liberal-humanist ethos of the western novel, individual fulfilment.

There are other respects in which La Guma's mode of presentation gives rise to a misleading superficial appearance. His technique is unevenly but in general somewhat stringently realistic, depending on a characteristic accumulation of the small physical details, each carefully qualified, to produce a homogenous scenic effect:

> In the dark a scrap of cloud struggled along the edge of Table Mountain, clawed at the rocks for a foothold, was torn away by the breeze that came in from the south-east, and disappeared. In the hot tenements the people felt the breeze through the chinks and cracks of loose boarding and broken windows and stirred in their sweaty sleep. Those who could not sleep sat by the windows or in doorways and looked out towards the mountain beyond the rooftops and searched for the sign of wind. The breeze carried the stale smells from passageway to passageway, from room to room, along lanes and back alleys, through the realms of the poor, until massed smells of stagnant water, cooking, rotting vegetables, oil, fish, damp plaster and timber, unwashed curtains, bodies and stairways, cheap per-fume and incense, spices and half-washed kitchenware, urine, ani-mals and dusty corners became one vast, anonymous odour, so widespread and all-embracing as to become unidentifiable hardly noticeable by the initiated nostrils of the teeming, cramped world of poverty which it enveloped. (p. 48)

This passage could have occurred almost anywhere in La Guma's novels, and to say this is doubtless to voice a reservation about the essential monotony of his style. But the monotony serves two purposes, one obvious and the other more subtle. First, it embodies the chief characteristic of the quality of life which is being described; it thus provides a consonance between medium and matter that is artistically satisfying. But secondly, it serves to mask, to hide and partially to stifle exactly what this quality of life must mask, hide and partially stifle: the essential individuality of response on the part of the people involved, the characters in the novel, to the conditions of monotonous and overbearing poverty in which they exist.

Thus the surface of La Guma's novels is essentially deceptive, an aspect of the survival strategy that governs the guerilla struggle waged by life against the forces of negation. (Though this last may sound like a conventionally vague bit of rhetorical ballast, it is in fact fairly precisely related to the way La Guma structures his reality in his novels.) As far as *A Walk in the Night* is concerned, the monotonous overlay of drabness is heavy enough and in some respects pervasive, but it vanishes in relation to particular individuals. It is pervasive in that all the coloured characters share the same conditions of life, are surrounded by the same physical reality and faced by the same economic and political results of this reality. An interesting dichotomy emerges: the non-human factors seem to cluster on the one hand against the human on the other. Every one of the coloured characters presented more than momentarily is in a state of reaction against the physical-economic-political antagonist. Take for instance the insignificant watchman who guards the portals of a seamen's brothel:

> The look-out in front of the house halfway up an alleyway that was half stone steps and half cobbles was an old decrepit ghost of a man that sat in a ruined grass chair beside the doorway in the darkness of the high stoep facing the entrance of another street.
>
> He saw Willieboy emerge from the lemon-coloured light of a street-lamp, recognised him, and relaxed, but maintaining an expression of officiousness with which he tried to hide his identity as another of the massed nonentities to which they both belonged. He nursed a sort of pride in his position as the look-out for a bawdy house, a position which raised him a dubious degree out of the morass into which the dependent poor had been trodden. (p. 49)

Significantly, the images, both real and metaphorical, surrounding the old man are natural and physical: the stone steps and cobbles, the grass chairs, the morass. Although he is part of this set-up, his relationship to his surroundings is filled with tension (which is stressed by the nature of his occupation): and his purpose in life seems to be to distinguish himself from this all-absorbent environment.

Obviously, this situation of tension between the individual and his environment bears closely on a problem that is central to the orthodox liberal tradition of the modern western novel — that of identity; and La Guma confronts this problem in a manner suggestive of the same orthodoxy. His main characters are without exception afflicted by grave difficulties over identity, which are conveyed through two basic modes, one of which, again, is more subtle — and effective — than the other.

One of these — the less effective — is the mode of direct statement:

He was feeling muzzy and his head ached. And felt angry and humiliated by the manhandling he had received at Gipsy's shebeen. He clenched his fists in his pockets and thought, They can't treat a man like that, where can they treat a juba like that? Hell, I'm a shot, too. I'll show those sonsa bitches. He was also aware of his inferiority. All his youthful life he had cherished dreams of becoming a big shot. He had seen others rise to some sort of power in the confined underworld of this district and found himself left behind. He had looked with envy at the flashy desperadoes who quivered across the screen in front of the eightpenny gallery and had dreamed of being transported wherever he wished in great black motorcars and issuing orders for the execution of enemies. And when the picture faded and he emerged from the vast smoke-laden cinema mingling with the noisy crowd he was always aware of his inadequacy, moving unnoticed in the mob. He had affected a slouch, wore gaudy shirts and peg-bottomed trousers, brushed his hair into a flamboyant peak. He had been thinking of piercing one ear and decorating it with a gold ring. But even with these things he continued to remain something less than nondescript, part of the blurred face of the crowd, inconspicuous as a smudge on a grimy wall. (p. 72)

The character being described is Willieboy, an aimless — and workless — young thug who has spent time in a reformatory. La Guma takes pains to spell out in the cant of middlebrow psychologising his exact problem. The result is blatant and irritating: for while it would be wrong to say that the specific instance is inconvincing, because within the given context there is nothing improbable in what La Guma actually says about Willieboy, there is no particular reason why one should accept this mode, which is essentially extraneous to the fictive process, from a novelist whose only credential as anything but a fiction writer is the easiest kind of authorial omniscience. Nothing is 'told' about

Willieboy in the above extract that the averagely sensitive reader could not have extrapolated from the events that have taken place up to this point. The technique is exceedingly reductive, since it narrows the range of Willieboys' potential behaviour within absurdly rigid limits, while at the same time imprisoning what he has done up to now within a cast-iron interpretational scheme. Besides, La Guma in no way succeeds in conveying how Willieboy was 'aware of his inadequacy'—what form this 'awareness' took; it is insufficient to render it in terms of a taste for flamboyant dress, in other words, only in terms of its external symptoms.

The more satisfying mode that La Guma uses to convey his characters' identity crises forges the structural kingpins that maintain the plot. This is the way in which La Guma demonstrates the precariousness of the separate identities of his characters by making them, as it were, overrun each others' boundaries. The process is particularly clear in the schematic relationship between Michael Adonis and Willieboy. They have one physical encounter in the book: this takes place close to the beginning, in the cafe where Michael Adonis goes to eat on his way home in the evening, after having been dismissed from his job. From that time the development of the plot is almost entirely dependent on their unconscious interaction, and in the process La Guma's more profound preoccupations emerge. In simple topographical terms, their take is told thus: they meet at the café of the Portuguese where Michael Adonis goes after losing his job. After Michael leaves the café he encounters first Joe, a saintly young beggar who lives by the sea, then two policemen, who search him for dagga (marijuana); he enters a pub, drinks, and goes on to the tenement building where he lives, where he meets Doughty the broken-down actor in the corridor, helps him into his room, drinks some of his wine and kills him on impulse, by mistake. He then takes refuge in his own room.

Meanwhile Willieboy has decided to try to cadge 'a couple of bob' from Michael Adonis, and he sets off for the tenement. On the way he meets the gangsters whom Michael Adonis has already encountered, both in the café and in the pub, in their restless quest for Sockies. At the door of the tenement he gives a match to a stranger; he ascends the stairs and tries the door of Michael Adonis's room. It is locked; Michael, who is within, makes no response. So Willieboy decides to try Mister Doughty in the room opposite for a loan; he knocks, twice, and receiving no response, opens the door and discovers Doughty's corpse. He shouts and slams the door, and is seen by a woman who has gone to get water from the communal tap at the end of the corridor. He escapes. Shortly after, Michael Adonis hears the woman's scream when she opens Doughty's door and sees the corpse; and he, too, escapes from the building at the first opportunity.

From this time on, while their physical paths appear to diverge, they are all the time moving towards one another so that, in the end, they constitute a metaphysical continuity.

Willieboy is seen on his way out of the building by Abrahams, the man to whom he has given a match—and who later betrays him to the police. Then he goes to Gipsy's shebeen, where he gets into a fight with some sailors and is thrown out by the redoubtable Gipsy. On his recovery he mugs the pathetic Mr Greene, and is seen in the headlamps of the police van; his yellow shirt gives him away to the police and he is hunted down over the rooftops, shot and stuffed into the back of the van where he lies dying, while the policemen go for cigarettes and a coke into the same Portuguese café where the reader was introduced to Willieboy at the beginning of the novel. He dies while they are in the café.

Michael Adonis leaves the tenement shortly after Willieboy, by a back window, because by this time a crowd has gathered at the entrance. He is seen by the three gangsters, searching, as ever, for Sockies, as he flits up a dark alleyway. Then he walks about aimlessly for an hour before going into an Indian café, where Joe, the beggar-boy saint, is completing a meal he has bought with money Michael had given him at their first encounter. Michael orders a cup of tea and sits down with him; they talk, but are interrupted by the gangsters who by this time are prepared to find a substitute for Sockies and invite Michael to join them later at their rendezvous. Joe tries to prevent this but Michael brusquely, if guiltily, rejects him and goes to the snooker club, where the gangsters await him. There he is initiated into the smoking of dagga (which he had earlier truthfully denied taking, to the policemen who had searched him) and finally, as Willieboy dies in the back of the police car, Michael steps into his place in the petty underworld, emerging from the snooker club with his new comrades to 'pull' his first 'job'.

The connections between Michael Adonis and Willieboy are evoked chiefly through the use of minute detail. For example, at the time of their first encounter, we are given this introductory description of Willieboy:

Willieboy was young and dark and wore his kinky hair brushed into a point above his forehead. He wore a sportscoat over a yellow T-shirt and a crucifix around his neck, more as a flamboyant decoration than as an act of religious devotion. He had yellowish eyeballs and big white teeth and an air of nonchalance, like the outward visible sign of his distorted pride in the terms he had served in a reformatory and once in prison for assault. (p. 3)

The yellowish eyeballs are a hint from South African folklore, that he is addicted to dagga; whereas Michael Adonis, a short time later, accosted by the police, searched, and asked, 'Where's your dagga?' replies: 'I don't smoke it'. Thus a distinction is suggested, early on, between Michael and Willieboy, which may not appear all that significant in itself, except that at the very end of the book it is converted into an identity: Michael Adonis is not, at first, accepted by the two gangsters who do not know him personally, and they put him to the test:

He took two long puffs at the dope and let the smoke out through his nostrils in long twin jets. Then he looked at Michael Adonis and said, 'Pull a skuif, pal?' The other boy had stopped working at the billiard balls, poised over the table about to make a shot, but not finishing it, standing quite still as if a motion picture of him had suddenly been stopped, looking at Michael Adonis.
'Take a pull, pally,' the boy with the skull-and-crossbones ring said again.
'Why not, man?' Michael Adonis said, meeting his look, and reached out. He took a deep puff at the dagga and felt the floor move under him and the walls tilt, then settle back, and there was a light feeling in his head. He took another puff and handed it back to the boy. (pp. 76–7)

Thus the link is established between Willieboy at the beginning of the book and Michael at the end. Dagga is a most conventional symbol in South African literature of moral weakness, of a tendency to corruption; and when Michael succumbs to it he abandons the precarious hold on respectability that has distinguished him in terms of identity from Willieboy.

The most fundamental effect of the almost complete switch of identity that takes place between the two is, of course, that Willieboy 'becomes' the murderer of Uncle Doughty. There is no question of innocence or guilt, or justice and injustice: the characters are in a situation in which only a tenuous hold on identity is available in any event, and that hold has to be maintained against environmental forces of unrelieved, and arbitrary, hostility. Thus there is no question in any of the characters' minds that Willieboy had committed the murder; the relationship between the individual and the environment is on this level a matter of primitive balance, and Willieboy becomes, almost, a random sacrifice to restore the balance and appease the gods. Thus there is no difference between Michael and Willieboy since there is no difference between guilty and innocent; and in circumstances like these the problem of action, so dear to the liberal sensibility, has not yet even arisen.

This fluidity of identity exists on several levels at once. Apart from 'becoming' Willieboy, Michael Adonis also fills the role of the absent Sockies in becoming the new look-out for the gang. The gangsters function as a sort of refrain to the action of the book; they appear on almost every significant occasion—in the café where Michael Adonis goes after work, next in the pub, then to Willieboy on his way to Michael Adonis's home; they are near enough to the tenement to see Michael Adonis escape, then they meet him again in the Indian café, where he goes after the murder, and where he decides to join them. Up to and including this penultimate encounter, each time they appear they are hunting for Sockies, their look-out; so slender is *his* claim to distinct identity that he never turns up, existing only as a role, which Michael Adonis is able to fill without difficulty or objection, 'becoming', as I have said, Sockies in almost the same way as he 'becomes' Willieboy.

The position is not quite the same in each case: Willieboy has to lose his adult identity, such as it is, before Michael Adonis can claim it. La Guma makes this clear through the manner in which he treats Willieboy's death. This is a rather complex performance, and at this stage, the relevant point is that La Guma achieves this effect of vacating, as it were, Willieboy's adult identity by causing him to regress, mentally, to his childhood as he lies bleeding to death in the police van. La Guma presents his mental death-agony as a delirious flow of repetition of images from a painful childhood; and it is as a bewildered and hurt child that Willieboy dies.

The almost schematic interchange of identities between Willieboy and Michael Adonis is underpinned by the persistent theme of the difficulty of communication that runs through the book. There is a clear structural connection between the two notions of the precariousness of personal identity and the near-impossibility of communication, and this is demonstrated on many occasions. La Guma seems to be saying that the one is the prerequisite for the other—people without identity cannot communicate effectively or intelligibly. This is a point which has powerful, albeit negative, political implications, as we shall see: it is about as near as La Guma comes in this novel to treating the problem of action.

The first example of this pervasive difficulty in communication occurs with some appropriateness in the only direct encounter between Willieboy and Michael Adonis in the café at the beginning of the book.

[Willieboy] grinned, showing his big teeth as Michael Adonis strolled up, and said, 'Hoit, pally,' in greeting. He had finished a meal of steak and chips and was lighting a cigarette. 'Howzit,' Michael Adonis said surlily, sitting down opposite him. They were not very close friends, but had been thrown together in the whirlpool of poverty, petty crime and violence of which that café was an outpost.

'Nice boy, nice You know me, mos. Always take it easy. How goes it with you?'

'Strolling again. Got pushed out of my job at the factory.'

'How come then?'

'Answered back to an effing white rooker Foreman.'

'Those whites. What happened?'

'That white bastard was lucky I didn't pull him up good. He had been asking for it a long time. Every time a man goes to the pisshouse he starts moaning. Jesus Christ, the way he went on you'd think a man had to wet his pants rather than take a minute off. Well, he picked on me for going for a leak and I told him to go to hell.'

'Ja,' Willieboy said. 'Working for whites. Happens all the time, man. Me, I never work for no white john. Not even brown one. To hell with work. Work, work, work, where does it get you? Not me, pally.'

The Swahili waiter came over, dark and shiny with perspiration, his white apron grimy and spotted with egg-yolk. Michael Adonis said: 'Steak and chips, and bring the tomato sauce, too'. To Willieboy he said: 'Well, a juba's got to live. Called me a cheeky black bastard. Me, I'm not black. Anyway I said he was a no-good pore-white and he calls the manager and they gave me my pay and tell me to muck off [sic] out of it. White sonofabitch. I'll get him.'

'No, man, me I don't work. Never worked a bogger yet. Whether you work or don't, you live anyway, somehow. I haven't starved to death , have I? Work. Eff work.'

'I'll get him,' Michael Adonis said. His food came, handed to him on a chipped plate with big slices of bread on the side. He began to eat, chewing sullenly. Willieboy got up and strolled over to the juke-box, slipping a sixpenny piece into the slot. Michael Adonis ate silently, his anger mixing with a resentment for a fellow who was able to take life so easy. (pp. 4–5)

At this point an interruption occurs in their contact, as Michael Adonis is approached for the first time by the little group of gangsters who are in such persistent search of Sockies. By the time Willieboy turns back, he is no longer there:

Inside the café the juke-box had stopped playing and Willieboy turned away from it, looking for Michael Adonis, and found that he had left. (p. 7)

The illustrative disjunction with which the chapter ends is continuous with the process of their conversation, which begins by looking like genuine communication but quickly turns into an exercise in mutual incomprehension. The marginal, but essential, distinction between them still holds at this point, because Michael regards himself as committed to the conventional struggle for existence on the only legitimate terms the society seems to offer. The importance of this difference is clear at the end of their conversation, by which time each is talking to himself. Michael Adonis is interested in his own situation, in what has just happened to him, and does not relate it to a broader context, while Willieboy's airy generalities show him to be cut off from any sort of social pattern. So while Michael at this stage continues to function in terms of the only available polity, though it has just rejected his participation, Willieboy does not belong to that polity; he does not recognise its existence. Thus genuine verbal communication between the two is impossible; and La Guma uses this fact to establish the topography of Michael Adonis's slide into alienation.

Communication is then the thematic tool which La Guma manipulates in charting his territory within South African reality. The exploration takes place mainly through the peregrinations of Michael Adonis and his communicative behaviour carries the most significance, though there are other episodes which bear upon this theme. Michael is placed in 'communication situations' with a handful of people: Willieboy (as we have seen), Doughty, Joe, a girl he chats to at the door of his tenement house, the police and the gangsters.

His two encounters with Joe take place before and after the crucial episode in which he kills Doughty, and they constitute the outlines of the interesting moral dialectic La Guma inserts into the plot. Joe's saintliness is adumbrated without delay:

> Nobody knew where Joe came from, or anything about him. He just seemed to have happened, appearing in the District like a cockroach emerging through a floorboard. Most of the time he wandered around the harbour gathering fish discarded by fishermen and anglers, or along the beaches of the coast, picking limpets and mussels. He had a strange passion for things that came from the sea. (p. 9)

His personal orientation is away from the society of the District, towards a force which La Guma tries (and fails) to produce as the symbolic embodiment of affirmation, in antagonism to the negation and chaos that prevails in the lives of the land-dwellers. In this first encounter he and Michael Adonis communicate fairly naturally and efficiently, in a way that is impossible between Michael and Willieboy:

> 'How you, Joe?' Michael Adonis asked.
> 'Okay, Mikey.'
> 'What you been doing today?'
> 'Just strolling around the docks. York Castle came in this afternoon.'
> 'Ja?'
> 'You like mussels, Mikey? I'll bring you some.'
> 'That's fine, Joe.'
> 'I got a big starfish out on the beach yesterday. One big big one. It was dead and stank.'
> 'Well, it's a good job you didn't bring it into town. City Council would be on your neck.'
> 'I hear they're going to make the beaches so only white people can go there,' Joe said.
> 'Ja. Read it in the papers. Damn sonsabitches.'
> 'It's going to get so's nobody can go nowhere,'
> 'I reckon so,' Michael Adonis said.
> They were some way up the street now and outside the Queen Victoria. Michael Adonis said, 'You like a drink, Joe?' although he knew that the boy did not drink.
> 'No thanks, Mikey.'
> 'Well, so long.'

'So long, man.'

'You eat already?'

'Well . . . no . . . not yet.' Joe said, smiling humbly and shyly, moving his broken shoes gently on the rough cracked paving.

'Okay, here's a bob. Get yourself something. Parcel of fish and chips.'

'Thanks, Mikey.'

'Okay. So long, Joe.'

'See you again.'

'Don't forget those mussels,' Michael Adonis said after him, knowing that Joe would forget anyway.

'I'll bring them,' Joe said, smiling back and raising his hand in a salute. He seemed to sense the other young man's doubt of his memory, and added a little fiercely, 'I won't forget. You'll see. I won't forget.' (pp. 9–10)

This meeting contrasts not only with Michael's encounter with Willieboy: it is virtually the only unstrained, natural human communication in the book. Two things stand out: the first, of course, is the generosity of Michael Adonis, who, having just lost his job, has sufficient insight to recognise Joe's greater need, and enough moral force to act on this recognition. The implications of this act are somewhat surprising, as indeed is the whole moral pattern La Guma weaves in the book; but these will be examined later. The second point of interest is the manner in which the characters are defined in relation to each other, at the end of their exchange: 'he seemed to sense the other young man's doubt of his memory'. This is the only occasion in the book where characters enjoy such freedom from context; that this is the effect of some quality of Joe's becomes clear from referring the episode to the rest of the book. Michael Adonis exists for an instant as a young man, talking to another young man, free of the qualifications of colour, poverty, insecurity and lack of identity.

The two points are related to each other: Michael's act of generosity liberates him momentarily from his isolation and consequent moral anonymity, and the writer withdraws from the situation far enough—or angles his vision with sufficient selectivity—to obscure the context of action, so that we are left with an almost playful interchange between two youths who understand each other well enough to communicate in nuances. It is a moment of light in the moral and actual darkness of the book; it looks suspiciously like a moment of grace.

This episode is contrasted, structurally, with Michael's second encounter with Joe, which takes place after he has committed murder and commenced the life of existential despair that is successfully realised in the gangsters' never-ending wanderings in search of Sockies, or some idea or state of being the fact of whose existence they cannot even grasp.

The episode is the central point in a complex web of structural design. Michael meets Joe in an Indian café: he has been walking aimlessly since his escape from the building in which he has committed murder. The theme of the tenuousness of identity is evoked. Michael's sense of homelessness, of not having a resting place in the matrix of human relations, draws him across the ineffectual boundaries of his own individuality into a sort of invasion of the vagrant Joe's state of being; and indeed, before the episode has ended, the dominance of Michael enjoyed in their first encounter, as we shall see, has been altogether reversed.

Michael Adonis had seen the café as he came into the short, grey, yellow lamp-lighted street with its scarred walls and cracked pavements, and had headed towards it because he had been walking about for an hour and wanted to sit down. He saw the pale glow of the café light behind the greasy window piled with curry-balls and Indian sweetmeats and headed for it like a lost ship sighting a point of land for the first time after a long and hopeless voyage. (p. 64)

In the jumbled imagery that renders the experience, the metaphorical association of Michael Adonis with the sea indicates the level of identification with Joe, who lives by the sea and through his fascination for it; but the other, negative element in the same metaphor, that of continuous, aimless wandering the lost ship pre-figures the ultimately stronger level on which he is identified with the emptiness of the search for Sockies, the kind of existence led by Willieboy, the inevitability of damnation arising out of Michael's sole act of choice, joining the gang.

The situation is fraught with ironies that we might as well call theological, thereby letting the cat out of the bag. Joe is finishing a meal, which he has bought 'with the shilling what you gave me' (p. 65). Thus Michael's act of grace is still potent, even after he has committed murder: whether he is capable of being saved through it or is not one of those nice, teasing Greenian points. At first such a possibility seems to exist. Michael sits with Joe, who asks him: 'What are you walking about for, Mikey? You look sick, too'. (p. 65). Indeed, Michael is in a state of egocentric self-pity that makes it impossible for him to imagine that anyone but himself may be in any way afflicted:

'. . . We all got troubles. Don't I say.'
'You. Troubles,' Michael Adonis said, looking at him with some derision. 'What troubles you got?' He was suddenly pleased and proud of his own predicament. He felt as if he was the only man who had ever killed another and through himself a curiosity at which people should wonder . . . The rights and wrongs of the matter did not occur to him then. It was just something that to himself, placed him above others, like a poor beggar who suddenly found himself the heir to vast riches . . . He said surlily: 'Where the hell you get troubles from?' (pp. 65–6)

Joe's rejoinder is interrupted before it begins by the incursion of the three gangsters in search of Sockies; ironically, it is at this point that Michael is presented with his most specific temptation. 'You feel like doing something with us?' Foxy asked Michael Adonis. (p. 66). It is not quite as simple as it sounds.

The old Indian came back with the cup of tea Michael Adonis had ordered and put it down on the table . . . The boy with the scarface looked around him and said:
'Okay, baas, we going. We want nothing.'
He looked at Michael Adonis again, while the old Indian went away. Then he said: 'We saw some law going into your place. Heard a rooker got chopped or something.'
'And we seen you come out the side lane, too,' the boy with the skull-and-crossbones ring said, with smiling malice.
Michael Adonis stared at them and felt suddenly trapped. (pp. 67–8)

This leads Joe to conclude that Michael's troubles are indeed serious. He has been ignored by the gangsters throughout the exchange—a point which La Guma lays some emphasis upon, not merely out of adherence of his customary level of narrative realism. 'They looked with some disgust at the ragged boy and then immediately ignored him . . .' (p. 66) In the confrontation between good and evil that this represents, the appearance of the character who embodies the 'good' forces is so 'ragged' that his antagonists feel they can disregard him. But when the gangsters leave, with their invitation to Michael potent but as yet unaccepted, Joe intervenes again.

> 'Listen, Michael,' Joe said, speaking seriously now and feeling
> awkward about it at the same time. 'Listen, maybe you got big
> troubles. Bigger than I got.' He felt somewhat ashamed of the
> comparison, but he went on. 'Like I said, we all got troubles. But
> johns like them don't help you out of them. They in trouble them-
> selves. You'd only add to the whole heap of troubles. I don't know
> how to tell it, but you run away with them and you got another
> trouble. Like those rookers. They started a small trouble, maybe, and
> they run away from it and it was another trouble, so they run away
> all the time, adding up the troubles. Hell, I don't know.' He felt
> desperate and a little sad, and did not know quite what to say.
>   Michael Adonis scowled at him and asked: 'What the blerry hell
> you know? What troubles you got?' (pp. 68–9)

Joe goes into his 'troubles' at length: 'No house, no people, no place.
Maybe that's troubles. Don't I say?' (p. 69) He fills in the inevitable
background of poverty, desertion, flight from problems that cannot be
evaded. There is nothing explicitly political in what he says, though of
course his situation relates to the political context evoked by the novel.
The fundamental point of the exercise is not, it seems to me, political at
all. Michael's reaction to Joe's story indicates this: it should be read as
both contrastive and complementary to his response to Joe's hunger at
their first encounter. (pp. 9–10: see pp. 178–9 above)

> Michael Adonis stared at him for a moment. He felt a little embar-
> rassed now in the presence of this boy. He had never said anything as
> lengthy and as serious as this and he wondered whether the boy had
> spoken the truth or was a little queer. Then he picked up his neglected
> cup and drank. The tea was quite cold now and a scum of milk had
> started to form on the surface. He said, uncomfortably: 'You like
> some tea?'
>   'No thanks, man. It's okay.'
>   Michael Adonis put his cup down and took out his cigarettes. He
> shoved the packet over to Joe and said gruffly: 'Well, have a smoke,
> then.'
>   Joe shook his head and smiled gently and somewhat shyly. He
> said: 'No thanks, I don't mos smoke.' Then he added, serious again:
> 'You musn't go with those gangsters, Mikey. You leave those
> gangsters alone.'

'What's it to you?' Michael Adonis asked, feeling both angry and embarrassed. 'What's it to you?'

'Nothing. Nothing. I reckon. But they mean boys.'

'Ah, hell.' Michael Adonis said and got up. He went over to the counter where the old Indian dozed and got some money out. He paid for his tea, feeling the ragged boy's eyes on him, and did not look back when he went out. (pp. 70–1)

At this point there is a strategic interruption, before the encounter reaches its climax: the fourteenth chapter shifts the focus onto Willieboy in his purgatorial wanderings as he goes away from the shebeen whence he has been ejected, feeling acutely his humiliation and sense of inferiority: he encounters Green, the ineffectual drunkard who had earlier stood belching uncomprehendingly with Michael Adonis (Willieboy's alter ego) and the taxi-driver at the bar: Willieboy 'mugs' him, but as he comes to the end of the street he is caught flatfooted in the headlamps of the police van, and has almost reached the end of his suffering on earth.

The effect of placing this interruption of the narrative concerning Michael at this juncture is to heighten the anticipatory tension regarding the outcome of his relationship with Joe. The actual content of chapter fourteen functions so as to complete the theological picture at a crucial moment in Michael's career. La Guma, in presenting Willieboy at this moment at the beginning of the final chapter in his life, prefigures Michael's probable fate: the outcome will depend on how he concludes with Joe. The structural connection between Michael and Willieboy is elicited here through the figures of both Green and Raalt, the policeman who is to execute judgment on Willieboy for Michael's sin. Willieboy is left hesitant, caught in the glare of the police van's headlights; even at this juncture he may not be doomed, and it seems possible to argue that La Guma's structural approach suggests that what happens to Willieboy may in a sense depend on Michael's behaviour, streets away, in the coming few moments. Michael's *moral* posture is similarly undecided.

Michael Adonis was almost at the end of the street when he heard Joe coming after him. One of Joe's shoelaces was loose and it flick-flicked on the asphalt as he ran. He came beside the young man and said, a little breathless:

'Mike, Mikey, listen here . . .'

Walking along the dark street Michael Adonis did not look at him, but thought, Well, what do you want now. You reckon you going to be around me for the rest of my blerry life? You spook.

Somewhere up ahead people were singing.

'Mike,' Joe was saying, 'Mike, maybe it isn't my business, you see? Maybe it got nothing to do with me, but you like my brother. I go to mos think about you. Jesus, man, why, you even gave me money for food. There's not a lot of people give me money for food. Awright, maybe now and then. But most of the time I do what I can out on the rocks.'

He was getting out of breath again because Michael Adonis was quickening his pace and the boy, Joe, had to step out to keep up with him. He spoke quickly as if he had very little time in which he had to say what he wanted to say. (p. 74)

Joe goes on to catalogue the gang's known misdeeds — rape, robbery and stabbing — and concludes:

'Christ, I don't want to see you end up like that, Mike. Hell, a man'd rather starve. They'll murder somebody and get hanged, Mikey. You want to get hanged?'

Michael Adonis suddenly stopped in his stride and looked at Joe. 'What the hell you following me around like a blerry tail for?' he asked angrily. 'What's it got to do with you what I'm going to do?'

Please, Mike,' Joe said. He looked as if he was going to cry. 'I'm your pal. A man's got a right to look after another man. Jesus, isn't we all people?'

'Ah, go to hell,' Michael Adonis shouted at him. 'Go to hell. Leave me alone.'

He turned his back and went on down the street, leaving Joe staring after him, his face puckering with the beginning of weeping.

Blerry young squashy, Michael Adonis thought as he turned up another street. For what's he got to act like a blerry godfather? (pp. 74–5)

Michael's attempt, at the end of the thirteenth chapter, to console Joe by offering him various forms of material sustenance — a cup of tea or a cigarette are rejected, which is the obvious structural aspect of the contrast between this encounter and their first one. What Joe has just described is his spiritual situation, from which in the circumstances Michael's own cannot be very different, and the point is that difficulties of this kind are not susceptible to material alleviation. Then the interpolated fourteenth chapter describes Willieboy's situation sufficiently general manner to apply to all three—Willieboy, Michael and Joe himself. The effect of this is to complete the description of the range of alternatives open to Michael Adonis as he moves half-consciously towards his movement of choice.

The rest of the encounter between Michael Adonis and Joe, which takes place in the street as Michael walks with ever-increasing speed towards the club where the gangsters wait, is remarkable above all for the implied frame of reference contained in its vocabulary. The signals are out almost from the beginning: 'Somewhere up ahead people were singing'. The apparently simple statement is pregnant with implication. The Hollywoodian rhetorical echo of 'Somewhere up ahead'—note the apparently redundant 'up', as well as certain connotations of the word 'ahead'—is followed by the comforting sense of community in 'people were singing', the simple affirmative nature of the statement against the context of Michael Adonis's guilty, bitter indecision and Joe's eager, but helpless, inarticulacy. The surface effect may be a variant of the cinematic realism of La Guma's technique; but the rhetorical results is to indicate an almost churchlike frame of reference for what follows. Joe's vocabulary is littered with casual expletives that constitute, at the same time, virtual invocations of the Deity—prayers, even. 'Jesus' is used twice, on both occasions juxtaposed with an affirmative proposition of the brotherhood of man, and of the personal responsibility arising from that, that Cain denied. 'Christ' comes into it once, as a prayerful expression of Joe's wish to save Michael from evil and damnation. In a contrast which acts as a corollary within the moral structure, Michael uses the word 'hell' three times in his last four sentences, once associated fairly precisely with a denial of the brotherhood of man, and on the next occasion almost as the second part of an oxymoron to Joe's invocation of Jesus.

Thus adumbrated in this scene is a simple but powerful and comprehensive moral system, resting on certain basic Judaeo-Christian precepts: one should love one's neighbour and try to help him because one is one's brother's keeper and one is involved in his fate. Put another way, it is a system based on shared responsibility, mutual recognition between human beings of their obligations to each other in a hostile environment. The world of La Guma's novels is without doubt a vale of tears. Within it, human beings are presented with various opportunities of choice: it is reasonable to suppose that these occasions imply meaningful consequences.

Within this scheme the characters attain to various degrees of awareness or self-knowledge. Joe talks to Michael on this occasion:

> . . . as if he had very little time in which he had to say what he wanted to say.

The possible analogy of a priest trying to administer the Last Rites to a dying man is coupled with the suggestion that Joe knows, somehow, that time is running out for Michael, or at least for his prospects of saving him. Again, Michael acknowledges to himself the nature and validity of Joe's function in relation to himself, though he explicitly denies its effect: 'For what's he got to act like a blerry godfather?' Thus Joe offers Michael Adonis the chance of salvation, but at this point, despite the grace conferred by his earlier act of generosity towards Joe, Michael is unwilling and unable to accept the opportunity: this is shown through the contrast between the two episodes, through Michael's inability on this occasion to communicate with Joe and his final, angry rejection of him. The nature of this rejection is intimately connected with the theme of communication: '"Ah, go to hell," Michael Adonis shouted at him. "Go to hell. Leave me alone."' It is the classic situation of the damned: because solace is for him the ultimate torment, since it is impossible, in its place he must demand the very essence of his torment—which is, in the cases of both Michael Adonis and Willieboy, isolation. Thus, on this occasion their contact breaks off with Michael imprisoned within the context of his life and the consequences of his acts, in direct contrast to the corresponding, climactic moment of his *first* encounter with Joe.

And Joe's tears obviously signify on two levels: he weeps for Michael Adonis as much as or more than for his own hurt at being rejected.

The middle step in this theological dialectic is, of course, Michael's murder of Doughty, which symbolically transforms his relationship with the saintly Joe from one of mutual trust and communication to one characterised on Michael's side by resentment, hostility and rejection. Michael's whole encounter with Doughty may be read as a symbolic challenge to certain commonly-held notions about the composition of South African society, and the influence of a particular world view on the pattern of relationships within that society. Doughty is a broken-down actor, who tries to declaim the first speech of Hamlet's father's ghost to the uncomprehending Michael Adonis. The symbolic significance of Doughty's relationship to English culture is obvious, and La Guma lays it on thickly in the choice of means of identification he makes for his character. The point being established is that the nature of Doughty's relationship with Michael arises out of Doughty's physical and spiritual decay, not out of a desire to communicate—in other words, out of need, a need which did not exist when the actor was in his prime, touring 'England and Australia with Dame Clara Bright'. There is a grotesque irony in his offer to recite the speech to Michael in exchange for a drink from his own bottle of port, which Michael is teasingly keeping from him; but the content of the speech offends Michael. Appropriately enough to the whole moral tenor of the book, Doughty gives the passages dealing with purgatory:

> He broke off and grinned at Michael Adonis, and then eyed the bottle. 'That's us, us, Michael, my boy. Just ghosts, doomed to walk in the night. Shakespeare.'
> 'Bull,' Michael Adonis said, and took another swallow at the bottle. 'Who's a blerry ghost?' He scowled at the old man through a haze of red that swam in front of his eyes like thick oozing paint, distorting the ancient face staring up at him.
> 'Michael, my boy. Spare a drop for your old uncle.'
> 'You old bastard,' Michael Adonis said angrily. 'Can't a boy have a bloody piss without getting kicked in the backside by a lot of effing law?'
> 'Now, now, Michael. I don't know what you're talking about, God bless my soul. You take care of that old port, my boy.'
> The old man tried to get up and Michael Adonis said, 'Take your effing port,' and struck out at the bony, blotched, sprouting skull, holding the bottle by the neck so that the wine splashed over his hand. The old man made a small, honking, animal noise and dropped back on the bed. (pp. 28–9)

Doughty becomes the focus of all Michael's resentment against whites, which has been intensified that day by his dismissal and subsequent encounter with the policemen. What provokes Michael to his sudden act of violence seems to be Doughty's halting recitation of the speech from *Hamlet*. Doughty may suggest a whole culture in decay, weak in its final ugliness, suddenly and much too late trying to convey something of value out of the store of its creations to a subject group. But the subject group is accustomed to a different sort of role; the sudden change is confusing and provokes an irrational, dangerous response. Doughty may thus be seen as representative of the English-speaking (or Anglo-centric) tradition in South African affairs. Once great, now in decline, its powers gone beyond recovery, it no longer possesses a viable role: in its weakness it may approach other subservient groups within the society, offering gifts out of the glories of its past; but the recipient groups are historically unequipped to deal with the change in relationships, and their reactions, influenced by just resentment, may be dangerous and destructive; one ground for resentment is that their very inability to benefit from the kind of 'offering' Doughty is making is the result of a deliberate policy of deprivation by the representatives of the English tradition in its period of cultural and political dominance. Thus Michael's crime—or 'sin'— is closely related to the historical circumstances that have produced the present reality he must endure. Up to this point he is not really aware of the nature of spiritual suffering that is, however, just what the speech of Hamlet's father's ghost is all about, and it is very difficult for Michael to accept a formulation of his own problems.

The only other white characters of significance in the novel are the two policemen on patrol in the district that night, Constable Raalt and the driver of his van. Each is a highly representative figure, though this is achieved at the expense of realistic effect. Raalt is obsessed with his wife's unfaithfulness, and the energy of frustration engendered by this is expressed as aggression towards the coloured people on his beat. Thus Raalt is in the paradoxical situation of having to protect and enforce an order in the outer world, while his inner life is in a state of turmoil and chaos—a neat paradigm for the situation of his group, whose moral confusion, the author suggests, is complete, contradicting the external insistence on a rigidly ordered social structure based on the hierarchic subservience of non-white to white, Englishman to Afrikaner. The ineffectual driver of the van is perhaps of greater interest than Raalt because through him La Guma expresses his scorn for another, well-publicised but fundamentally somewhat obscure tradition in South African life, that apparently easy-going but easily rattled form of benevolent paternalism known as 'Cape liberalism'. Thus Raalt worries the driver because the extremity of his behaviour detracts from the dignity of the white man (p. 39): but at the same time the driver himself believes that coloured people should be trained 'like dogs to have respect for you'. (p. 79). Both Raalt and the driver fulfil important functions within the metaphysical structure of the novel, linking the penultimate and final stages of its moral dialectic.

The nature of Willieboy's death (which is described with lavish attention to detail), constitutes this final stage in the theological dialectic within which the major moral significance of the book is, surprisingly, located. There is no point in lengthy quotation: but certain images establish the connection with the general moral scheme:

> The driver was worried, and he said: 'Come on, man, let's go. Let's go.'
> He looked down at the boy who had been shot. The front of the yellow shirt was dark with blood and there was some blood on the edge and lapels of his coat. He had fainted and in the light of the headlamps his face bore a stark, terrible look, the skin coarse and drawn tight so that the bone structure of the adolescent, undeveloped face showed gauntly, covered with a film of sweat.
> The driver said: 'Christ, man, we'd better hurry up. Get him out of here. We ought to call an ambulance, I say.' (p. 88)

But Raalt refuses to allow an ambulance to be called, and the suffering Willieboy is thrust rudely into the back of the police van to be taken to the station. The imagery of suffering describing Willieboy's condition carries powerful connotations of youth and innocence, and the visual suggestions of the crucified Christ are confirmed in the driver's exclamation. Thus Willieboy moves closer, in terms of identity, to Joe, and away from Michael; and in the end he establishes a perfect antithesis with Raalt, in whose eyes, just prior to the shooting, the driver had seen 'what he thought were the fires of hell'. (p. 81) This takes place at the same time as Michael Adonis moves towards *his* corruption and inevitable damnation, and his identification with Raalt is thus obvious. The spiritual antithesis between Raalt and Willieboy is consummated in the last moments of Willieboy's life — it is another of La Guma's little moral surprises. As Willieboy lies bleeding, Raalt insists in stopping for cigarettes and a Coke at the café of the Portuguese where Willieboy and Michael had first encountered each other, occupying very different moral situations, at the beginning of the evening. Most of Willieboy's delirium is conveyed as flashbacks to the same sort of deprived childhood as Joe describes to Michael Adonis, only Willieboy's is the more vicious; but he has a couple of moments of clarity as well. The first of these occurs when the van stops at the café:

> In the back of the van Willieboy had come to with the small jolt the stopping had made. He awoke with the faint smell of petrol and carbon-monoxide in his nostrils. It made him retch again and he shook until the retching turned to weeping and he cried, the sobs wrenching at him, jerking the pain through his abdomen. He reached down to where the pain was worse and felt the wet stickiness of his

clothes and then the bleeding mouth of the wound where the bullet had torn through him, smashing into his insides. Then he seemed to realise for the first time what had happened to him.

'Help! Oh, God, help me! Oh, mamma, oh, mamma. Oh, Lord Jesus, save me. Save me. I'm dying! I'm dying! Save me. Save me. Oh, Christ, help me. Help me. Help me. Please. Help me. God. Jesus. Mother. Help me! Help me!'

His screams crashed against the sides of the van, confined within the metal walls. His father's leather belt whistled and snapped through the air, its sharp edge ripping at his legs and buttocks, the pain jumping through him. (pp. 91–2)

Again, the qualities of youth, even childhood, defencelessness, and, essentially, innocence predominate in the description; and, of course, the theological implications of the last-named quality are clear. These are reinforced, moreover, by what Willieboy actually says in the consciousness of his discovery of the nearness of death.; there can be no doubt that on one level the meaning of his words is God-directed, a cry for salvation. Coupled with the strong suggestions of innocence just mentioned, this amounts to an only slightly ambiguous resolution of his spiritual affairs, along the lines of the younger Graham Greene. Thus Willieboy *may* be regarded as dying 'saved', in a sort of state of grace, even though La Guma's world-view would ostensibly deny such a possibility; the convenience of this particular teleological frame of reference, however, comes out of Willieboy's last words: '"They're always kicking a poor bastard around," he said, and was surprised at the loudness and clarity of his voice.' (pp. 93–4)

This is a political statement, indicative of a final awareness of the nature of life at the moment of death: its 'grace' or validity is confirmed by the 'loudness and clarity' with which it is enunciated. In this way the political and 'religious' or moral frameworks are linked: La Guma suggests the redemptive and redeeming possibility of full political awareness, and that even though it might come late, who is to say that it is too late?

If the 'liberal' provenance of this novel were to be judged on these indications alone, the result would be exceedingly negative; either no justification would be established for regarding it as coming within the definition, or at best it might be regarded as falling in the same category as a book like Mrs Millin's *God's Stepchildren*. Where, then, is the genuine liberal affirmation to be found in *A Walk in the Night*?

The answer lies in the novel's carefully-planned and controlled but dominant concentration on the very opposite of fulfilment-deprivation. This points, of course, to the essential distinction between the attitude of Mrs Millin and that of La Guma. In the work of the former, as has been pointed out, fulfilment exists as the great illusion obsessively pursued by her characters, to their grave disadvantage; for La Guma, it is the great impossibility. It never enters his characters' minds, except as a fleeting, barely comprehended daydream. La Guma consciously presents a version of life utterly remote from the experience of his readers, and fairly distinct from the general run of what Western novelists usually choose to imitate; but he manages the presentation, in his first novel, effectively enough, sustaining the illusion of total deprivation, both material and spiritual, in a manner reminiscent of Solzhenitsyn's *One Day in the Life of Ivan Denisovitch*, another novel in which basic issues such as identity and communication are treated in a context of total deprivation of the normal appurtenances—both moral and physical—of life. Like Solzhenitsyn, La Guma bases his decision to focus on the obverse of fulfilment on the assumption that it *is*, in fact, an obverse—that not only the idea of fulfilment but all the preconditions for its existence, material and other, do exist and exist in order to be participated in by all men—exist, that is, as standards by which the quality of the life of a man or a group of men may be judged. Thus an implicit judgment runs throughout *A Walk in the Night*: if the focus is on deprivation, then the judgment is made on the basis of what the characters in the novel are deprived of; and, as has been demonstrated, their deprivation is rendered in terms of concepts characteristic of the liberal vision in the fiction of the last hundred and fifty years: identity, communication, personal fulfilment.

Thus the implied attribution of unorthodoxy, of a sort of virtuous and conscious artistic naivety contained in Bunting's introduction to *And a Threefold Cord* cannot hold for as heavily structured a work as *A Walk in the Night*, with its intricate dance along the strands of a preconceived moral web, and the regular and rhythmic interchange of positions between characters within the pattern of the web. The deliberate selection of a central human activity as major theme suggests that purpose as much as method should be seen as primarily aesthetic rather than political: and that the strength of *A Walk in the Night* lies in its effective rendition and interpretation of a specific area of human experience, while the effectiveness is flawed mainly by a current of somewhat simplistic politico-moral truisms flowing rather weakly beneath the toughly realistic surface texture.

Notes

NOTES TO PREFACE

1. J. P. L. Snyman, *The South African Novel in English, 1880–1930,* (Potchefstroom, South Africa: The University of Potchefstroom, Potchefstroom, 1952).
2. Vladimir Klima, *South African Prose Writing in English,* (Prague, Czechoslovakia: Czechoslovak Academy of Sciences, 1971).
3. Ezekiel Mphahlele, *The African Image* (London: Faber and Faber, 1974).

NOTES TO CHAPTER 1

1. Harry Bloom, *Transvaal Episode,* (Berlin: Seven Seas, 1959) p. 200.
2. For further reading on the history of the period to the coming to power of the Nationalist Party, see H. J. and R. E. Simons, *Class and Colour in South Africa 1850–1950* (Harmondsworth; Penguin, 1969). For a critical appraisal of the immediate past and of the contemporary position, see R. W. Johnson, *How Long Will South Africa Survive* (London: Macmillan, 1977).
3. For useful bibliographical material, see Donald J. Weinstock, 'The Two Boer Wars and the Jameson Raid', in *Research in African Literatures,* vol. 2, no. 1 (Spring 1971) pp. 39–43 for novels in Dutch and Afrikaans, and, again, vol. 3, no. 1 (Spring 1972) pp. 60–7, for novels in English.
4. Francis Brett Young 'South African Literature', *The London Mercury,* vol. XIX, no. 113 (March 1929).
5. Laurens van der Post, *In a Province* (New York: Coward and McCann, 1934) pp. 258–9.
6. *Contrast,* vol. 1, no. 1 (Summer 1960).
7. *The Classic,* vol. 1, no. 1 (1963).
8. *Contrast,* vol. 2, no. 3 (Summer 1963–4).
9. In P. Wastberg (ed.), *The Writer in Modern Africa* (New York: Africana Publishing Corporation, 1969) p. 24.
10. From 'Thoughts on South Africa', quoted from Uys Krige (ed.), *Olive*

Schreiner: A Selection (Cape Town: Oxford University Press, 1968) pp. 122–3.

11. *The New African*, vol. 4, no. 1 (March 1963).
12. John Coetzee, *In the Heart of the Country* (London: Secker & Warburg, 1975).
13. William Plomer, *Turbott Wolfe* (London: Hogarth Press, 1965).
14. Dan Jacobson, *A Dance in the Sun* (London: Weidenfeld & Nicolson, 1956).
15. Dan Jacobson, *The Evidence of Love* (London: Weidenfeld & Nicolson, 1960).
16. Peter Abrahams, *Wild Conquest* (New York: Harper, 1952).
17. Peter Abrahams, *Return to Goli* (London: Faber & Faber, 1953).
18. Ibid., p. 14.
19. Ibid., pp. 153–4.
20. *Wild Conquest*, op cit., p. 21.
21. *Return to Goli*, op. cit., p. 22.
22. *Wild Conquest*, op. cit., p. 286.
23. Alex la Guma, *A Walk in the Night* (Ibadan, Nigeria: Mbari Publications, 1962; London: Heinemann Educational Books, 1967).
24. Alex la Guma, *And a Threefold Cord* (Berlin: Seven Seas Books, 1964).
25. Alex la Guma, *The Stone Country* (Berlin: Seven Seas Books, 1967).
26. Ibid., p. 11.
27. Alex la Guma, *In the Fog of the Seasons' End* (London: Heinemann Educational Books, 1972).
28. David Rabkin, 'La Guma and Reality in South Africa', *Journal of Commonwealth Literature*, vol. VIII, no. 1 (June 1973) p. 66.

NOTES TO CHAPTER 2

1. All page references in this article are to the Chapman & Hall edition of 1892.
2. Olive Schreiner, *Undine* (London: Ernest Benn, 1929).
3. Olive Schreiner, *From Man to Man* (London: T. Fisher Unwin, 1926).
4. W. H. Nevinson, *The Fire of Life* (Nesbitt, 1924) p. 123.
5. S. C. Cronwright-Schreiner, *The Life of Olive Schreiner* (London: T. Fisher-Unwin, 1924) p. 87.
6. S. C. Cronwright-Schreiner (ed.), *The Letters of Olive Schreiner*, 1876–1920 (London: T. Fisher Unwin, 1924) p. 112.
7. Ibid., p. 57.
8. Ibid., p. 65. Olive Schreiner's italics.
9. Ibid., p. 17.
10. *Life*, p. 184, op. cit.
11. A. James and N. Hills (eds.), *Mrs John Brown: 1847–1935* (Edinburgh: Murray, 1937) p. 189.
12. Olive Schreiner, *Woman and Labour*, (London: T. Fisher Unwin, 1911).
13. Ibid., p. 33.
14. Ibid., p. 283.
15. D. L. Hobman, *Olive Schreiner, Her Friends and Times* (London: Watts & Co., 1915) p. vii.

16. *Life,* p. 215, op. cit.
17. Ibid., p. 251.
18. *Letters,* p. vii, op. cit.
19. Ibid., p. 321.
20. Ibid., p. 257.
21. Ibid., p. 283.
22. Olive Schreiner, *Trooper Peter Halkett of Mashonaland* (London: T. Fisher Unwin, 1897).
23. Ibid., p. 29.
24. Ibid., p. 55.
25. Ibid., p. 77.
26. Olive Schreiner, *A South African's View of the Situation* or *Words in Season* (London: Hodder & Stoughton, 1898).
27. Olive Schreiner, *Thoughts on South Africa* (London: T. Fisher Unwin, 1923 posthumous) p. 243.
28. Ibid., p. 323.
29. Olive Schreiner, *Closer Union: a Letter on the South African Union and the Principles of Government* (Fifield, 1909).
30. Ibid., p. 17.
31. Ibid., p. 44.
32. Ibid., p. 45.
33. *Letters,* p. 37, op. cit.
34. Ralph Waldo Emerson, *Essays,* vol. 1, (London: Geo. Bell, 1884), p. 167.
35. *Letters,* p. 323, op. cit.
36. *Essays,* p. 169, op. cit.
37. *Life,* p. 185, op. cit.
38. Olive Schreiner, *Dreams* (London: T. Fisher Unwin, 1891); *Dream Life and Real Life* (London: T. Fisher Unwin, 1893); *Stories Dreams and Allegories* (London: T. Fisher Unwin, 1923).
39. Ibid., *Stories, Dreams and Allegories,* p. 69.
40. *Letters,* p. 185, op. cit.
41. Olive gave the manuscript to Havelock Ellis, with whom she had had frequent discussions about her youth. After her death Ellis sent it to Cronwright-Schreiner. He had been unaware of its existence.
42. *Undine,* p. 194, op. cit.
43. *From Man to Man,* p. 440, op. cit.
44. Olive Schreiner, *The Story of an African Farm* (London: Chapman & Hall, 1892) p. 4.

NOTES TO CHAPTER 3

1. *The Journals of Arnold Bennett,* edited by Newman Flower (1932) vol. 1, pp. 300–1.
2. Pauline Smith, *A.[rnold] B.[ennett]* (1933) p. 15.
3. Parish records, St. Jude's Church, Oudtshoorn.
4. Pauline Smith, *School.* A note in the Magazine of the Girls' High School, Oudtshoorn, March 1932.
5. Pauline Smith, *Platkops Children* (1935).

6. Letter to A. Ravenscroft, 28 March 1952.
7. *A.B.*, p. 13.
8. Ibid., p. 18.
9. Ibid., pp. 53–4.
10. Pauline Smith, *The Little Karoo* (1925) (4 impressions). New edition (1930) with two additional stories, 'Desolation' and 'The Father'. Reprinted 1936, 1950, 1951, 1956, 1957, 1958, 1959, 1960, 1961 (twice), 1972; not including U.S. editions.
11. Pauline Smith, *The Beadle*, (1926) and *The Beadle* (Cape Town: Balkema, 1956) limited edition of 1500 copies, reprinted once.
12. *A.B.*, p. 45, op. cit.
13. *New York Times*, 3 June 1959.

NOTES TO CHAPTER 4

1. J. P. L. Snyman, *The South African Novel in English 1880–1930* (U. of Potchefstroom, Potchefstroom, S.A., 1952) p. 141.
2. M. Tucker, *Africa in Modern Literature*, (New York: Ungar, 1968) p. 257.
3. J. Jahn, *A History of Neo-African Literature*, (London: Faber, 1966) p. 90.
4. J. Jahn, *Muntu* (London: Faber, 1961) p. 200.
5. T. D. Mweli Skota, *The African Yearly Register, Being an Illustrated National Biographical Dictionary (Who's Who) of Black Folks in Africa*, (Johannesburg: Orange Press, 1931 [?]) p. 245.
6. Public Record Office, London. Colonial Office Series CO 417/629, Letter from Plaatje to the Administrator of Southern Rhodesia, 6 April 1919.
7. J. Jahn, *A History of Neo-African Literature*, p. 105.
8. S. Plaatje, *Native Life in South Africa* (London, 1916) p. 68.
9. *Sechuana Proverbs with Literal Translations and their European Equivalents* (London: Kegan Paul, Trench, Trubner and Co., 1916) p. 11. He makes this point in a slightly different way in *Mhudi* (p. 94) when he says one could describe Mzilikazi's wife, Umnandi, perfectly in terms of the Song of Songs by changing one word only, 'vineyards' to 'cornfields'.
10. S. Plaatje, *Mhudi* (Lovedale, C. P., South Africa, 1930) p. 122.
11. Ibid., p. 12.
12. Ibid., p. 45.
13. Ruth Finnegan, *Oral Literature in Africa* (Oxford: Clarendon Press, 1970) p. 393.
14. *Mhudi*, pp. 121–5.
15. *Oral Literature in Africa*, p. 411.
16. *Mhudi*, p. 120.
17. *Oral Literature in Africa*, p. 407.
18. *Mhudi*, p. 46.
19. *Sechuana Proverbs* . . . p. 13.
20. J. D. Omer-Cooper, *The Zulu Aftermath* (Longman, 1966) p. 20.
21. *Sechuana Proverbs* . . . p. 1.
22. G. W. Stow, *The Native Races of South Africa* (Swan Sonneschein & Co., 1905) p. 489.
23. G. M. Theal, *History of South Africa Since 1795*, vol. V (London: Allen &

Unwin, 1915 edn.) p. 456.
24. C. W. De Kiewiet, *A History of South Africa* (O.U.P., 1957 edn.) p. 73.
25. *Mhudi*, p. 135.
26. *A History of South Africa*, p. 86.
27. *The Zulu Aftermath*, p. 7.
28. V. Klima, *South African Prose Writing in English* (Prague: Academia, 1971) p. 41.
29. *Native Life in South Africa*, p. 136.
30. *Mhudi*, p. 85.
31. *Native Life in South Africa*, p. 91.
32. Ibid., p. 338.
33. *Mhudi*, p. 77.
34. Ibid., p. 132.
35. *Native Life in South Africa*, p.111.
36. *Mhudi*, p. 129, op. cit.
37. *Native Life in South Africa*, p. 100.
38. *Mhudi*, p. 208.
39. Ibid., p. 159.
40. *The Rhodesia Herald*, Salisbury, 22 April 1910.
41. *The Rhodesia Herald*, 29 April 1910.
42. Peter Walshe, *The Rise of African Nationalism in South Africa* (London: Hurst, 1970) p. 73.
43. *Native Life in South Africa*, p. 225.

NOTES TO CHAPTER 5

1. Sarah Gertrude Millin, *God's Stepchildren* (London, 1924) p. 263, in the undated Central News Agency (Johannesburg) edition with a Preface (dated 1 January 1951) by the author. All references are to this edition.
2. William Plomer, *Turbott Wolfe* (1926; 2nd edition, 1965) p. 68; all references in this article are to the 1965 edition.
3. J. P. L. Snyman, *The South African Novel in English 1880-1930* (U. of Potchefstroom, Potchefstroom S.A. 1952).
4. Michael Wade, 'William Plomer, English Liberalism, and the South African Novel', *The Journal of Commonwealth Literature*, VIII, 1, p. 22.
5 Quoted in Snyman, op. cit.
6. S. G. Millin, *The Night is Long* (London, 1950) quoted in Snyman op. cit., p. 98.
7. V. Klima, *South African Prose Writing in English* (Prague, 1971) p. 73.
8. William Plomer, *Double Lives* (London: Jonathan Cape, 1943) p. 9.
9. Laurens van der Post, 'Introduction', *Turbott Wolfe*, 1965 edition, pp. 32-3.
10. Cosmo Pieterse, 'Conflict in the Germ', *Protest and Conflict in African Literature*, ed. C. Pieterse and D. Munro (London, 1969) pp. 1-26.
11. Michael Wade, op. cit.
12. *Double Lives*, p. 186.
13. Ibid., p. 187.
14. Ibid.

NOTES 197

15. Ibid.
16. *Turbott Wolfe*, Appendix I, pp. 212–13.
17. Michael Wade, op. cit.
18. Nadine Gordimer, 'The Novel and the Nation in South Africa', *African Writers on African Writing*, ed. G. D. Killam (London, 1973) p. 39.

NOTES TO CHAPTER 6

1. William Empson, *Some Versions of Pastoral* (London: Peregrine, 1966) Chapter 1.
2. Peter Abrahams, *Mine Boy* (London: Heinemann Educational Books, 1963).
3. Mphahlele draws the comparison in African Image (London: Faber & Faber, 1962) p. 177.

NOTES TO CHAPTER 7

1. 'The English Novel in South Africa', from *The Novel and the Nation*, National Union of South African Students (Cape Town, 1960) p. 16.
2. Ibid., p. 17.
3. 'A Writer in South Africa', *The London Magazine*, vol. 5, no. 2 (May 1965) pp. 22–3.
4. Her contribution to the debate continues. See, for instance, 'English-language Literature and Politics in South Africa' in *Aspects of South African Literature*, ed. Christopher Heywood (London: Heinemann, 1976).
5. 'Towards a Desk-Drawer Literature', *The Classic*, vol. 2, no. 4 (1968) pp. 73–4.
6. Nadine Gordimer, *A World of Strangers* (London: Gollancz, 1958).
7. Nadine Gordimer, *Occasion for Loving* (London: Gollancz, 1963).
8. 'A Writer in South Africa', *The London Magazine*, vol. 5, no. 2 (May 1965) p. 23.
9. Nadine Gordimer, *The Late Bourgeois World* (London: Gollancz, 1966).

NOTES TO CHAPTER 8

1. Nadine Gordimer, *A Guest of Honour* (London: Jonathan Cape, 1971).

NOTES TO CHAPTER 9

1. Alex La Guma, *A Walk in the Night* (Ibadan: Mbari Publications, 1962).
2. Alex La Guma, *And a Threefold Cord* (Berlin: Seven Seas Books, 1964).
3. Alex La Guma, *The Stone Country* (Berlin: Seven Seas Books, 1967).
4. Alex La Guma, *A Walk in the Night and other stories* (London: Heinemann, 1967). Page references in the text are to the African Writers

Series edition (London, Heinemann, 1968).

5. Brian Bunting, Foreword to *And a Threefold Cord*.
6. Bunting, op. cit. p. 10.
7. Lewis Nkosi, 'Fiction by Black South Africans', in *Home and Exile* (London: Longmans, 1965) p. 135.
8. S. G. Millin, *What Hath a Man?* (London: Chatto and Windus, 1938).

Index